# F THE
# DONNER PARTY
## A Tragedy of the Sierra

By C. F. McGLASHAN

*With Foreword, Notes, and a Bibliography*
By GEORGE H. HINKLE AND
BLISS McGLASHAN HINKLE

STANFORD UNIVERSITY PRESS
*Stanford, California*

STANFORD UNIVERSITY PRESS
STANFORD, CALIFORNIA

PUBLISHED IN GREAT BRITAIN, INDIA, AND
PAKISTAN BY GEOFFREY CUMBERLEGE,
OXFORD UNIVERSITY PRESS,
LONDON, BOMBAY, AND KARACHI

———

THE BAKER AND TAYLOR COMPANY
HILLSIDE, NEW JERSEY

HENRY M. SNYDER & COMPANY, INC.
440 FOURTH AVENUE, NEW YORK 16

W. S. HALL & COMPANY
457 MADISON AVENUE, NEW YORK 22

———

COPYRIGHT 1940 AND 1947 BY THE BOARD OF TRUSTEES
OF THE LELAND STANFORD JUNIOR UNIVERSITY

PRINTED AND BOUND IN THE UNITED STATES
OF AMERICA BY STANFORD UNIVERSITY PRESS

———

First printing, May 1940
Revised edition, December 1947
Third printing, October 1949
Fourth printing, May 1954
Fifth printing, October 1957

*Library of Congress Catalog Card Number: 40-10251*

# TABLE OF CONTENTS

Sole of John Denton's Shoe (from the McGlashan Collection)

Relics of the Donner Party (from the McGlashan Collection)

# EDITORS' FOREWORD, 1947

IT IS DIFFICULT to account for the enduring reputation of a book, in the face of changing taste and fashions of thought, when its subject is one of minor appeal and demands a rather special interest in the reading public. In the book here freshly presented, the problem is complicated by an extensive body of material on its subject from other hands.

McGlashan's *History of the Donner Party* appeared in its final and revised form in 1880. The first printing of the edition sold out in something less than two weeks—a record for a day when tourist traffic was still a thin trickle and when busy editors printed book notices only when news of boom camps, land feuds, political brawls, and local shootings ran a bit below par. Since 1880 the book has run through twelve large printings, has been widely quoted, and remains prominent in the minds of many readers for its contribution to their knowledge of Western history.

The book appeared at a most propitious time. People in California in the early 'eighties were still restless and venturesome, and the land they occupied was still raw. Many were still living who had lively recollections of gold-rush days and who remembered the disaster of the Donner party as a sensational illustration of their own hardships. Eldorado was still turbulent. Its legend had not yet hardened. In the hurly-burly of the day, however, Californians were already becoming conscious of the past and of its monuments and episodes as a field for study—even if those who worked in that field were not native sons. The 'eighties were about to witness that surprising outburst of literary activity which followed the vast work of Bancroft.

vii

The Donner party had received considerable attention from early writers, for the most part attracted by the sensational aspects of its story. Conscientious chroniclers such as Bryant, Mrs. Farnham, and Thornton had interviewed Eddy, the Breens, the Donners, and the Reeds. But their accounts were relatively brief, written more or less as "intelligence from California." Moreover, having been written but a short time after the events themselves, the most reliable of them, that by Thornton, lacked critical perspective. In 1880, records, diaries, and correspondence were widely scattered and in private hands. The exact relationship between the episodes of the expedition and its leading characters had become lost to view in the chronicle of its hardships. And almost from the beginning loose gossip and dense folklore tended to gather about the events: long before McGlashan wrote his book, other survivors had suffered as much as the unfortunate Keseberg from the impertinent curiosity of idle chatterboxes and sensation-mongers.

Against such a background the McGlashan book appeared at precisely the right moment to rescue the essential facts from oblivion. It became the first serious attempt to consult sources, weigh evidence, marshal detached episodes into an organized whole, and extend the story of the Donner party from a sensational incident to a full-length chapter in California history. From every point of view, it was calculated to appeal to the widest circle of readers; and it did so.

But neither the primacy of McGlashan's *History* nor the interest in its subject can wholly explain its place in public esteem. Considered as a history, it leaves much to be desired: It frequently leaves vital questions concerning dates, places, and the exact sequence of events unanswered—indeed, it confidently asserts that such details are "of slight importance." Judged by current theories of psychology, its view of human motives seems quaintly prejudiced: it continually asserts that the copybook virtues of loyalty, courage, generosity, and chivalry are controlling influences upon character under the stress of misery and terror; and it finds that these virtues, once hallowed by suffering, are sufficient to whitewash a character which otherwise has been base. Its language is saturated with sentiment, and great stretches of the narrative are written in the pressed-flower-and-keepsake style of a young lady's album of the period. These are the worst things that can be said about the book. And, despite all of them, it still stands as a moving chronicle of human despair, dissension, and defeat.

In order to comprehend the eccentricities of this book and to appraise its contribution to the history of California, a reader needs to identify the author rather fully in his relation to his work. As the author himself humorously observed, the *History* was a book that had to be written. It is more exact to say that it was inevitable that he should write it.

C. F. McGlashan, born in Janesville, Wisconsin in 1847, was two years old when his family came over the trail to California, thus qualifying as a contemporary in age and experience with the younger children of the Donner Party. When he attended Sotoyome Institute at Healdsburg, Lovina Graves was still in school at Calistoga, and George Donner had just started his suit for repossession of a San Francisco town lot. While he was growing up, McGlashan heard of the Reeds at San Jose, of the Fosters on the Yuba, and of the Breens at San Juan Bautista. He grew into California with the surviving families of the Party, a circumstance which accounted in no small part for the successful undertaking of his *History*. He taught school in Hangtown and during the 'sixties he had a varied experience in the diggings of the Lode, from Michigan Bar to Yankee Jim's. He finally settled in Truckee in 1871, where he lived for sixty years as attorney and publisher, combining a gusty public career with a series of intense and unpredictable hobbies.

In 1874 McGlashan wrote a classic series of dispatches from Utah on the Mountain Meadow Massacre, a factual chronicle which later formed the basis of the government's case against John D. Lee. He plunged into state politics as publisher of the *Santa Barbara Press,* succeeding Theodore Glancy, who had been shot to death in an editorial feud. He was a member of the California Assembly during the early 'eighties, in the tense days of the antihydraulic-mining legislation. In 1885, still frontier-minded, he joined the rush to the Cœur d'Alene diggings. But these activities were only interludes in a long residence in Truckee, and merely supplemented the long line of private enthusiasms which occupied him there.

At various times McGlashan plunged into rather than dabbled in entomology, astronomy, geology, and the hydrography of the Sierra watershed. He discovered the rare butterfly of the Truckee Basin, *Euphydryas chalcedona Macglashanae,* published a series of practical planetary maps, and built a museum around Truckee's famous geological curiosity, the Rocking Stone. His intimate knowledge of the watershed led him to odd plans—at one time for the large-scale raising of frogs on a mountain top, at another for the playing of twenty-six fountains on the shores of Donner Lake. At the time of his death, in 1931, he had accumulated a score of actual or pending patents on such a diversity of gadgets as a railroad telegraph, an improvement on the Roman catapult, a collapsible bird-feeding tray, and a device for the controlled breeding of moths and butterflies. The author of *History of the Donner Party* was, in short, a man of considerable eccentricity and virtuosity, qualities conspicuous in his day. They were also the qualities of his book, in the circumstances of its publication and in its final form.

McGlashan had taken over the publication of the *Truckee Republican* in 1876, when the possibility of a fully documented Donner Party history first occurred to him. The paper was in a rickety state, having changed hands several times over the poker table, and one of its editors had already met a violent death by gunshot. McGlashan filled the early issues with local lore and issued a prospectus for a Sierra guidebook in which the Donner Party episode was to have a prominent place. One A. D. Rock had projected a Donner Party history in 1866, for the *San Francisco Examiner,* but the plan fell through when the survivors, with the exception of James Reed, refused to give Rock any information. McGlashan's announcement, in 1878, of a forthcoming serialized version of the story was made frankly as a circulation booster. He had no more to go on at the time than Rock had had before him. He knew only the published works of Thornton, Bryant, and Reed, and two of these were secondhand accounts. Local sources of information were vague, and local interest was lukewarm. At Donner Lake, three miles out of town, a tangle of underbrush hid some still-substantial remains of the emigrants' shelters, but few could give any approximate location and no one was anxious to explore. The place and the episode had a somewhat sinister reputation: vague traditions of the Donner Party were kept alive in Truckee through the fireside yarns of old settlers and by a local character who had appropriated the name of Keseberg and who boasted, when he could get an audience, of having eaten great quantities of human flesh.

McGlashan's announcement brought a swift and uncalculated response. New subscribers at widely scattered points inside and outside the state wrote enthusiastically, many of them enclosing money. In the spring of 1879, McGlashan had to meet the situation by printing in a special edition a synopsis of the history which he had not yet begun to write,

## CHART OF EVENTS

| 1846 | Events at Alder Creek | Events at Donner Lake | Chronology of Relief Parties | Chronology of Refugee Parties | Storms |
|---|---|---|---|---|---|
| Oct. 28 | | | | | Oct. 28 to Nov. 11 |
| Nov. 4 | | | Reed reaches Sutter's | | |
| Nov. 8 | | First attempt to cross summit | | | |
| Nov. 12 | | | Reed and McCutchen leave Johnson's | | |
| Nov. 16 | | | They reach Dry Valley; turn back | | Nov. 25 to Dec. 3 |
| Nov. 21 | | Second attempt to cross | Cache food | | |
| Dec. 2 | | Last of cattle lost | Reed seeks further aid at Sutter's | | |
| Dec. 9 | | Milton Elliot and Noah James go to Alder Creek | | | Dec. 9–13 |
| Dec. 14 | Jacob Donner, Sam Shoemaker, Joseph Rinehart, and James Smith die (?) | Death of Bayliss Williams | | | |
| Dec. 16 | | Departure of "Forlorn Hope" | | | |
| Dec. 20 | | Milton and Noah return | | | |
| Dec. 22 | | | | Food of "Forlorn Hope" gone; Stanton dies | Dec. 23–25 |
| Dec. 24 | | Lewis Keseberg, Jr., dies | | "Camp of Death": Antoine and F. W. Graves die | |
| Dec. 25 | | | | Dolan dies; body eaten; Lemuel Murphy dies | |
| Dec. 28 | | | | Leave "Camp of Death" | |
| Dec. 29 | | Charles Burger dies | | Reach deep canyon | |
| Dec. 30 | | | | | |
| **1847** | | | | | |
| Jan. 1 | | | | Thongs are eaten | |
| Jan. 3 | | John L. Murphy dies | | | |
| Jan. 4 | | Mrs. Reed, Virginia, and Elliot try to cross | | Shooting of the deer; Fosdick dies | |
| Jan. 6 | | | | North Fork of American River | Jan. 9–13 |
| Jan. 8 | | | | Lewis and Salvador killed | |
| Jan. 10 | | | | Reach Indian camp | |
| Jan. 17 | | | | Party reaches Johnson's | |
| Jan. 18 | | | | Rhodes carries news to Sutter's | Jan. 22–27 |
| Jan. 31 | | | Tucker's party leaves Sutter's | | |
| Feb. 2 | | Harriet McCutchen dies | | | |
| Feb. 3 | | Margaret Eddy dies | Yerba Buena meeting | | |
| Feb. 5 | | Augustus Spitzer and Mrs. E. Eddy die | First relief leaves Johnson's; Reed leaves Yerba Buena for Sonoma and Napa | | Feb. 2–6 |
| Feb. 7 | | Milt Elliot dies | | | |
| Feb. 9 | | | Coon and Tucker left at Mule Springs | | |
| Feb. 11 | | | Cache of Nov. 16 gone | | |
| Feb. 13 | | | | | |
| Feb. 14 | | Children of Eddy and Foster | | | |

| Date | | | | | |
|---|---|---|---|---|---|
| Feb. 19 | | Relief party arrives | Party reaches Donner Lake | | |
| Feb. 20 | Tucker, Moultry, and Rhoads rescue Noah James, Mrs. Wolfinger, Leanna, Elitha, and George Donner, Jr. | Catherine Pike dies | | | |
| Feb. 22 | All food gone except one hide | Relief party leaves with 18. Patty and Tommy Reed return with Moultry and Glover; Breen shoots dog | Second relief leaves with Reed | Second relief leaves | |
| Feb. 23 | | | | | |
| Feb. 24 | | | Reed reaches Mule Springs | Find cache gone; Ada Keseberg and Denton die | |
| Feb. 25 | | Resort to cannibalism | Refugees met at Bear Valley | At Bear Valley | |
| Feb. 26 | | | | | |
| Feb. 27 | | | | William Hook dies | |
| Feb. 28 | | Root left by passing Indian | | | |
| Mar. 1 | | | Meets 10 Indians | | |
| Mar. 2 | Clark and Cady stay with Donners; Isaac and Mary leave; Clark kills bear | | Arrives at Donner Lake | Reach Mule Springs and safety | |
| Mar. 3 | | Second relief leaves with 23 | | Third group camp on shores of Donner Lake | |
| Mar. 4 | Stone returns; he and Cady leave with Frances, Eliza, and Georgia | | | Mrs. Graves buries money | |
| Mar. 5 | | | | | |
| Mar. 7 | Lewis Donner dies; Mrs. Elizabeth Donner dies (?) | | Eddy and Foster leave Johnson's | Dofar, Jondro, Turner sent ahead; party reaches Yuba | Mar. 6–8 |
| Mar. 8 | Cady and Stone abandon Donner children | | Eddy and Foster meet Woodworth in Bear Valley | Isaac Donner, Elizabeth and F. W. Graves, Jr., die | |
| Mar. 9 | | | Meet Reed and return with him to Bear Valley; Leave Bear Valley | Breen and Graves left at "Starved Camp"; Reed pushes on; Cady and Stone overtake them | |
| Mar. 11 | Clark goes to Donner; reports children in danger | | | | |
| Mar. 12 | Tamsen Donner goes to Donner Lake | | Reach "Starved Camp"; Stark, Oakley, and Stone lead refugees | Refugees set out with Stark, Oakley, and Stone | |
| Mar. 13 | Tamsen returns to Alder; finds Clark and Baptiste gone; Samuel and George Donner die(?) | | Eddy and Foster reach Donner Lake; leave with all except Mrs. Murphy, Keseberg, and Alder camp members; Overtake Stark's party | | |
| Mar. 16 | | | | Overtaken by Eddy and Foster | |
| Mar. 17 | | | | Meet Glover and Moultry, who have food | |
| Mar. 19 | | Mrs. Murphy dies (?) | | | |
| Mar. 23 | | | | Reach Sutter's | |
| Mar. 26 | Tamsen goes to Donner Lake | Tamsen arrives at Keseberg's cabin | Fallon's party leaves Johnson's | | |
| Apr. 16 | Keseberg goes to Alder Creek | | | Keseberg finds his child's body | Mar. 28 to Apr. 3 |
| Apr. 17 | | Fallon's party arrives | | | |
| Apr. 19 | | | Arrives at Donner Lake | | |
| Apr. 21 | | Fallon's party leaves | | | |

promising an early publication of the expanded version in forthcoming issues.

The first tentative chapters were undertaken even while the author was feverishly busy trying to track down eye-witnesses. In fact, many of his close friendships with survivors originated during this period, when he had to answer the frequent protests of members who had been listed as dead. As the editor gained the confidence of the Reed, Donner, Breen, Graves, Murphy, and Tucker families, his correspondence mounted to hundreds of letters. He supplemented his fresh information with intensive reading of published accounts and with preliminary researches at the Donner Lake cabin sites. But, by May 1879, the early chapters were interrupted by a somewhat sensational incident—which ultimately, had much to do with establishing the authority of the McGlashan history in the public mind.

The *Sacramento Daily Record-Union* of May 17 announced the discovery by McGlashan of an initialed whetstone which had belonged to James Reed. The same issue carried a letter from Benjamin Wilder, the husband of Elitha C. Donner, criticizing the serialized story, berating the author for poor taste in writing it, and suggesting that survivors meet and review the facts. McGlashan replied quickly in the issue of the *Republican* of May 20:

I confess surprise at reading Mr. B. W. Wilder's letter in last Saturday's *Record-Union*. Mr. Wilder's wife, Elitha C. Donner, left the mountains with the first relief party and personally knows nothing whatever of the calamities which befell her mother and younger sisters. These sisters have been among my most valued correspondents. That they do not regret this I am led to believe from the fact that I have been the first to ferret out information which fully disproves the oft-repeated and oft-published story that their mother, Tamsen Donner, was murdered. I have received from all sources 1000 letters relating to the history. I have personally interviewed a majority of the survivors who were old enough to remember the fatal journey. I have letters and correspondence of James F. Reed, Captain Sutter, C. T. Stanton, and many others. I have every scrap that ever was published, as can be ascertained. Finally, I am publishing all the important facts of history in the *Truckee Republican,* and as an error appears it is corrected forthwith by every survivor who deems it an error. All concede that the truth is far better than the crude, false, exaggerated accounts which in bygone days have been made public. If Mr. Wilder is appalled at any fact I have published, I sympathize with his feelings. This, however, does not prevent the truthfulness of the History. Were I to write the history of the Eve of St. Bartholomew, I should not be deterred from telling the truth, though someone who was a descendant should be appalled or should prefer the tale not to be made public.

But this was only a preliminary skirmish. Wilder, acting as he said for the Donner family and for his wife, suddenly filed suit to enjoin from publication further chapters. Obviously, by the wording of the complaint and in the light of subsequent events, Elitha Donner-Wilder had received from an unnamed source the transcript of an allegedly libelous statement which her informant declared would appear in a subsequent chapter of the *Republican* serialized story. The Wilder complaint, indicating as it does how little the reading public of the 'seventies knew of the common sources of information and misinformation on the subject, is worth quoting in full:

That the defendants herein have now in press and threaten to publish and unless restrained by the Honorable Court will publish a book entitled *The History of the Donner Party,* meaning the parties above described, including the plaintiff Elitha C. Donner and family; that plaintiffs are informed and believe that said book will contain statements of and concerning the Donner Party showing that while they were in camp in the mountains they subsisted upon human flesh and devoured the bodies of their dead comrades. And upon information and belief, the

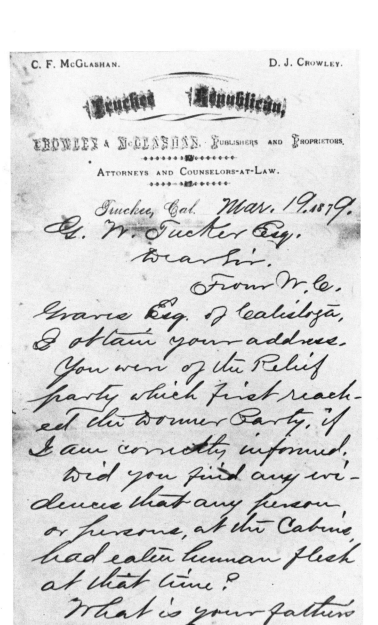

C. F. McGlashan.                    D. J. Crowley.

**Truckee Republican,**

CROWLEY & McGLASHAN, Publishers and Proprietors.

ATTORNEYS AND COUNSELORS-AT-LAW.

Truckee, Cal. Mar. 19, 1879.

G. W. Tucker Esq.
    Dear Sir.
        From W. C.
Graves Esq. of Calistoga,
I obtain your address.
You were of the Relief
party which first reach-
ed the Donner Party, if
I am correctly informed.
Did you find any evi-
dences that any person
or persons, at the Cabins
had eaten human flesh
at that time?
    What is your fathers

(Courtesy of Mr. G. H. Tucker, Burlingame, California)

accusers. Indeed, the author's oral reminiscences of his visits to the grotesque Keseberg household made the worst of the hearsay evidence seem quite frivolous. The lumbering and tortured bulk of Keseberg, the bareness and squalor of his quarters, his passionate outbursts joined by the screams and babblings of his deformed and idiot daughters, formed a scene of misery and terror calculated to make the deposition of Fallon sound like an old wives' tale.

McGlashan held further fire until the Wilder complaint had been disallowed in the court. In his issue of the *Republican* of June 7, he produced his trump, managing at the same time to sharpen public interest in his forthcoming "first edition."

We feel warranted in laying the full text of the complaint before our readers because they will be both surprised and edified at Mr. Wilder's version of the Donner Party. The Keseberg statement was to have concluded the history this week. Lewis Keseberg's narration will doubtless prove interesting, yet we cannot promise such a sensational repast as the one given above.

Dropping to the serious—Mr. Wilder's version is copied boldly from Judge J. Quinn Thornton's *Oregon and California,* a book published in 1847. Among numerous questions asked the survivors was one enquiring as to the truth or falsity of the quotation from Thornton. A large number of answers were received, denouncing it as false. Mr. Wilder was personally informed of this fact.

This injunction suit is one of the best arguments ever adduced for the publication of a true history of the Donner Party. Just such false and sensational articles as Mr. Wilder gives in his version above have appeared year after year, dished up in one form or another and labelled "The History of the Donner Party." Hon. J. F. Breen was the first one who ever gave us an intimation that the true history had never been written. We appeal to him to know if the sketch of the Starved Camp, published in the *Republican* or given by Mr. Wilder, be the truth.

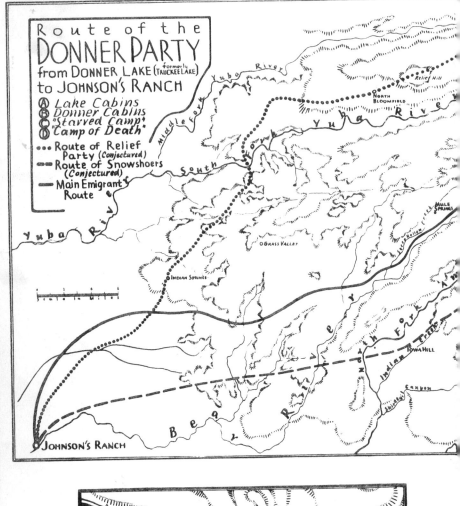

Route of the
DONNER PARTY
from DONNER LAKE (formerly TRUCKEE LAKE)
to JOHNSON'S RANCH

Ⓐ Lake Cabins
Ⓑ Donner Cabins
Ⓒ "Starved Camp"
Ⓓ "Camp of Death"
••• Route of Relief Party (Conjectured)
--- Route of Snowshoers (Conjectured)
— Main Emigrant Route

JOHNSON'S RANCH

DONNER
LAKE
CABIN
SITES

The DONNER
PARTY in the
SIERRA
Ⓐ Donner Cabins
Ⓑ Lake Cabins
— — — Route of 1st Attempt
———— Later Route

So far as the case was concerned, it was virtually decided upon submission. Upon the *ex parte* motion of Wilder, the court refused to grant the restraining order. Even if all were true which is contained in Mr. Wilder's complaint, the whole line of decisions declares that no injunction should issue. If Mr. Wilder or anyone else is libelled by the book which will issue to subscribers the first day of July, he will have ample remedy at law.

But the revised draft of the *Republican* serialized version did not appear until December. By this time, McGlashan had managed to win the confidence of most of the survivors, only to meet increased difficulties: nearly two thousand letters had accumulated, and others were arriving daily. The Reed family, with whom the author had formed what came to be a lifelong friendship, had furnished the Reed and Tucker-Ritchie diaries and personal recollections of the greatest importance; exploration of camp sites had thrown new light on the situation and movements of the emigrants; Franklin Graves had guided McGlashan to the Alder Creek camp site of the Donners; and George Murphy and Eliza Donner-Houghton, together with the author and a committee of thirteen well-known residents of Truckee, had systematically cleared the Donner Lake cabin sites, sifted the debris, and identified and catalogued the scattered remains. A complete reorganization was now in order; and in 1880 the second edition appeared, advertised as "corrected and revised by present survivors."

The publication of the *History* was after all merely an incident, with unforeseen complications, in a crowded and episodic life. McGlashan went on from it to experiment with willow wands and gold finders and to associate himself in a highly diverting way with a syndicate of Guatemalan treasure hunters. But events seemed to conspire throughout his life to associate him with the Truckee district primarily as the historian of the Donner Party. In 1891 he assisted in the recovery of the Graves money, buried on the shores of Donner Lake since 1847; in 1893 he directed the salvaging of the remaining fragments of the foundation log of the Murphy cabin; and in 1918 he stood with the last aged survivors as an honored guest to witness the dedication of a pioneer monument on the Breen cabin site. Its location might never have been established had not his compelling curiosity drawn him through the trackless undergrowth covering it nearly forty years before. He died in Truckee on January 6, 1931.

The question of the value of the *History* as a contribution to Californiana must depend to a large extent upon a knowledge of the sources and resources at the command of the author when he wrote it.

Of the twenty-six survivors who were still living in 1879, McGlashan obtained information from twenty-four. Three of his informants had been of mature years at the time of the disaster and their faculties were unimpaired in 1879. Nine had been at most impressionable ages—from fourteen to eighteen. Ten had been mere children, although those from six to twelve might well have preserved clear recollections; two had been infants, whose later contributions must have come from family traditions. It would thus appear that he had at his disposal a fairly reliable majority of available witnesses.

In the 'seventies the terrain of the district remained relatively undisturbed, and public knowledge of the Donner party was still too meager to have caused destruction of landmarks or the disturbance of cabin sites. Members of the Graves, Murphy, and Reed families were able to give intelligent co-operation in fixing the locale of various episodes.

In his reading of published works and manuscript sources, McGlashan seems to have anticipated much of the labor and research of writers on the subject who came after him. He certainly made detailed use of the published accounts by Breen, Bryant, Tamsen Donner, Dunbar, Mrs. Farnham, Graves, Virginia and James Reed, Power, and Thornton. Extensive manuscript material, the fate of much of which is now unknown, came to him from the Graves, Murphy, Foster, and Reed families. He closely followed the records of the relief parties in the files of the *California Star*, used the transcript of Fallon's diary, and had access to many of the letters and reports since incorporated in the collection of Fort Sutter records. These latter materials were supplemented by conversations with McCutchen, by material in the manuscripts of the Reed, Ritchie, and Tucker diaries, and by correspondence with Cady and Clark.

The extent of these labors appears the more remarkable when one remembers that the author worked without the advantages of rapid communication and without the organization and apparatus of great libraries; moreover, the examination of this mass of oral and written testimony, together with the actual task of writing his book, was completed during odd portions of a year and a half of one of the busiest and most eventful periods of the writer's life.

McGlashan brought to his task another advantage. Few men had a more extensive knowledge of the topography of the Truckee basin and its western watershed. No one knew better the overpowering physical forces of a Sierra winter. He knew from experience what it meant to be caught in the open before the paralyzing and stifling strength of blizzards which even today can and do bring all the machinery of man to a complete standstill.

Such knowledge and experience gave him a natural and deeply sympathetic understanding of the dire circumstances of the characters in his story. The secret of his narrative is its complete subjectivity. He may know much more than he tells, about many things; but he can report only that which was seen through the eyes of his characters, in their situation as he knew it to have been.

It is certainly true that men brought to the extremities of privation and despair will scarcely be able to halt and coolly take stock of the evidences of their own plight, so that they can make a statistical survey of them later on. They are apt to remember their own reactions of hate, anger, or revulsion, and to describe their surroundings only as they were seen through the haze of these emotions. This obvious truth forms a principle from which the author never departs. He says nothing of the gruesome remains at the Alder Creek camp (although he certainly knew about them), because there was no testimony on the situation except that of two outsiders, Cady and Stone, and the runaway Jean Baptiste. He chronicles events at "Starved Camp" as they struck the half-numbed brains of Patrick and Margaret Breen, instead of describing the evidences of these events as the relief parties later found them. He describes scenes at Donner Lake briefly though adequately, but from testimony of the sympathetic Tucker and Foster rather than from that in the sensational diary of the somewhat bumptious Fallon. McGlashan himself was not squeamish by nature, and he had seen his share of life in the raw. But it must be remembered that he was writing a narrative of the sufferings of the Donner party, and not a coroner's report.

One other characteristic of the book, its apparently over-sentimentalized view of life, can cause great distress to some readers, especially to the very young. The legend of pioneer life in the West is of course misleading and absurd in many ways. Restlessness may look from a distance like versatility when more often than not it may arise from mere hunger; impulsiveness may look like noble courage when it really arises from surface excitement; prodigality, in a land of free and easy enterprise, may look like generosity;

A survivor of the Donner Party, Patty Reed's doll. (Courtesy of Sutter's Fort Museum and Mr. Robert Handsaker, Sacramento, California)

and resignation may resemble sacrifice when it is often the purely physical slump of the tired body that can go on no longer.

It is permissible for one to challenge an arbitrary statement of human motives when one knows all of the facts. Yet McGlashan does not deny that there was much of the ungenerous and unheroic in the expedition of the Donner party. He freely admits that there was lack of foresight in the acceptance of Hastings' route, great folly in the banishment of Reed, selfishness in the extremities of starvation at Donner Lake, and dissension throughout. But the critical analysis of human motives becomes rather frivolous when applied to Dan'l Rhodes, who carried Naomi Pike over the Pass at a time when it was a case of every man for himself; or to Tamsen Donner, who certainly did have to choose between husband and children; or to the outcast Keseberg, who dug his child's body out of the snow. The historian Bancroft, perhaps the most impartial of all writers on the Donner party, made a comprehensive statement of the case:

Doubtless many committed errors of judgment, were moved by their trouble to do or say foolish things, or were driven in the insanity of starvation to petty acts of apparent cruelty and selfishness; but on the other hand, there were few, if any, who did not, on one occasion or another, show traits of heroic self-sacrifice. Most of them ate human flesh, and they did right; it was the necessity, not the act, that was deplorable. The emigrants acted as others would have done under like circumstances, though under a competent leader and with unity of purpose and action they might have escaped the worst of their misfortunes. I think McGlashan has done wisely in suppressing disagreeable details and dwelling on the noble deeds of each member.

A short time before he died, McGlashan systematically burned all papers and correspondence relating to the writing and publication of his book rather than risk presuming upon a friendship or violating a confidence. This holocaust of the author's files, regardless of the curiosities of manuscript that disappeared in it, was a significant epilogue to the publication of the *History*. McGlashan was much more than the mere historian of the Donner party: he was its confessor; and, as such, he was concerned with the harrowings of the spirit rather than with those of the flesh.

In this edition, reproduced photographically from a printing of the Second Edition made in 1881, notes and a bibliography have been supplied at the end of the text. The notes (with corresponding parenthetical numbers in margins of text) have been designed to supplement the text with factual information and to avoid, as far as possible, any discussion of controversial questions. The bibliography has been designed to aid the reader who seeks more detailed information. It has been arranged to show the important chronological relationship of the McGlashan text to other accounts written before and after the revival of public interest in the subject.

The tracing of main emigrant routes is based upon well-established data on numerous early maps. The dating in the legends on the map "Route of the Donner Party from Fort Bridger to Donner Lake" (on page xx) follows wherever possible that of McGlashan; when McGlashan fails to give a date, it follows that of Thornton. The location of the Alder Creek camp, that of "Starved Camp," and that of "Camp of Death," and the route of the snowshoe party from Cisco Butte to Johnson's Ranch are conjectural, the last being based upon the careful study of the subject made by George Stewart (*Ordeal by Hunger*, pp. 122–50 and 316 n.).

The editors wish to express their gratitude for the invaluable assistance and co-operation extended to them during the preparation of this edition by the staffs of the following libraries: The California State Library at Sacramento; the Bancroft Library at the University of California; the Huntington Library at San Marino; the Nevada State Library at Carson City, Nevada; and the Public Library at Reno, Nevada. They also wish to thank Mr. Carroll Hall, Curator of the Sutter's Fort Historical Museum, for permission to cite passages from the important Milt Elliott diary and to produce a photograph of the Reed doll; and Mr. and Mrs. George H. Tucker of Burlingame for their generous loan of the rare McGlashan-Tucker letter.

G. H. H.
B. McG. H.

THE SECOND (1881) EDITION OF McGLASHAN'S "HISTORY OF THE DONNER PARTY" REPRODUCED COMPLETE BY PHOTOLITHOGRAPHY ON THE FOLLOWING PAGES (1–261)

DONNER LAKE.

(From a Photograph by H. K. Gage, June 12, 1879.)

# HISTORY

## OF THE

# DONNER PARTY.

---

## A Tragedy of the Sierra.

---

By C. F. McGlashan,
PUBLISHER " PRESS," SANTA BARBARA, CAL.

---

FOURTH EDITION—ILLUSTRATED.

SAN FRANCISCO:
A. L. BANCROFT & COMPANY, PRINTERS.
1881.

TO

MRS. ELIZABETH A. KEISER,

ONE OF THE

PIONEER MOTHERS OF CALIFORNIA,

THIS BOOK

IS

RESPECTFULLY DEDICATED BY THE AUTHOR.

# PREFACE.

—

THE delirium preceding death by starvation, is full of strange phantasies. Visions of plenty, of comfort, of elegance, flit ever before the fast-dimming eyes. The final twilight of death is a brief semi-consciousness in which the dying one frequently repeats his weird dreams. Half rising from his snowy couch, pointing upward, one of the death-stricken at Donner Lake may have said, with tremulous voice: "Look! there, just above us, is a beautiful house. It is of costliest walnut, inlaid with laurel and ebony, and is resplendent with burnished silver. Magnificent in all its apartments, it is furnished like a palace. It is rich with costly cushions, elegant tapestries, dazzling mirrors; its floor is covered with Oriental carpets, its ceiling with artistic frescoings; downy cushions invite the weary to repose. It is filled with people who are chatting, laughing, and singing, joyous and care-free. There is an abundance of warmth, and rare viands, and sparkling wines. Suspended among the storm-clouds, it is flying along the face of the precipice at a marvelous speed. Flying? no! it has wheels and is gliding along on a smooth, steel pathway. It is sheltered from the wind and snow by large beams and huge posts, which are bolted to the cliffs with heavy, iron rods. The avalanches, with their burden of earth and rocks and crushed pines, sweep harmlessly above this beautiful house and its happy inmates. It is drawn by neither oxen nor horses, but by a fiery, hot-breathed monster, with iron limbs and thews of steel. The mountain trembles beneath his tread, and the rocks for miles re-echo his roar."

If such a vision was related, it but indicates, prophetically, the progress of a few years. California's history is replete with tragic, startling events. These events are the landmarks by which its advancement is traced. One of the most mournful of these is recorded in this work—a work intended as a contribution, not to the literature, but to the history of the State. More thrilling than romance, more terrible than fiction, the sufferings of the Donner Party form a bold contrast to the joys of pleasure-seekers who to-day look down upon the lake from the windows of silver palace cars.

The scenes of horror and despair which transpired in the snowy Sierra in the winter of 1846-7, need no exaggeration, no embellishment. From all the works heretofore published, from over one thousand letters received from the survivors, from ample manuscript, and from personal interviews with the most important actors in the tragedy, the facts have been carefully compiled. Neither time, pains, nor expense have been spared in ferreting out the truth. New and fragmentary versions of the sad story have appeared almost every year since the unfortunate occurrence. To forever supplant these distorted and fabulous reports—which have usually been sensational newspaper articles—the survivors have deemed it wise to contribute the truth. The truth is sufficiently terrible.

Where conflicting accounts of particular scenes or occurrences have been contributed, every effort has been made to render them harmonious and reconcilable. With justice, with impartiality, and with strict adherence to what appeared truthful and reliable, the book has been written. It is an honest effort toward the truth, and as such is given to the world.

C. F. McGLASHAN.

Truckee, Cal., June 30, 1879.

# CONTENTS.

## CHAPTER XVI.

## CHAPTER XVII.

## CHAPTER XVIII.

## CHAPTER XIX.

## CHAPTER XXIV.

# LIST OF ILLUSTRATIONS.

# CHAPTER I.

THREE miles from Truckee, Nevada County, California, lies one of the fairest and most picturesque lakes in all the Sierra. Above, and on either side, are lofty mountains, with castellated granite crests, while below, at the mouth of the lake, a grassy, meadowy valley widens out and extends almost to Truckee. The body of water is three miles long, one and a half miles wide, and four hundred and eighty-three feet in depth.

Tourists and picnic parties annually flock to its shores, and Bierstadt has made it the subject of one of his finest, grandest paintings. In summer, its willowy thickets, its groves of tamarack and forests of pine, are the favorite haunts and nesting places of the quail and grouse. Beautiful, speckled mountain trout plentifully abound in its crystalline waters. A rippling breeze usually wimples and dimples its laughing surface, but in calmer moods it reflects, as in a polished mirror, the lofty,

overhanging mountains, with every stately pine, bounding
rivulet, blossoming shrub, waving fern, and—high above all,
on the right—the clinging, thread-like line of the snow-sheds
of the Central Pacific.   When the railroad was being constructed, three thousand people dwelt on its shores; the surrounding forests resounded with the music of axes and saws,
and the terrific blasts exploded in the lofty, o'ershadowing
cliffs, filled the canyons with reverberating thunders, and
hurled huge bowlders high in the air over the lake's quivering bosom.

In winter it is almost as popular a pleasure resort as during the summer.   The jingling of sleighbells, and the shouts
and laughter of skating parties, can be heard almost constantly.   The lake forms the grandest skating park on the
Pacific Coast.

Yet this same Donner Lake was the scene of one of the
most thrilling, heart-rending tragedies ever recorded in California history.   Interwoven with the very name of the lake
are memories of a tale of destitution, loneliness, and despair,
which borders on the incredible.   It is a tale that has been
repeated in many a miner's cabin, by many a hunter's camp-
fire, and in many a frontiersman's home, and everywhere it
has been listened to with bated breath.

The pioneers of a new country are deserving of a niche in
the country's history.   The pioneers who became martyrs to
the cause of the development of an almost unknown land,
deserve to have a place in the hearts of its inhabitants.   The
far-famed Donner Party were, in a peculiar sense, pioneer
martyrs of California.   Before the discovery of gold, before
the highway across the continent was fairly marked out,
while untold dangers lurked by the wayside, and unnumbered
foes awaited the emigrants, the Donner Party started for California.   None but the brave and venturesome, none but the

ELIZA P. DONNER.

energetic and courageous, could undertake such a journey. In 1846, comparatively few had dared attempt to cross the almost unexplored plains which lay between the Mississippi and the fair young land called California. Hence it is that a certain grandeur, a certain heroism seems to cling about the men and women composing this party, even from the day they began their perilous journey across the plains. California, with her golden harvests, her beautiful homes, her dazzling wealth, and her marvelous commercial facilities, may well enshrine the memory of these noble-hearted pioneers, pathfinders, martyrs.

The States along the Mississippi were but sparsely settled in 1846, yet the fame of the fruitfulness, the healthfulness, and the almost tropical beauty of the land bordering the Pacific, tempted the members of the Donner Party to leave their homes. These homes were situated in Illinois, Iowa, Tennessee, Missouri, and Ohio. Families from each of these States joined the train and participated in its terrible fate; yet the party proper was organized in Sangamon County, Illinois, by George and Jacob Donner and James F. Reed. Early in April, 1846, the party set out from Springfield, Illinois, and by the first week in May reached Independence, Missouri. Here the party was increased by additional members, and the train comprised about one hundred persons.

Independence was on the frontier in those days, and every care was taken to have ample provisions laid in and all necessary preparations made for the long journey. Ay, it was a long journey for many in the party! Great as was the enthusiasm and eagerness with which these noble-hearted pioneers caught up the cry of the times, "Ho! for California!" it is doubtful if presentiments of the fate to be encountered were not occasionally entertained. The road was difficult, and in places almost unbroken; warlike Indians

2

guarded the way, and death, in a thousand forms, hovered about their march through the great wilderness.

In the party were aged fathers with their trusting families about them, mothers whose very lives were wrapped up in their children, men in the prime and vigor of manhood, maidens in all the sweetness and freshness of budding woman-hood, children full of glee and mirthfulness, and babes nest-ling on maternal breasts. Lovers there were, to whom the journey was tinged with rainbow hues of joy and happiness, and strong, manly hearts whose constant support and en-couragement was the memory of dear ones left behind in home-land. The cloud of gloom which finally settled down in a death-pall over their heads was not yet perceptible, though, as we shall soon see, its mists began to collect al-most at the outset, in the delays which marked the journey.

The wonderment which all experience in viewing the scenery along the line of the old emigrant road was pecul-iarly vivid to these people. Few descriptions had been given of the route, and all was novel and unexpected. In later years the road was broadly and deeply marked, and good camping grounds were distinctly indicated. The bleaching bones of cattle that had perished, or the broken fragments of wagons or cast-away articles, were thickly strewn on either side of the highway. But in 1846 the way was through al-most trackless valleys waving with grass, along rivers where few paths were visible, save those made by the feet of buf-faloes and antelope, and over mountains and plains where little more than the westward course of the sun guided the travelers. Trading-posts were stationed at only a few widely distant points, and rarely did the party meet with any human beings, save wandering bands of Indians. Yet these first days are spoken of by all of the survivors as being crowned with peaceful enjoyment and pleasant anticipations. There were beautiful flowers by the roadside, an abundance of game in the meadows and mountains, and at night there were singing, dancing, and innocent plays. Several musical instruments, and many excellent voices, were in the party, and the kindliest feeling and good-fellowship prevailed among the members.

The formation of the company known as the Donner Party was purely accidental. The union of so many emigrants into one train was not occasioned by any preconcerted arrangement. Many composing the Donner Party were not aware, at the outset, that such a tide of emigration was sweeping to California. In many instances small parties would hear of the mammoth train just ahead of them or just behind them, and by hastening their pace, or halting for a few days, joined themselves to the party. Many were with the train during a portion of the journey, but from some cause or other became parted from the Donner company before reaching Donner Lake. Soon after the train left Independence it contained between two and three hundred wagons, and when in motion was two miles in length.

With much bitterness and severity it is alleged by some of the survivors of the dreadful tragedy that certain impostors and falsifiers claim to have been members of the Donner Party, and as such have written untruthful and exaggerated accounts of the sufferings of the party. While this is unquestionably true, it is barely possible that some who assert membership found their claim upon the fact that during a portion of the journey they were really in the Donner Party. Bearing this in mind, there is less difficulty in reconciling the conflicting statements of different narrators.

The members of the party proper numbered ninety, and were as follows:

George Donner, Tamsen Donner (his wife), Elitha C. Donner, Leanna C. Donner, Frances E. Donner, Georgia A. Donner and Eliza P. Donner. The last three were children of George and Tamsen Donner; Elitha and Leanna were children of George Donner by a former wife.

Jacob Donner, Elizabeth Donner (his wife), Solomon Hook, William Hook, George Donner, Jr., Mary M. Donner, Isaac Donner, Lewis Donner and Samuel Donner. Jacob Donner was a brother of George; Solomon and William Hook were sons of Elizabeth Donner by a former husband.

James Frazier Reed, Margaret W. Reed (his wife), Virginia E. Reed, Martha F. (Patty) Reed, James F. Reed, Jr., Thomas K. Reed, and Mrs. Sarah Keyes, the mother of Mrs. Reed.

The two Donner families and the Reeds were from Springfield, Illinois. From the same place were Baylis Williams and his half-sister Eliza Williams, John Denton, Milton Elliott, James Smith, Walter Herron and Noah James.

From Marshall County, Illinois, came Franklin Ward Graves, Elizabeth Graves (his wife), Mary A. Graves, William C. Graves, Eleanor Graves, Lovina Graves, Nancy Graves, Jonathan B. Graves, F. W. Graves, Jr., Elizabeth Graves, Jr., Jay Fosdick and Mrs. Sarah Fosdick (*née* Graves). With this family came John Snyder.

From Keokuk, Lee County, Iowa, came Patrick Breen, Mrs. Margaret Breen, John Breen, Edward J. Breen, Patrick Breen, Jr., Simon P. Breen, James F. Breen, Peter Breen, and Isabella M. Breen. Patrick Dolan also came from Keokuk.

William H. Eddy, Mrs. Eleanor Eddy, James P. Eddy, and Margaret Eddy came from Belleville, Illinois.

From Tennessee came Mrs. Lavina Murphy, a widow, and her family, John Landrum Murphy, Mary M. Murphy, Lemuel B. Murphy, William G. Murphy, Simon P. Murphy, William M. Pike, Mrs. Harriet F. Pike (*née* Murphy), Naomi

GEORGIA A. DONNER

(Mrs. W. A. Babcock.)

1879.

L. Pike, and Catherine Pike. Another son-in-law of Mrs. Murphy, William M. Foster, with his wife, Mrs. Sarah A. C. Foster, and infant boy George Foster, came from St. Louis, Missouri.

William McCutchen, Mrs. W. McCutchen, and Harriet McCutchen were from Jackson County, Missouri.

Lewis Keseberg, Mrs. Phillipine Keseberg, Ada Keseberg, and L. Keseberg, Jr., Mr. and Mrs. Wolfinger, Joseph Rhinehart, Augustus Spitzer, and Charles Burger, came from Germany.

Samuel Shoemaker came from Springfield, Ohio, Charles T. Stanton from Chicago, Illinois, Luke Halloran from St. Joseph, Missouri, Mr. Hardcoop from Antwerp, in Belgium, Antoine from New Mexico. John Baptiste was a Spaniard, who joined the train near the Santa Fé trail, and Lewis and Salvador were two Indians, who were sent out from California by Captain Sutter.

The Breens joined the company at Independence, Missouri, and the Graves family overtook the train one hundred miles west of Fort Bridger. Each family, prior to its consolidation with the train, had its individual incidents. William Trimble, who was traveling with the Graves family, was slain by the Pawnee Indians about fifty miles east of Scott's Bluff. Trimble left a wife and two or three children. The wife and some of her relatives were so disheartened by this sad bereavement, and by the fact that many of their cattle were stolen by the Indians, that they gave up the journey to California, and turned back to the homes whence they had started.

An amusing incident is related in the Healdsburg (Cal.) Flag, by Mr. W. C. Graves, of Calistoga, which occurred soon after his party left St. Joseph, Missouri. It was on the fourth night out, and Mr. Graves and four or five others were detailed to stand guard. The constant terror of the emigrants in those days was Indians.  Both the Pawnees, the Sioux, and the Snakes were warlike and powerful, and were jealous, revengeful, and merciless toward the whites.  That night a fire somehow started in the prairie grass about half a mile from camp.  The west wind, blowing fierce and strong, carried the flames in great surging gusts through the tall prairie grass.  A resin weed grows in bunches in this part of the country, generally attaining the height of four or five feet. The night being very dark, these weeds could be seen standing between the fire and the guards.  As the flames swayed past the weeds, the impression was very naturally produced upon the mind of a timid beholder that the weeds were moving in the opposite direction.  This optical illusion caused some of the guards to believe that the Indians had set fire to the grass, and were moving in immense numbers between them and the fire with intent to surround them, stampede the cattle, and massacre the entire party.  The watcher next to Mr. Graves discovered the enemy, and rushed breathlessly to his comrade to impart the intelligence.  Scarcely had Mr. Graves quieted him before it was evident that a general alarm had been spread in the camp.  Two other guards had seen the Indians, and the aroused camp, armed to the teeth, marched out to give battle to the imaginary foe.  It was a rich joke, and it was some time before those who were scared heard the last of the resin Indians.

Only once, before reaching Salt Lake, did death invade the joyous Donner company.  It was near the present site of Manhattan, Kansas, and Mrs. Sarah Keyes was the victim. This estimable lady was the mother of Mrs. J. F. Reed, and had reached her four score and ten years.  Her aged frame and feeble health were not equal to the fatigues and exposure of the trip, and on the thirtieth of May they laid her tenderly to rest.  She was buried in a coffin carefully fashioned from

the trunk of a cottonwood tree, and on the brow of a beautiful knoll overlooking the valley. A grand old oak, still
standing, guards the lonely grave of the dear old mother who
was spared the sight of the misery in store for her loved ones.
Could those who performed the last sad rites have caught a
vision of the horrors awaiting the party, they would have
known how good was the God who in mercy took her to
Himself.

# CHAPTER II.

PRESENTING, as they do, an interesting glimpse of
the first portion of the journey, the following letters
are here introduced. They were written by Mrs.
Tamsen Donner, and were published in the Springfield (Illinois) Journal. Thanks for copies of these
letters are due to Mrs. Eliza P. Houghton of San Jose, Mrs.
Donner's youngest daughter. Allusions are made in these
letters to botanical researches. Mrs. Donner, C. T. Stanton,
and perhaps one or two others who were prominent actors
in the later history, were particularly fond of botany. Mrs.
Donner made valuable collections of rare flowers and plants.
Her journal, and a full description of the contents of her
botanical portfolios, were to have been published upon her
arrival in California.

Though bearing the same date, the letters here presented
were written at different times. The following appeared in
the Springfield Journal, July 23, 1846:

Near the Junction of the North }
and South Platte, June 16, 1846. }

My Old Friend: We are now on the Platte, two hundred miles from Fort Laramie. Our journey so far has been pleasant, the roads have been good, and food plentiful. The water for part of the way has been indifferent, but at no time have our cattle suffered for it. Wood is now very scarce, but "buffalo chips" are excellent; they kindle quickly and retain heat surprisingly. We had this morning buffalo steaks broiled upon them that had the same flavor they would have had upon hickory coals.

We feel no fear of Indians, our cattle graze quietly around our encampment unmolested.

Two or three men will go hunting twenty miles from camp; and last night two of our men lay out in the wilderness rather than ride their horses after a hard chase.

Indeed, if I do not experience something far worse than I have yet done, I shall say the trouble is all in getting started. Our wagons have not needed much repair, and I can not yet tell in what respects they could be improved. Certain it is, they can not be too strong. Our preparations for the journey might have been in some respects bettered.

Bread has been the principal article of food in our camp. We laid in 150 pounds of flour and 75 pounds of meat for each individual, and I fear bread will be scarce. Meat is abundant. Rice and beans are good articles on the road; cornmeal, too, is acceptable. Linsey dresses are the most suitable for children. Indeed, if I had one, it would be acceptable. There is so cool a breeze at all times on the plains that the sun does not feel so hot as one would suppose.

We are now four hundred and fifty miles from Independence. Our route at first was rough, and through a timbered country, which appeared to be fertile. After striking the prairie, we found a first-rate road, and the only difficulty we have had, has been in crossing the creeks. In that, however, there has been no danger.

I never could have believed we could have traveled so far with so little difficulty. The prairie between the Blue and the Platte rivers is beautiful beyond description. Never have I seen so varied a country, so suitable for cultivation. Everything was new and pleasing; the Indians frequently come to see us, and the chiefs of a tribe breakfasted at our tent this morning. All are so friendly that I can not help feeling sympathy and friendship for them. But on one sheet what can I say?

Since we have been on the Platte, we have had the river on one side and the ever varying mounds on the other, and have traveled through the bottom lands from one to two miles wide, with little or no timber. The soil is sandy, and last year, on account of the dry season, the emigrants found grass here scarce. Our cattle are in good order, and when proper care has been taken, none have been lost. Our milch cows have been of great service, indeed. They have been of more advantage than our meat. We have plenty of butter and milk.

We are commanded by Captain Russell, an amiable man. George Donner is himself yet. He crows in the morning and shouts out, "Chain up, boys—chain up," with as much authority as though he was "something in particular." John Denton is still with us. We find him useful in the camp. Hiram Miller and Noah James are in good health and doing well. We have of the best people in our company, and some, too, that are not so good.

Buffaloes show themselves frequently.

We have found the wild tulip, the primrose, the lupine, the eardrop, the larkspur, and creeping hollyhock, and a beautiful flower resembling the bloom of the beech tree, but in bunches as large as a small sugar-loaf, and of every variety of shade, to red and green.

I botanize, and read some, but cook "heaps" more. There are four hundred and twenty wagons, as far as we have heard, on the road between here and Oregon and California.

Give our love to all inquiring friends. God bless them.

Yours, truly,<br>Mrs. George Donner.

The following letter was published in the Journal of July 30, 1846:

South Fork of the Nebraska,<br>Ten Miles from the Crossing,<br>Tuesday, June 16, 1846.

Dear Friend: To-day, at nooning, there passed, going to the States, seven men from Oregon, who went out last year. One of them was well acquainted with Messrs. Ide and Cadden Keyes, the latter of whom, he says, went to California. They met the advance Oregon caravan about 150 miles west of Fort Laramie, and counted in all, for Oregon and California (excepting ours), 478 wagons. There are in our company over 40 wagons, making 518 in all, and there are said to be yet 20 behind. To-morrow we cross the river, and, by reckoning, will be over 200 miles from Fort Laramie, where we intend to stop and repair our wagon wheels. They are nearly all loose, and I am afraid we will have to stop sooner, if there can be found wood suitable to heat the tires. There is no wood here, and our women and children are out now gathering "buffalo chips" to burn, in order to do the cooking. These chips burn well.

Mrs. George Donner.

At Fort Laramie a portion of the Donner Party celebrated the Fourth of July, 1846. Arriving there on the evening of the third, they pitched camp somewhat earlier than usual, and prepared a grand dinner for the Fourth. At the Fort were a large party of Sioux who were on the war-path against the Snakes or Pawnees. The Sioux were, perhaps, the most warlike Indian nation on the great prairies, and when dressed in their war paint and mounted on their fleet ponies, presented a truly imposing appearance. The utmost friendliness prevailed, and there was a mutual interchange of gifts and genial courtesies. When the Donner Party pursued their march, and had journeyed half a day from the Fort, they were overtaken and convoyed quite a distance by about three hundred young warriors. The escort rode in pairs alongside the train in true military fashion. Finally halting, they opened ranks, and as the wagons passed, each warrior held in his mouth a green twig or leaf, which was said to be emblematic of peacefulness and good feeling.

The train was never seriously molested by the Sioux. On one occasion, about fifty warriors on horseback surrounded a portion of the train, in which was the Graves family. While generally friendly, a few of the baser sort persisted in attempting to steal, or take by force, trivial articles which struck their fancy. The main body of Indians were encamped about half a mile away, and when the annoyances became too exasperating, W. C. Graves mounted a horse, rode to the encampment, and notified the Chief of the action of his followers. Seizing an old-fashioned single-barreled shotgun, the Chief sprang upon his horse and fairly flew over the plain toward the emigrant wagons. When within about a hundred yards of the train he attracted attention by giving an Indian whoop, which was so full of rage and imprecation that the startled warriors forthwith desisted from their petty persecutions and scattered in every direction like frightened quail. One of the would-be marauders was a little tardy in mounting his pony, and as soon as the Chief got within range, the shotgun was leveled and discharged full at the unruly subject. Three of the buckshot entered the pony's side and one grazed the warrior's leg. As if satisfied that his orders to treat the emigrants in a friendly manner would not be again disregarded, the Chief wheeled his horse about, and in the most grave and stately manner rode back to his encampment.

On another occasion, Mary Graves, who was a very beautiful young lady, was riding on horseback accompanied by her brother. They were a little in the rear of the train, and a band of Sioux Indians, becoming enamored with the maiden, offered to purchase her. They made very handsome offers, but the brother not being disposed to accept, one of the Indians seized the bridle of the girl's horse and attempted to carry her away captive. Perhaps the attempt was made in half jest. At all events the bridle was promptly dropped when the brother leveled his rifle at the savage.

On the twentieth of July, 1846, George Donner was elected Captain of the train at the Little Sandy River. From that time forward it was known as the Donner Party.

One incident, not at all unusual to a trip across the plains, is pointedly described in a letter written by C. T. Stanton to his brother, Sidney Stanton, now of Cazenovia, New York. The incident alluded to is the unfriendliness and want of harmony so liable to exist between different companies, and between members of the same company. From one of Mr. Stanton's letters the following extract is made:

"At noon we passed Boggs' company on the Sweetwater; a mile further up the river, Dunlavy's; a mile further, West's; and about two miles beyond that, was Dunbar's. We encamped about half way between the two latter. Thus, within five miles were encamped five companies. At Indian

Creek, twenty miles from Independence, these five companies all constituted one, but owing to dissensions and quarreling they became broken into fragments. Now, by accident, we all again once more meet and grasp the cordial hand; old enmities are forgot, and nothing but good feeling prevails. * * * * * The next morning we got rather a late start, owing to a difference of opinion arising in our company as to whether we should lie by or go ahead. Those wishing to lie by were principally young men who wished to have a day's hunting among the buffaloes, and there were also a few families out of meat who wished to lay in a supply before they left the buffalo country. A further reason was urged that the cattle were nearly fagged out by hard travel, and that they would not stand the journey unless we stopped and gave them rest. On the other side it was contended that if we stopped here the other companies would all get ahead, the grass would all be eaten off by their thousand head of cattle, and that consequently, when we came along, our cattle would starve. The go-ahead party finally ruled and we rolled out."

As will presently be seen, the dissension existing in the company, and the petty differences of opinion and interest, were the fundamental causes of the calamities which befell the Donner Party.

When the company was near Fort Bridger, Edward Breen's leg was broken by a fall from a horse. His mother refused to permit amputation, or rather left the question to Edward's decision, and of course, boy-like, he refused to have the operation performed. Contrary to expectation, the bone knitted, and in a month he walked without a crutch.

At Fort Bridger, which was at this time a mere camp or trading post, the party heard much commendation bestowed upon a new route via Salt Lake. This route passed along the southern shore of the Lake, and rejoined the old Fort Hall emigrant road on the Humboldt. It was said to shorten the distance three hundred miles. The new route was known as the Hastings Cut-off, and was named after the famous Lansford W. Hastings, who was even then piloting a small company over the cut-off. The large trains delayed for three or four days at Fort Bridger, debating as to the best course to pursue. It is claimed that but for the earnest advice and solicitation of Bridger and Vasquez, who had charge of the fort, the entire party would have continued by the accustomed route. These men had a direct interest in the Hastings Cut-off, as they furnished the emigrants with supplies, and had employed Hastings to pilot the first company over the road to Salt Lake.

After mature deliberation, the party divided, the greater portion going by Fort Hall and reaching California in safety. With the large train, which journeyed the old road, this narrative is no longer interested. Eighty-seven persons, however, took the Hastings Cut-off. Their names are included in the ninety mentioned in the preceding chapter, it being remembered that Mrs. Sarah Keyes had died, and that Lewis and Salvador were not yet members of the party. For several days the party traveled without much difficulty. They reached Weber River near the head of the well-known Weber Canyon. At the first crossing of this river, on the third of August, they found a letter from Hastings stuck in the split of a stick, informing them that the road down the Weber Canyon was in a terrible condition, and that it was doubtful if the sixty-six wagons which L. W. Hastings was then piloting through the canyon would ever succeed in reaching the plain. In the letter, Hastings advised all emigrants to avoid the canyon road, and pursue over the mountains a course which he faintly outlined. In order to obtain further information,

and, if possible, to induce Hastings to return and act as
(2) guide, Messrs. Reed, Stanton, and Pike were sent forward to
overtake the advance company.   This was accomplished after
a fatiguing trip, which so exhausted the horses of Stanton
and Pike that these gentlemen were unable to return to the
Donner Party.   Hastings was overtaken at a point near the
southern end of Great Salt Lake, and came back with Reed
to the foot of the bluffs overlooking the present city of Salt
Lake.   Here he declared that he must return to the company
he was piloting, and despite the urgent entreaties of Reed,
decided that it was his duty to start back the next morning.
He finally consented, however, to ascend to the summit of
the Wahsatch Mountains, from which he endeavored, as best
he could, to point out the direction in which the wagons
must travel from the head of Weber Canyon.   Reed proceeded alone on the route indicated, taking notes of the
country and occasionally blazing trees to assist him in re-
tracing the course.

Wm. G. Murphy (now of Marysville, Cal.) says that the wagons remained in the meadows at the head of Weber Canyon
until Reed's return.   They then learned that the train which
preceded them had been compelled to travel very slowly down
the Weber River, filling in many irregular places with brush
and dirt; that at last they had reached a place where vast
perpendicular pillars of rock approached so closely on either
side that the river had barely space to flow between, and just
here the water plunged over a precipice.   To lower the wagons down this precipice had been a dreadful task.

The Donner Party unanimously decided to travel across
the mountains in a more direct line toward Salt Lake.   They
soon found rolling highlands and small summit valleys on
the divide between Weber River and Salt Lake.   Following
down one of the small streams, they found a varying, irregu-

lar canyon, down which they passed, filling its small stream with brush and rocks, crossing and recrossing it, making roads, breaking and mending wagons, until three weeks' time had expired. The entire country was heavily covered with timber and underbrush. When the party arrived at the outlet of this stream into Salt Lake Valley, they found it utterly impassable. It was exceedingly narrow, and was filled with huge rocks from the cliffs on either side. Almost all the oxen in the train were necessary in drawing each wagon out of the canyon and up the steep overhanging mountain. While in this canyon, Stanton and Pike came up to the company. These gentlemen encountered great hardships after their horses gave out, and were almost starved to death when they reached the train.

Instead of reaching Salt Lake in a week, as had been promised, the party were over thirty days in making the trip. No words can describe what they endured on this Hastings Cut-off. The terrible delay was rendering imminent the dangers which awaited them on the Sierra Nevada. At last, upon ascending the steep rugged mountain before mentioned, the vision of Great Salt Lake, and the extensive plains surrounding it, burst upon their enraptured gaze. All were wild with joy and gratitude for their deliverance from the terrible struggle through which they had just passed, and all hoped for a prosperous, peaceful journey over pleasant roads throughout the remainder of the trip to California. Alas! there were trials in the way compared with which their recent struggles were insignificant. But for the fatal delay caused by the Hastings Cut-off, all would have been well, but now the summer was passed, their teams and themselves were well-nigh exhausted, and their slender stock of provisions nearly consumed.

3

# CHAPTER III.

NEAR the southern shore of great Salt Lake the Donner Party encamped on the third or fourth of September, 1846. The summer had vanished, and autumn
had commenced tinting, with crimson and gold, the
foliage on the Wahsatch Mountains. While encamped here, the party buried the second victim claimed by
death. This time it was a poor consumptive named Luke Halloran. Without friend or kinsman, Halloran had joined the
train, and was traveling to California in hopes that a change
of climate might effect a cure. Alas! for the poor Irishman,
when the leaves began to fall from the trees his spirit winged
its flight to the better land. He died in the wagon of Captain George Donner, his head resting in Mrs. Tamsen Donner's lap. It was at sundown. The wagons had just halted
for the night. The train had driven up slowly, out of respect
to the dying emigrant. Looking up into Mrs. Donner's face,
he said: "I die happy." Almost while speaking, he died.
In return for the many kindnesses he had received during the

journey, he left Mr. Donner such property as he possessed,
including about fifteen hundred dollars in coin. Hon. Jas. F.
Breen, of South San Juan, writes: "Halloran's body was
buried in a bed of almost pure salt, beside the grave of one (3)
who had perished in the preceding train. It was said at the
time that bodies thus deposited would not decompose, on account of the preservative properties of the salt. Soon after
his burial, his trunk was opened, and Masonic papers and
regalia bore witness to the fact that Mr. Halloran was a member of the Masonic Order. James F. Reed, Milton Elliott,
and perhaps one or two others in the train, also belonged to
the mystic tie."

On the sixth day of September they reached a meadow in
a valley called "Twenty Wells," as there were that number of
wells of various sizes, from six inches to several feet in diam-
eter. The water in these wells rose even with the surface
of the ground, and when it was drawn out the wells soon re-
filled. The water was cold and pure, and peculiarly welcome
after the saline plains and alkaline pools they had just passed.
Wells similar to these were found during the entire journey
of the following day, and the country through which they
were passing abounded in luxuriant grass. Reaching the
confines of the Salt Lake Desert, which lies southwest of the
lake, they laid in, as they supposed, an ample supply of water
and grass. This desert had been represented by Bridger and
Vasquez as being only about fifty miles wide. Instead, for a
distance of seventy-five miles there was neither water nor
grass, but everywhere a dreary, desolate, alkaline waste.
Verily, it was

"A region of drought, where no river glides,
 Nor rippling brook with osiered sides;
 Where sedgy pool, nor bubbling fount,
 Nor tree, nor cloud, nor misty mount

Appears to refresh the aching eye,
But the barren earth and the burning sky,
And the blank horizon round and round
Spread, void of living sight or sound."

When the company had been on the desert two nights and one day, Mr. Reed volunteered to go forward, and, if possible, to discover water. His hired teamsters were attending to his teams and wagons during his absence. At a distance of perhaps twenty miles he found the desired water, and hastened to return to the train. Meantime there was intense suffering in the party. Cattle were giving out and lying down helplessly on the burning sand, or frenzied with thirst were straying away into the desert. Having made preparations for only fifty miles of desert, several persons came near perishing of thirst, and cattle were utterly powerless to draw the heavy wagons. Reed was gone some twenty hours. During this time his teamsters had done the wisest thing possible, unhitched the oxen and started to drive them ahead until water was reached. It was their intention, of course, to return and get the three wagons and the family, which they had necessarily abandoned on the desert. Reed passed his teamsters during the night, and hastened to the relief of his deserted family. One of his teamster's horses gave out before morning and lay down, and while the man's companions were attempting to raise him, the oxen, rendered unmanageable by their great thirst, disappeared in the desert. There were eighteen of these oxen. It is probable they scented water, and with the instincts of their nature started out to search for it. They never were found, and Reed and his family, consisting of nine persons, were left destitute in the midst of the desert, eight hundred miles from California. Near morning, entirely ignorant of the calamity which had befallen him in the loss of his cattle, he reached his family.

All day long they looked and waited in vain for the returning teamsters. All the rest of the company had driven ahead, and the majority had reached water. Toward night the situation grew desperate. The scanty supply of water left with the family was almost gone, and another day on the desert would mean death to all he held dear. Their only way left was to set out on foot. He took his youngest child in his arms, and the family started to walk the twenty miles. During this dreadful night some of the younger children became so exhausted that, regardless of scoldings or encouragements, they lay down on the bleak sands. Even rest, however, seemed denied the little sufferers, for a chilling wind began sweeping over the desert, and despite their weariness and anguish, they were forced to move forward. At one time during the night the horror of the situation was changed to intense fright. Through the darkness came a swift-rushing animal, which Reed soon recognized as one of his young steers. It was crazed and frenzied with thirst, and for some moments seemed bent upon dashing into the frightened group. Finally, however, it plunged madly away into the night, and was seen no more. Reed suspected the calamity which had prevented the return of the teamsters, but at the moment, the imminent peril surrounding his wife and children banished all thought of worrying about anything but their present situation. God knows what would have become of them had they not, soon after daylight, discovered the wagon of Jacob Donner. They were received kindly by his family, and conveyed to where the other members of the party were camped. For six or eight days the entire company remained at this spot. Every effort was made to find Reed's lost cattle. Almost every man in the train was out in the desert, searching in all directions. This task was attended with both difficulty and danger; for when the sun

shone, the atmosphere appeared to distort and magnify objects so that at the distance of a mile every stone or bush
would appear the size of an ox. Several of the men came
near dying for want of water during this search. The desert
mirage disclosed against the horizon, clear, distinct, and perfectly outlined rocks, mountain peaks, and tempting lakelets.
Each jagged cliff, or pointed rock, or sharply-curved hill-top,
hung suspended in air as perfect and complete as if photographed on the sky. Deceived, deluded by these mirages,
in spite of their better judgment, several members of the
company were led far out into the pathless depths of the
desert.

The outlook for Reed was gloomy enough. One cow and
one ox were the only stock he had remaining. The company were getting exceedingly impatient over the long delay,
yet be it said to their honor, they encamped on the western
verge of the desert until every hope of finding Reed's cattle
was abandoned. Finally, F. W. Graves and Patrick Breen
each lent an ox to Mr. Reed, and by yoking up his remaining cow and ox, he had two yoke of cattle. "Cacheing," or
concealing such of his property on the desert, as could not
be placed in one wagon, he hitched the two yoke of cattle to
(4) this wagon and proceeded on the journey. The word cache
occurs so frequently in this history that a brief definition of
the interesting process of cacheing might not be amiss. The
cache of goods or valuables was generally made in a wagon
bed, if one, as in the present instance, was to be abandoned.
A square hole, say six feet in depth, was dug in the earth,
and in the bottom of this the box or wagon bed containing
the articles was placed. Sand, soil, or clay of the proper
stratum was filled in upon this, so as to just cover the box
from sight. The ground was then tightly packed or tram-
pled, to make it resemble, as much as possible, the earth in its

natural state. Into the remaining hole would be placed such useless articles as could be spared, such as old tins, cast-off clothing, broken furniture, etc., and upon these the earth was thrown until the surface of the ground was again level. These precautions were taken to prevent the Indians from discovering and appropriating the articles cached. It was argued that the Indians, when digging down, would come to the useless articles, and not thinking there was treasure further down would abandon the task. "But," says Hon. James F. Breen, in speaking on this subject, "I have been told by parties who have crossed the plains, that in no case has the Indian been deceived by the emigrant's silent logic." The Indians would leave nothing underground, not even the dead bodies buried from time to time. One of the trains in advance of the Donner Party buried two men in one grave, and succeeding parties found each of the bodies unearthed, and were compelled to repeat the last sad rites of burial.

Before the Donner Party started from the Desert camp, an inventory of the provisions on hand was accurately taken, and an estimate was made of the quantity required for each family, and it was found that there was not enough to carry the emigrants through to California. As if to render more emphatic the terrible situation of the party, a storm came during their last night at the camp, and in the morning the hill-tops were white with snow. It was a dreadful reminder of the lateness of the season, and the bravest hearts quailed before the horrors they knew must await them. A solemn council was held. It was decided that some one must leave the train, press eagerly forward to California, and obtaining a supply of provisions, return and meet the party as far back on the route as possible. It was a difficult undertaking, and perilous in the extreme. A call was made for volunteers, and after a little reflection two men offered their services. One was Wm. McCutchen, who had joined the train from Missouri, and the other was C. T. Stanton, of Chicago, a man who afterwards proved himself possessed of the sublimest heroism. Taking each a horse, they received the tearful, prayerful farewells of the doomed company, and set out upon their solitary journey.

Would they return? If they reached the peaceful, golden valleys of California, would they turn back to meet danger, and storms, and death, in order to bring succor to those on the dreary desert? McCutchen might come, because he left dear ones with the train, but would Stanton return? Stanton was young and unmarried. There were no ties or obligations to prompt his return, save his plighted word and the
(5) dictates of honor and humanity.

They bore letters from the Donner Party to Captain Sutter, who was in charge at Sutter's Fort. These letters were prayers for relief, and it was believed would secure assistance from the generous old Captain. Every eye followed Stanton and McCutchen until they disappeared in the west. Soon afterward the train resumed its toilsome march.

# CHAPTER IV.

GRAVELLY FORD, on the Humboldt River, witnessed a tragedy which greatly agitated the com- (6)
pany. Its results, as will be seen, materially affected
the lives not only of the participants, but of several
members of the party during the days of horror on
the mountains, by bringing relief which would otherwise
have been lacking. The parties to the tragedy were James
F. Reed and John Snyder. Reed was a man who was
tender, generous, heroic, and whose qualities of true nobility
shone brilliantly throughout a long life of usefulness. His
name is intimately interwoven with the history of the Donner Party, from first to last. Indeed, in the Illinois papers of
1846–7 the company was always termed the "Reed and
Donner Party." This title was justly conferred at the time,
because he was one of the leading spirits in the organization
of the enterprise. In order to understand the tragedy which
produced the death of John Snyder, and the circumstances

resulting therefrom, the reader must become better acquainted with the character of Mr. Reed.

The following brief extract is from " Powers' Early Settlers of Sangamon County:" "James Frazier Reed was born November 14, 1800, in County Armagh, Ireland. His ancestors were of noble Polish birth, who chose exile rather than submission to the Russian power, and settled in the north of Ireland. The family name was originally Reednoski, but in process of time the Polish termination of the name was dropped, and the family was called Reed. James F. Reed's mother's name was Frazier, whose ancestors belonged to Clan Frazier, of Scottish history. Mrs. Reed and her son, James F., came to America when he was a youth, and settled in Virginia. He remained there until he was twenty, when he left for the lead mines of Illinois, and was engaged in mining until 1831, when he came to Springfield, Sangamon County, Illinois."

Among the papers of Mr. Reed is a copy of the muster roll of a company which enlisted in the Blackhawk war, and in this roll are the names of Abraham Lincoln, Stephen A. Douglas, and James F. Reed. At the termination of this war, Mr. Reed returned to Springfield, engaged in the manufacture of cabinet furniture, and amassed a considerable fortune. He was married in 1835 to Mrs. Margaret Backenstoe, whose maiden name was Keyes. The death of his wife's mother, Mrs. Sarah Keyes, has already been mentioned as occurring on the Big Blue River, near Manhattan, Kansas.

During the progress of the train, Mr. Reed was always a prominent, active member. Full of life and enthusiasm, fearless of danger, he was ready at all times to risk his life for the company's welfare. On the desert, we have seen that his lonely expedition in search of water cost him his valuable oxen, and left him and his family almost destitute.

The deplorable affair about to be narrated was only the natural outgrowth of the trying circumstances in which the company were placed. The reader must bear in mind that many petty causes combined to produce discord and dissension among the members of the Donner Party. Coming from so many different States, being of different nationalities and modes of thought, delayed on the road much longer than was expected, rendered irritable by the difficulties encountered on the journey, annoyed by losses of stock, fearful of unknown disasters on the Sierra, and already placed on short allowances of provisions, the emigrants were decidedly inharmonious.

The action of the company, moreover, was doubtless influenced in a greater or less degree by Snyder's popularity. A young man, not over twenty-three years old, he was tall, straight, and of erect, manly carriage, and his habits of life as a frontiersman had developed him into a muscular, athletic being. He excelled and led in all the out-door sports most in favor with Western men, such as jumping, running, and wrestling. His manner was gentle, retired, and timid to a degree verging on bashfulness, until roused by the influence of passion. The lion in the man was dormant until evoked by the fiercer emotions. His complexion was dark, but as you studied his face you could not repress the suspicion that Nature had marked him for a blonde, and that constant exposure to the wind and sun and rain of the great plains of the West had wrought the color change, and the conviction was strong that the change was an improvement on Nature. His features were cast in a mold of great beauty — such beauty as we seldom look for in a man. He was never moody, despondent, or cast down, and at all times, and under all circumstances, possessed the faculty of amusing himself and entertaining others. In the evening camp, when other amusements failed, or when anticipated troubles depressed the spirits of the travelers, it was his custom to remove the "hindgate" of his wagon, lay it on the ground, and thereon perform the "clog dance," "Irish jigs," the "pigeon wing," and other fantastic steps. Many an evening the Donner Party were prevented from brooding over their troubles by the boyish antics of the light-hearted youth.

(7)      As stated above, the train had reached Gravelly Ford. Already the members of the company were beginning to scan eagerly the western plain in hopes of discovering the relief which it was believed Stanton and McCutchen would bring from Sutter's Fort. Of course there were the usual accidents and incidents peculiar to a journey across the plains. Occasionally a wagon would need repairing. Occasionally there would be a brief halt to rest and recruit the jaded cattle. The Indians had stolen two of Mr. Graves' oxen, and a couple of days later had stolen one of the horses.

In traveling, the Donner Party observed this rule: If a wagon drove in the lead one day, it should pass back to the rear on the succeeding day. This system of alternating allowed each his turn in leading the train. On this fifth of October, 1846, F. W. Graves was ahead, Jay Fosdick second, John Snyder third, and the team of J. F. Reed fourth. Milton Elliott was driving Reed's team. Arriving at the foot of a steep, sandy hill, the party was obliged to "double teams," that is, to hitch five or six yoke of oxen to one (8) wagon. Elliott and Snyder interchanged hot words over some difficulty about the oxen. Fosdick had attached his team to Graves' and had drawn Graves' wagon up the hill. Snyder, being nettled at something Elliott had said, declared

## THE BREEN FAMILY.

1. PATRICK, Sr.   2. MARGARET.   3. JOHN.   4. EDWARD P.   5. PATRICK, Jr.
6. SIMON P.   7. JAMES F.   8. PETER.   9. BELLA M.   10. WILLIAM M.

that his team could pull up alone. During the excitement
Snyder made use of very bad language, and was beating his
cattle over the head with his whip-stock. One account says
that Reed's team and Snyder's became tangled. At all
events, Snyder was very much enraged. Reed had been off
hunting on horseback, and arriving at this moment, remon-
strated with Snyder for beating the cattle, and at the same
time offered him the assistance of his team. Snyder refused
the proffered aid, and used abusive language toward both
Reed and Elliott. Reed attempted to calm the enraged man.
Both men were of fiery, passionate dispositions, and words
began to multiply rapidly. When Reed saw that trouble
was likely to occur, he said something about waiting until
they got up the hill and settling this matter afterwards.
Snyder evidently construed this to be a threat, and with an
oath replied, "We will settle it now." As Snyder uttered
these words, he struck Reed a blow on the head with the
butt-end of his heavy whip-stock. This blow was followed
in rapid succession by a second, and a third. As the third
stroke descended, Mrs. Reed ran between her husband and
the furious man, hoping to prevent the blow. Each time the
whip-stock descended on Reed's head it cut deep gashes.
He was blinded with the blood which streamed from his
wounds, and dazed and stunned by the terrific force of the
blows. He saw the cruel whip-stock uplifted, and knew
that his wife was in danger, but had only time to cry " John !
John !" when down came the stroke full upon Mrs. Reed's
head and shoulders. The next instant John Snyder was
staggering, speechless and death-stricken. Reed's hunting-
knife had pierced his left breast, severing the first and second
ribs and entering the left lung.

No other portion of the History of the Donner Party, as
contributed by the survivors, has been so variously stated

as this Reed-Snyder affair. Five members of the party, now living, claim to have been eye-witnesses. The version of two of these, Mrs. J. M. Murphy and Mrs. Frank Lewis, is the one here published. In the theory of self-defense they are corroborated by all the early published accounts. This theory was first advanced in Judge J. Quinn Thornton's work in 1849, and has never been disputed publicly until within the last two or three years. Due deference to the valuable assistance rendered by Wm. G. Murphy, of Marysville, and W. C. Graves, of Calistoga, demands mention of the fact that their accounts differ in important respects from the one given above. This is not surprising in view of the thirty-three years which have elapsed since the occurrence. The history of criminal jurisprudence justifies the assertion that eye-witnesses of any fatal difficulty differ materially in regard to important particulars, even when their testimony is taken immediately after the difficulty. It is not strange, therefore, that after the lapse of an ordinary life-time a dozen different versions should have been contributed by the survivors concerning this unfortunate tragedy. James F. Reed, after nearly a quarter of a century of active public life in California, died honored and respected. During his life-time this incident appeared several times in print, and was always substantially as given in this chapter. With the single exception of a series of articles contributed to the Healdsburg Flag by W. C. Graves, two or three years ago, no different account has ever been published. This explanatory digression from the narrative is deemed necessary out of respect to the two gentlemen who conscientiously disagree with Mrs. Murphy and Mrs. Lewis. On all other important subjects the survivors are harmonious or reconcilable.

W. C. Graves, now of Calistoga, caught the dying man in his arms, and in a few minutes he was carried a little way up the hill and laid upon the ground. Reed immediately regretted the act and threw the knife from him. His wife and daughters gathered about him and began to stanch the blood that flowed from the gashes on his head. He gently pushed them aside and went to the assistance of the dying man. He and Snyder had always been firm friends, and Snyder had been most active in securing a team for Reed after the latter had lost his cattle in the desert. Snyder expired in about fifteen minutes, and Reed remained by his side until the last. Patrick Breen came up, and Snyder said, " Uncle Patrick, I am dead." It is not certain that he spoke again, though Reed's friends claim that he said to Reed, " I am to blame."

Snyder's death fell like a thunderbolt upon the Donner Party.. Camp was immediately pitched, the Reed family being a little removed down the hill from the main body of emigrants. Reed felt that he had only acted in defense of his own life and in defense of the wife he adored. Nevertheless, it was evident that trouble was brewing in the main camp where Snyder's body was lying.

The Reed family were in a sad situation. They commenced the journey with a more costly and complete outfit than the other emigrants, and thereby had incurred the envy of some of their less fortunate companions. They had a fine race horse and good stock, and Virginia had a beautiful pony of her own, and was fond of accompanying her father on his horseback excursions. From these and other circumstances the Reeds had acquired the name of being "aristocratic." Ordinarily, this is a term which would excite a smile, but on this dreadful day it had its weight in inflaming the minds of the excited emigrants. On the desert Reed had cached many valuable articles, but all his provisions had been distributed among his companions. This, however, was forgotten in the turbulent camp, and the destitute, desolate. family could plainly catch the sound of voices clamoring for Reed's death.

Meantime, Virginia Reed was dressing the wounds on her father's head. Mrs. Reed was overwhelmed with grief and apprehension, and the father came to Virginia for assistance. This brave little woman was only twelve years old, yet in this and all other acts of which there is a record she displayed a nerve and skillfulness which would have done credit to a mature woman. The cuts in Reed's scalp were wide and deep. Indeed, the scars remained to his dying day. In San Jose, long years afterwards, as James F. Reed lay dead, the gentle breeze from an open window softly lifted and caressed his gray hair, disclosing plainly the scars left by these ugly wounds.

Reed entertained none but the friendliest sentiments toward Snyder. Anxious to do what he could for the dead, he offered the boards of his wagon-bed from which to make a coffin for Snyder. This offer, made with the kindliest, most delicate feeling, was rejected by the emigrants. At the funeral, Reed stood sorrowfully by the grave until the last clod was placed above the man who had been one of his best friends. A council was held by the members of the company. A council to decide upon Reed's fate. It was in the nature of a court, all-powerful, from whose decision there was no appeal. Breathlessly the fond wife and affectionate children awaited the verdict. The father was idolized by the mother and the little ones, and was their only stay and support.

The friendship of the Donner Party for John Snyder, the conflicting and distorted accounts of the tragedy, and the personal enmity of certain members of the company toward Reed, resulted in a decree that he should be banished from the train. The feeling ran so high that at one time the end of a wagon-tongue was propped up with an ox-yoke by some of the emigrants with the intention of hanging Reed thereon, but calmer counsel prevailed.

When the announcement was communicated to Reed that he was to be banished, he refused to comply with the decree. Conscious that he had only obeyed the sacred law of self-defense, he refused to accede to an unjust punishment. Then came the wife's pleadings! Long and earnestly Mrs. Reed reasoned and begged and prayed with her husband. All was of no avail until she urged him to remember the want and destitution in which they and the entire company were already participants. If he remained and escaped violence at the hands of his enemies, he might nevertheless see his children starve before his eyes, and be helpless to aid them. But if he would go forward, if he would reach California, he could return with provisions, and meet them on the mountains at that point on the route where they would be in greatest need. It was a fearful struggle, but finally the mother's counsels prevailed. Prior to setting out upon his gloomy journey, Mr. Reed made the company promise to care for his family.

At the time of the Snyder tragedy, George and Jacob Donner, with their wagons and families, were two days in advance of the main train. Walter Herron was with them, and, when Reed came up, Herron concluded to accompany him to California.

It was contemplated that Reed should go out into the wilderness alone, and with neither food nor ammunition. Happily this part of the programme was thwarted. The faithful Virginia, in company with Milton Elliott, followed Mr. Reed after he had started, and carried him his gun and ammunition. The affectionate girl also managed

4

to carry some crackers to him, although she and all the company were even then on short allowance.

The sad parting between Reed and his family, and the second parting with the devoted Virginia, we pass over in silence. James F. Reed, Jr., only five years old, declared that he would go with his father, and assist him in obtaining food during the long journey. Even the baby, only two and a half years old, would fret and worry every time the family sat down to their meals, lest father should find nothing to eat on his difficult way. Every day the mother and daughters would eagerly search for the letter Mr. Reed was sure to leave in the top of some bush, or in a split stick by the wayside. When he succeeded in killing geese or ducks, as he frequently did along the Humboldt and Truckee, he would scatter the feathers about his camping-ground, that his family might see that he was supplied with food. It is hardly necessary to mention that Mrs. Reed and the children regarded the father's camping-places as hallowed ground, and as often as possible kindled their evening fires in the same spot where his had been kindled.

But a day came when they found no more letters, no further traces of the father. Was he dead? Had the Indians killed him? Had he starved by the way? No one could answer, and the mother's cheek grew paler and her dear eyes grew sadder and more hopeless, until Virginia and Patty both feared that she, too, was going to leave them. Anxious, grief-stricken, filled with the belief that her husband was dead, poor Mrs. Reed was fast dying of a broken heart. But suddenly all her life, and energy, and determination were again aroused into being by a danger that would have crushed a nature less noble. A danger that is the most terrible, horrible, that ever tortured human breast; a danger—that her children, her babes, must starve to death!

# CHAPTER V.

STARVATION now stared the emigrants in the face. The shortest allowance capable of supporting life was all that was portioned to any member of the company. At times, some were forced to do without food for a day or more, until game was procured. The poor cattle were also in a pitiable condition. Owing to the lateness of the season, the grass was exceedingly scanty and of a poor quality. Frequently the water was bad, and filled with alkali and other poisonous deposits. George Donner, Jacob Donner, Wolfinger, and others, lost cattle at various points along the Humboldt. Mr. Breen lost a fine mare. The Indians were constantly hovering around the doomed train, ready to steal cattle, but too cowardly to make any open hostile attack. Arrows were shot into several of the oxen by Indians who slipped up near them during the night-time. At midnight, on the twelfth of October, the party reached the sink of the Humboldt. The cattle, closely guarded, were turned out to graze and recruit their wasted strength. About dawn on the morning of the thirteenth the guard came into camp to breakfast. During the night nothing had occurred to cause the least apprehension, and no indications of Indians had been observed. Imagine the consternation in camp when it was discovered that during the temporary absence of the guard twenty-one head of cattle had been stolen by the redskins. This left the company in terribly destitute circumstances. All had to walk who were able. Men, women, and children were forced to travel on foot all day long, and in many cases were compelled to carry heavy burdens in order to lessen the loads drawn by the weary cattle. Wm. G. Murphy remembers distinctly seeing his brother carrying a copper camp-kettle upon his head. The Graves family, the Breens, the Donners, the Murphys, the Reeds, all walked beside the wagons until overpowered with fatigue. The men became exhausted much sooner, as a rule, than the women. Only the sick, the little children, and the utterly exhausted, were ever allowed to ride. Eddy and his wife had lost all their cattle, and each carried one of their children and such personal effects as they were able. Many in the train were without shoes, and had to travel barefooted over the weary sands, and flinty, sharp-edged stones.

On the ninth of October a death had resulted from this necessity of having to walk. It was a case of desertion, which, under other circumstances, would have been unpardonably heartless. An old man named Hardcoop was traveling with Keseberg. He was a cutler by trade, and had a son and daughter in the city of Antwerp, in Belgium. It is said he owned a farm near Cincinnati, Ohio, and intended, after visiting California, to dispose of this farm, and with the proceeds return to Antwerp, for the purpose of spending his declining years with his children. He was a man of nearly three-score years, and the hardships of the journey had weakened his trembling limbs and broken down his health. Sick, feeble, helpless as he was, this old man was compelled to walk with the others. At last, when his strength gave way, he was forced to lie down by the roadside to perish of cold and hunger. Who can picture the agony, the horror, the dreary desolation of such a death? The poor old man walked until his feet actually burst!—walked until he sank utterly exhausted by the roadside! It was a terrible death! To see the train disappear in the distance; to know he was abandoned to die of exposure and starvation; to think that the wolves would devour his flesh and gnaw his bones; to lie down on the great desert, hungry, famished, and completely prostrated by fatigue—to meet death thus is too dreadful to contemplate.

No one made any attempt to return and find the poor old (9) fellow. This, however, is partially excused by the overwhelming dangers which now threatened the entire company. Each hour's delay rendered death in the Sierra Nevada Mountains more imminent.

About the fourteenth of October, beyond the present site of Wadsworth, another tragedy occurred. Wolfinger, who (10) was supposed to be quite wealthy, was in the rear of the train, traveling with Keseberg. At nightfall, neither of the Germans made his appearance. It happened that both their wives had walked ahead, and were with the emigrants. Considering it suspicious that the men did not arrive, and fearing some evil had befallen them, a party returned to ascertain the cause of the delay. Before proceeding far, however, Keseberg was met traveling leisurely along. He assured them that Wolfinger was only a little way behind, and

would be along in a few moments.   Reassured by this information, the party returned with Keseberg to camp and
awaited the arrival of Wolfinger.   The night passed, and the
missing man had not appeared.   Mrs. Wolfinger was nearly
frantic.   She was a tall, queenly-looking lady, of good birth
and much refinement.   She was recently from Germany, and
understood but little English, yet she was evidently a well-
bred lady.   Nearly all the survivors remember the elegant
dresses and costly jewelry she wore during the first part of
the journey.   Her grief at her husband's disappearance was
so heart-rending that three young men at last consented to
start back in the morning and endeavor to find Wolfinger.
W. C. Graves, from whom this information is obtained, was
one of the three who returned.   Five miles back the wagon
was found standing in the road.   The oxen had been unhitched, but were still chained together, and were quietly
grazing at a little distance.   There were no signs of Indians,
but Wolfinger was not to be found.   At the time it was
strongly conjectured that Keseberg had murdered Wolfinger
for his money, and had concealed the body.   This was doubtless unjust, for when Joseph Rhinehart was dying, some weeks
later, in George Donner's tent, he confessed that he (Rhinehart) had something to do with the murder of Wolfinger.
The men hitched the oxen to the wagon, and drove on until
they overtook the emigrants, who, owing to the dangers by
which they were encompassed, felt compelled to pursue their
onward journey.   The team was given to Mrs. Wolfinger,
and she employed a German by the name of Charles Burger
to drive it thereafter.   Little was said about the affair at the
time.   Mrs. Wolfinger supposed the Indians had killed her
husband.

On the nineteenth of October, C. T. Stanton was met returning with provisions.   The company was near the present

town of Wadsworth, Nevada. A great rejoicing was held over the brave man's return. McCutchen had been severely ill, and was unable to return with Stanton. But the latter, true to his word, recrossed the Sierra, and met the emigrants at a time when they were on the verge of starvation. He had brought seven mules, five of which were loaded with flour and dried beef. Captain Sutter had furnished these mules and the provisions, together with two Indian vaqueros, without the slightest compensation or security. The Indians, Lewis and Salvador, would assist in caring for the pack-animals, and would also be efficient guides. Without Stanton's aid the entire party would have been lost; not a single soul would have escaped. The provisions, though scant, were sufficient to entirely alter the situation of affairs. Had the party pressed immediately forward, they could have passed the summits before the storms began. For some cause, however, it was concluded to rest the cattle for a few days near the present site of Reno, preparatory to attempting to ascend the difficult Sierra. Three or four days' time was lost. This loss was fatal. The storms on the mountains generally set in about Thanksgiving, or during the latter days of November. The emigrants trusted that the storm season of 1846 would not begin earlier than usual. Alas! the terrible consequences of this mistaken trust!

After the arrival of Stanton, it was still deemed necessary to take further steps for the relief of the train. The generosity of Captain Sutter, as shown to Stanton, warranted them in believing that he would send still further supplies to the needy emigrants. Accordingly, two brothers-in-law, William Foster and William Pike, both brave and daring spirits, volunteered to go on ahead, cross the summits, and return with provisions as Stanton had done. Both men had families, and both were highly esteemed in the company. At the encampment near Reno, Nevada, while they were busily preparing to start, the two men were cleaning or loading a pistol. It was an old-fashioned "pepper-box." It happened, while they were examining it, that wood was called for to replenish the fire. One of the men offered to procure it, and in order to do so, handed the pistol to the other. Everybody knows that the "pepper-box" is a very uncertain weapon. Somehow, in the transfer, the pistol was discharged. William Pike was fatally wounded, and died in about twenty minutes. Mrs. Pike was left a widow, with two small children. The youngest, Catherine, was a babe of only a few months old, and Naomi was only three years of age. The sadness and distress occasioned by this mournful accident, cast a gloom over the entire company, and seemed an omen of the terrible fate which overshadowed the Donner Party.

(11)

Generally, the ascent of the Sierra brought joy and gladness to weary overland emigrants. To the Donner Party it brought terror and dismay. The company had hardly obtained a glimpse of the mountains, ere the winter storm clouds began to assemble their hosts around the loftier crests. Every day the weather appeared more ominous and threatening. The delay at the Truckee Meadows had been brief, but every day ultimately cost a dozen lives. On the twenty-third of October, they became thoroughly alarmed at the angry heralds of the gathering storm, and with all haste resumed the journey. It was too late! At Prosser Creek, three miles below Truckee, they found themselves encompassed with six inches of snow. On the summits, the snow was from two to five feet in depth. This was October 28, 1846. Almost a month earlier than usual, the Sierra had donned its mantle of ice and snow. The party were prisoners. All was consternation. The wildest confusion prevailed. In their eagerness, many went far in advance of the main train. There was little concert of action or harmony of plan. All did not arrive at Donner Lake the same day. Some wagons and families did not reach the lake until the thirty-first day of October, some never went further than Prosser Creek, while others, on the evening of the twenty-ninth, struggled through the snow, and reached the foot of the precipitous cliffs between the summit and the upper end of the lake. Here, baffled, wearied, disheartened, they turned back to the foot of the lake.

Several times during the days which succeeded, parties attempted to cross the mountain barrier. W. C. Graves says the old emigrant road followed up Cold Stream, and so crossed the dividing ridge. Some wagons were drawn up this old road, almost to the top of the pass, others were taken along the north side of Donner Lake, and far up toward the summit. Some of these wagons never were returned to the lake, but were left imbedded in the snow. These efforts to cross the Sierra were quite desultory and irregular, and there was great lack of harmony and system. Each family or each little group of emigrants acted independently.

At last, one day, a determined and systematic attempt was made to cross the summit. Nearly the entire train was engaged in the work. The road, of course, was entirely obliterated by the snow. Guided only by the general contour of the country, all hands pressed resolutely forward. Here, large bowlders and irregular jutting cliffs would intercept the way; there, dizzy precipices, yawning chasms, and deep, irregular canyons would interpose, and anon a bold, impassable mountain of rock would rear its menacing front directly across their path. All day long the men and animals floundered through the snow, and attempted to break and trample a road. Just before nightfall they reached the abrupt precipice where the present wagon-road intercepts the snow-sheds of the Central Pacific. Here the poor mules and oxen had been utterly unable to find a foothold on the slippery; snow-covered rocks. All that day it had been raining slightly—a dismal, drizzling, discouraging rain. Most of the wagons had been left at the lake, and the mules and oxen had been packed with provisions and necessary articles. Even at this day some of the survivors are unable to repress a ripple of merriment as they recall the manner in which the oxen bucked and bellowed when the unaccustomed packs were strapped upon their backs. Stanton had stoutly insisted upon taking the mules over the mountains. Perhaps he did not wish to return to Capt. Sutter without the property which he had borrowed. Many in the train dissented from this proposition, and endeavored to induce the Indians, Lewis and Salvador, to leave Stanton, and guide them over the summits. The Indians realized the imminent danger of each hour's delay, and would probably have yielded to the solicitations of these disaffected parties, had not Stanton made them believe that Capt. Sutter would hang them if they returned to the Fort without the mules. This incident is mentioned to illustrate the great differences of opinion and interest which prevailed. (Never, from the moment the party encountered the first difficulties on the Hastings Cut-off until this fatal night in November, did the members of the company ever agree upon any important proposition.) This night all decided upon a plan for the morrow. The great and overwhelming danger made them forget their petty animosities, and united them in one harmonious resolve. On the morrow the mules and cattle were all to be slain, and the meat was to be stored away for future emergency. The wagons, with their contents, were to be left at the lake, and the entire party were to cross the summits on foot. Stanton had become perfectly satisfied that the mules could not reach the mountain-top, and readily consented to the proposed plan.

Returning to the lake they sought their weary couches, comforted with the thought that to-morrow should see all the Donner Party safely over the summit. That night a heavy snow fell at the lake. It was a night of untold terror! The emigrants suffered a thousand deaths. The pitiless snow came down in large, steady masses. All understood that the storm meant death. One of the Indians silently wrapped his blanket about him and in deepest dejection seated himself beside a tall pine. In this position he passed the entire night, only moving occasionally to keep from being covered with snow. Mrs. Reed spread down a shawl, placed her four children, Virginia, Patty, James, and Thomas, thereon, and putting another shawl over them, sat by the side of her babies during all the long hours of darkness. Every little while she was compelled to lift the upper shawl and shake off the rapidly accumulating snow.

With slight interruptions, the storm continued several days. The mules and oxen that had always hovered about camp were blinded and bewildered by the storm, and straying away were literally buried alive in the drifts. What pen can describe the horror of the position in which the emigrants found themselves! It was impossible to move through the deep, soft snow without the greatest effort. The mules were gone, and were never found. Most of the cattle had perished, and were wholly hidden from sight. The few oxen which were found were slaughtered for beef. All were not killed during any one day, but the emigrants gave this business their immediate attention, because aside from the beef and a few slight provisions, the entire party were completely destitute. Mrs. Breen was compelled to attend personally to the slaughtering of their cattle, because her husband was an

Breens

invalid. This family had by far the largest stock of meat. Too great praise can not be ascribed to Mrs. Breen for the care and forethought with which she stored up this food for her children. The meat was simply laid away in piles, like cordwood, and by the action of the frost was kept fresh until consumed. Mrs. Reed had no cattle to kill. She succeeded, however, in purchasing two beeves from Mr. Graves, and two from Mr. Breen, pledging herself to pay when the journey was ended. Mr. Eddy also purchased one ox of Mr. Graves.

The flesh of many of the cattle which strayed away, and were buried several feet under the snow, was nevertheless recovered by their owners. It was soon ascertained that the cattle had endeavored to seek shelter from the fury of the storm by getting under the branches of the bushiest trees. Going to these trees, the emigrants would thrust down long poles with sharpened nails in the ends of them. By thus probing about in the snow, the whereabouts of a number of cattle was discovered, and the bodies were speedily dug out of the drifts.

Realizing that the winter must be passed in the mountains, the emigrants made such preparations as they could for shelter. One cabin was already constructed. It was located about a quarter of a mile below the foot of the lake. It had been built in November, 1844, by Moses Schallenberger, Joseph Foster, and Allen Montgomery. Moses Schallenberger now resides three and a half miles from San Jose, and when recently interviewed by Mrs. S. O. Houghton, *née* Eliza P. Donner, gave a very complete and interesting account of the building of this cabin, and the sufferings endured by his party. This cabin, known as the Breen cabin, is so intimately connected and interwoven with future chapters in the History of the Donner Party, that the following items, taken from Mr. Schallenberger's narration, can not prove uninteresting:

"Mr. Schallenberger's party reached Donner Lake about the middle of November, 1844, having with them a large quantity of goods for California. Their cattle being very poor, and much fatigued by the journey, the party decided to remain here long enough to build a cabin in which to store their goods until spring. They also decided to leave some one to look after their stores, while the main portion of the party would push on to the settlement. Foster, Montgomery, and Schallenberger built the cabin. Two days were spent in its construction. It was built of pine saplings, and roofed with pine brush and rawhides. It was twelve by fourteen feet, and seven or eight feet high, with a chimney in one end, built "western style." One opening, through which light, air, and the occupants passed, served as a window and door. A heavy fall of snow began the day after the cabin was completed and continued for a number of days. Schallenberger, who was only seventeen years old, volunteered to remain with Foster and Montgomery. The party passed on, leaving very little provisions for the encamped. The flesh of one miserably poor cow was their main dependence, yet the young men were not discouraged. They were accustomed to frontier life, and felt sure they could provide for themselves. Bear and deer seemed abundant in the surrounding mountains. Time passed; the snow continued falling, until it was from ten to fifteen feet deep. The cow was more than half consumed, and the game had been driven out of the mountains by the storms.

"The sojourners in that lonely camp became alarmed at the prospect of the terrible fate which seemed to threaten them, and they determined to find their way across the mountains. They started and reached the summit the first night after leaving their camp. Here, young Schallenberger was taken ill with severe cramps. The following day he was unable to proceed more than a few feet without falling to the ground.   It was evident to his companions that he could go no farther.   They did not like to leave him, nor did they wish to remain where death seemed to await them.   Finally Schallenberger told them if they would take him back to the cabin he would remain there and they could go on.   This they did, and after making him as comfortable as possible, they bade him good-by, and he was left alone in that mountain wild.   A strong will and an unflinching determination to live through all the threatening dangers, soon raised him from his bed and nerved him to action.   He found some steel traps among the goods stored, and with them caught foxes, which constituted his chief or only article of food, until rescued by the returning party, March 1, 1845."

The Breen family moved into the Schallenberger cabin. Against the west side of this cabin, Keseberg built a sort of half shed, into which he and his family entered.   The Murphys erected a cabin nearer the lake.   The site of this cabin is plainly marked by a large stone about ten or twelve feet high, one side of which rises almost perpendicularly from the ground.   Against this perpendicular side the Murphys erected the building which was to shelter them during the winter. It was about three hundred yards from the shore of Donner Lake, and near the wide marshy outlet.   The Breen and Murphy cabins were distant from each other about one hundred and fifty yards.   The Graves family built a house close by Donner Creek, and half or three quarters of a mile further down the stream.   Adjoining this, forming a double cabin, the Reeds built.   The Donner brothers, Jacob and George, together with their families, camped in Alder Creek Valley, six or seven miles from Donner Lake.   They were, if possible, in a worse condition than the others, for they had only brush sheds and their tents to shield them from the wintry

weather. Mrs. John App (Leanna C. Donner), of Jamestown, Tuolumne County, writes: "We had no time to build
a cabin. The snow came on so suddenly that we had barely
time to pitch our tent, and put up a brush shed, as it were,
one side of which was open. This brush shed was covered
with pine boughs, and then covered with rubber coats, quilts,
etc. My uncle, Jacob Donner, and family, also had a tent,
and camped near us."

Crowded in their ill-prepared dwellings, the emigrants
could not feel otherwise than gloomy and despondent. The
small quantity of provisions became so nearly exhausted that
it is correct to say they were compelled to live on meat alone,
without so much as salt to give it a relish. There was an
abundance of beautiful trout in the lake, but no one could
catch them. W. C. Graves tells how he went fishing two or
three different times, but without success. The lake was not
frozen over at first, and fish were frequently seen; but they (13)
were too coy and wary to approach such bait as was offered.
Soon thick ice covered the water, and after that no one attempted to fish. In fact, the entire party seemed dazed by the
terrible calamity which had overtaken them.

# CHAPTER VI.

Endeavors to Cross the Mountains—Discouraging Failures—Eddy Kills a Bear —Making Snow-Shoes—Who Composed the "Forlorn Hope"—Mary A. Graves—An Irishman—A Generous Act—Six Days' Rations—Mary Graves' Account—Snow-Blind—C. T. Stanton's Death—"I am Coming Soon"— Sketch of Stanton's Early Life—His Charity and Self-Sacrifice—The Diamond Breastpin—Stanton's Last Poem.

ALL knew that death speedily awaited the entire company unless some could cross over the mountain barrier and hasten back relief parties. Out of the list of ninety persons mentioned in the first chapter, only Mrs. Sarah Keyes, Halloran, Snyder, Hardcoop, Wolfinger, and Pike had perished, and only three, Messrs. Reed, Herron, and McCutchen, had reached California. This left eighty-one persons at the mountain camps. It was resolved that at the earliest possible moment the strongest and ablest of the party should endeavor to cross the summits and reach the settlements. Accordingly, on the twelfth of November, a party of twelve or fifteen persons set out from the cabins. It was found impossible, however, to make any considerable headway in the soft, deep snow, and at midnight they returned to the cabins. They had not succeeded in getting more than a mile above the head of the lake. In this party were Mr. F. W. Graves and his two daughters, Mary A.

Graves, and Mrs. Sarah Fosdick. The rest, with the exception of Jay Fosdick and Wm. H. Eddy, were young, unmarried men, as, for instance, Stanton, Smith, Spitzer, Elliott, Antoine, John Baptiste, and the two Indians. It was comparatively a trifling effort, but it seemed to have the effect of utterly depressing the hopes of several of these men. With no one in the camps dependent upon them, without any ties of relationship, or bonds of affection, these young men were the first to attempt to escape from their prison walls of snow. Failing in this, many of them never again rallied or made a struggle for existence. Not so, however, with those who were heads of families. A gun was owned by William Foster, and with it, on the fourteenth of November, three miles north of Truckee, near the present Alder Creek Mill, Mr. Eddy succeeded in killing a bear. This event inspired many hearts with courage; but, alas! it was short-lived. No other game could be found except two or three wild ducks. What were these among eighty-one people! Mr. F. W. Graves was a native of Vermont, and his boyhood days had been spent in sight of the Green Mountains. Somewhat accustomed to snow, and to pioneer customs, Mr. Graves was the only member of the party who understood how to construct snow-shoes. The unsuccessful attempt made by the first party proved that no human being could walk upon the loose snow without some artificial assistance. By carefully sawing the ox-bows into strips, so as to preserve their curved form, Mr. Graves, by means of rawhide thongs, prepared very serviceable snow-shoes. Fourteen pair of shoes were made in this manner. It was certain death for all to remain in camp, and yet the first attempt had shown that it was almost equally certain death to attempt to reach the settlements. There was not food for all, and yet the ones who undertook to cross the mountains were undoubtedly sacri-

5

ficing their lives for those who remained in camp. If some should go, those who were left behind might be able to preserve life until spring, or until relief came. The stoutest hearts quailed before the thought of battling with the deep drifts, the storms, and the unknown dangers which lurked on the summits. The bravest shuddered at the idea of leaving the cabins and venturing out into the drear and dismal wilderness of snow. Yet they could count upon their fingers the days that would elapse before the provisions would be exhausted, and starvation would ensue, if none left the camps.

Day after day, with aching hearts and throbbing brows, the poor imprisoned wretches gazed into each other's faces in blank despair. Who should be sacrificed? Who would go out and seek a grave 'neath the crashing avalanche, the treacherous drifts, or in the dreary famished wilderness, that those left behind might live? Who would be the forlorn hope of the perishing emigrants?

Once, Messrs. Patrick Breen, Patrick Dolan, Lewis Keseberg, and W. H. Eddy, are said to have attempted to reach the summit. On another occasion these same parties, with Mrs. Reed and family, Mr. Stanton and the two Indians, made an unsuccessful attempt. Still another time, a large party, among whom were Mrs. Murphy and the older members of her family, made the effort, and even succeeded in crossing the topmost ridge and reaching Summit Valley, one and a half miles west of the summit. But all these parties were forced to return to the cabins, and each failure confirmed the belief that no living being could cross the mountains. In this manner time dragged wearily along until the tenth, or, as some say, the sixteenth of December. The mere matter of the date is of trifling importance. At all events a forlorn hope was organized. Seventeen names were enrolled as vol-

VIRGINIA E. REED.

(Mrs. J. M. Murphy)

1880.

unteers. Of these, Charles Burger went only a short distance, turning back weary and exhausted. Wm. G. Murphy, who is described as a most brave and resolute boy of eleven years of age, accompanied the party as far as the head of Donner Lake. He and his brother Lemuel were without snow-shoes. It was expected they would step in the beaten tracks of those who had shoes, but this was soon proven to be utterly impracticable. The party made snow-shoes for Lemuel on the first night, out of the *aparajos* which had been brought by Stanton from Sutter's Fort. Wm. G. Murphy saved his life by returning to the cabins. No human being could have endured the trip without snow-shoes. Fifteen remained in the party, and these pressed forward without so much as daring to look back to the dear ones whose lives depended upon this terrible venture. Without forgetting William G. Murphy and Charles Burger, who started with this little band, the first party who crossed the Sierra will in future be termed the fifteen. Who composed this party? Mothers, whose babes would starve unless the mothers went; fathers, whose wives and children would perish if the fathers did not go; children, whose aged parents could not survive unless the children, by leaving, increased the parents' share of food. Each were included in the forlorn hope.

It was time for some one to leave the cabins. During the days that had elapsed, no word had been received from the Donner brothers at Alder Creek, nor from the emigrants who camped with them. Alder Creek is a branch of Prosser (14) Creek, and the Donners encamped on the former stream about a mile and a half above the junction.

On the ninth of December, Milton Elliott and Noah James started back to learn some tidings of these people. Soon after they left the camps at the lake, a terrific storm came down from the mountains, and as nothing had been heard from them, it was considered certain they had perished.

About this time, starvation and exposure had so preyed upon one of the company, Augustus Spitzer, that one day he came reeling and staggering into the Breen cabin and fell prostrate and helpless upon the floor.   Poor fellow, he never rallied, although by careful nursing and kindest attentions he lingered along for some weeks.   The emigrants were no longer on short allowance, they were actually starving!   Oh! the horror!  the dread alarm which prevailed among the company!   C. T. Stanton, ever brave, courageous, lion-hearted, said, "I will bring help to these famishing people or lay down my life."   F. W. Graves, who was one of the noblest men who ever breathed the breath of life, was next to volunteer. Mr. and Mrs. Graves had nine children, the youngest being only nine months old.   Generously had they parted with the cattle which they brought to the lake, dividing equally with those families who had no food.   Mary A. Graves and her elder sister, Mrs. Sarah Fosdick, determined to accompany their father, and as will presently be seen, their hearts failed not during trials which crushed strong men.   Mary Graves was about nineteen years old.   She was a very beautiful girl, of tall and slender build, and exceptionally graceful carriage. Her features, in their regularity, were of classic Grecian mold.   Her eyes were dark, bright, and expressive.   A fine mouth and perfect set of teeth, added to a luxuriant growth of dark, rebelliously wavy hair, completed an almost perfect picture of lovely girlhood.   Jay Fosdick resolved to share with his wife the perils of the way.   Mrs. Murphy offered to take care of the infant children of her married daughters, Mrs. Foster and Mrs. Pike, if they would join the party.   The dear, good mother argued that what the daughters would eat would keep her and the little ones from starving.   It was

nobly said, yet who can doubt but that, with clearer vision,
the mother saw that only by urging them to go, could she
save her daughters' lives.   With what anguish did Mrs. Harriet F. Pike enroll her name among those of the "Forlorn
Hope," and bid good-by to her little two-year-old Naomi and
her nursing babe, Catherine!   What bitter tears were shed
by Mr. and Mrs. Foster when they kissed their beautiful baby
boy farewell!   Alas! though they knew it not, it was a long,
long farewell.   Mrs. Eddy was too feeble to attempt the journey, and the family were so poorly provided with food that
Mr. Eddy was compelled to leave her and the two little children in the cabins, and go with the party.   Mrs. McCutchen
also had an infant babe, and Mrs. Graves employed the same
reasoning with her that Mrs. Murphy had so effectively used
with Mrs. Pike and Mrs. Foster.   That these three young
mothers left their infant children, their nursing babes, with
others, and started to find relief, is proof stronger than words,
of the desperate condition of the starving emigrants.   The
Mexican Antoine, the two Indians Lewis and Salvador, and
an Irishman named Patrick Dolan, completed the fifteen.
This Patrick Dolan deserves more than a passing word.   He
had owned a farm in Keokuk, Iowa, and selling it, had taken
as the price, a wagon, four oxen, and two cows.   With these
he joined the Donner Party, and on reaching the lake had
killed his cattle and stored them away with those killed by
the Breens.   Dolan was a bachelor, and about forty years of
age.   He was possessed of two or three hundred dollars in
coin, but instead of being miserly or selfish, was characterized
by generous open-heartedness.   "When it became apparent
that there was to be suffering and starvation" (this quotation
is from the manuscript of Hon. James F. Breen), "Dolan determined to lighten the burden at the camps, and leave with
the party that was to attempt the passage of the summit, so

that there should be less to consume the scant supply of provisions. Previous to his departure, he asked my father (Patrick Breen) to attend to the wants of Reed's family, and to give of his (Dolan's) meat to Reed's family as long as possible." Accordingly, Mrs. Reed and her children were taken into Breen's cabin, where, as mentioned above, Dolan's meat was stored. Was ever a more generous act recorded? Patrick Dolan had no relative in the Donner Party, and no friends, save those whose friendship had been formed upon the plains. With the cattle which belonged to him he could have selfishly subsisted until relief came, but, whole-souled Irishman that he was, he gave food to the mothers and the children and went out into the waste of snow to perish of starvation! How many who live to-day owe their existence to Patrick Dolan's self-sacrifice! This blue-eyed, brown-haired Irishman is described as being of a jovial disposition, and inclined to look upon the bright side of things. Remembering how he gave his life for strangers, how readily can we appreciate Mr. Breen's tender tribute: "He was a favorite with children, and would romp and play with a child." As a token of appreciation for his kindness, Mrs. Reed gave Patrick Dolan a gold watch and a Masonic emblem belonging to her husband, bidding him to keep them until he was rewarded for his generosity. The good mother's word had a significance she wot not of. When Mrs. Reed reached Sutter's Fort she found these valuables awaiting her. They had been brought in by Indians. Patrick Dolan had kept them until his death—until the angels came and bore him away to his reward.

This party of fifteen had taken provisions to last only six days. At the end of this time they hoped to reach Bear Valley, so they said, but it is more than probable they dared not take more food from their dear ones at the cabins. Six days' rations! This means enough of the poor, shriveled beef to allow each person, three times a day, a piece the size of one's two fingers. With a little coffee and a little loaf sugar, this was all. They had matches, Foster's gun, a hatchet, and each a thin blanket. With this outfit they started to cross the Sierra. No person, unaccustomed to snow-shoes, can form an idea of the difficulty which is experienced during one's first attempt to walk with them. Their shoes would sink deep into the loose, light snow, and it was with great effort they made any progress. They had been at Donner Lake from forty-two to forty-six days, and on this first night of their journey had left it four miles behind them. After a dreadful day's work they encamped, in full sight of the lake (15) and of the cabins. This was harder for the aching hearts of the mothers than even the terrible parting from their little ones. To see the smoke of the cabins, to awake from their troubled dreams, thinking they heard the cry of their starving babes, to stifle the maternal yearnings which prompted them to turn back and perish with their darlings clasped to their breasts, were trials almost unbearable. The next day they traveled six miles. They crossed the summit, and the camps were no longer visible. They were in the solemn fastnesses of the snow-mantled Sierra. Lonely, desolate, forsaken apparently by God and man, their situation was painfully, distressingly terrible. The snow was wrapped about cliff and forest and gorge. It varied in depth from twelve to sixty feet.

Mrs. M. A. Clarke (Mary Graves), now of White River, Tulare County, speaking of this second day, says: " We had a very slavish day's travel, climbing the divide. Nothing of interest occurred until reaching the summit. The scenery was too grand for me to pass without notice, the changes being so great; walking now on loose snow, and now stepping on a hard, slick rock a number of hundred yards in length. Being a little in the rear of the party, I had a chance to observe the company ahead, trudging along with packs on their backs. It reminded me of some Norwegian fur company among the icebergs. My shoes were ox-bows, split in two, and rawhide strings woven in, something in form of the old-fashioned, split-bottomed chairs. Our clothes were of the bloomer costume, and generally were made of flannel. Well do I remember a remark one of the company made here, that we were about as near heaven as we could get. We camped a little on the west side of the summit the second night."

Here they gathered a few boughs, kindled a fire upon the surface of the snow, boiled their coffee, and ate their pitiful allowance of beef; then wrapping their toil-worn bodies in their blankets, lay down upon the snow. As W. C. Graves remarks, it was a bed that was soft, and white, and beautiful, and yet it was a terrible bed—a bed of death. The third day they walked five miles. Starting almost at dawn, they struggled wearily through the deep drifts, and when the night shadows crept over crag and pine and mountain vale, they were but five miles on their journey. They did not speak during the day, except when speech was absolutely necessary. All traveled silently, and with downcast eyes. The task was beginning to tell upon the frames of even the strongest and most resolute. The hunger that continually gnawed at their vitals, the excessive labor of moving the heavy, clumsy snow-shoes through the soft, yielding snow, was too much for human endurance. They could no longer keep together and aid each other with words of hope. They struggled along, sometimes at great distances apart. The fatigue and dazzling sunlight rendered some of them snow-blind. One of these was the noble-hearted Stanton. On this third day he was too blind and weak to keep up with the rest, and staggered into the camp long after the others had finished their pitiful supper. Poor, brave, generous Stanton! He said little, but in his inner heart he knew that the end of his journey was almost at hand.

Who was this heroic being who left the beautiful valleys of the Sacramento to die for strangers? See him wearily toiling onward during the long hours of the fourth day. The agony and blindness of his eyes wring no cry from his lips, no murmur, no word of complaint. With patient courage and heroic fortitude he strives to keep pace with his companions, but finds it impossible. Early in the morning he drops to the rear, and is soon lost to sight. At night he drags his weary limbs into camp long after his comrades are sleeping 'neath the silent stars. It must be remembered that they had been accustomed to short allowance of food for months, while he had been used to having an abundance. Their bodies had been schooled to endure famine, privations, and long, weary walks. For many days before reaching the mountains, they had been used to walking every day, in order to lighten the burdens of the perishing oxen. Fatigues which exhausted them crushed Stanton. The weather was clear and pleasant, but the glare of the sun during the day had been like molten fire to their aching eyes.

On the morning of the fifth day Stanton was sitting smoking by the smoldering fire when the company resumed its journey. Mary Graves, who had a tender heart for the suffering of others, went kindly up to him, and asked him if he were coming. "Yes," he replied, "I am coming soon." Was he answering her, or the unseen spirits that even then were beckoning him to the unknown world? "Yes, I am coming soon!" These were his last words. His companions were too near death's door to return when they found he came not,

and so he perished.   He had begged them piteously to lead
him, during the first days of his blindness, but seeming to
realize that they were unable to render assistance, he ceased
to importune, and heroically met his fate.   He did not blame
his comrades.   They were weak, exhausted, and ready to die
of starvation.   With food nearly gone, strength failing, hope
lost, and nothing left but the last, blind, clinging instinct of
life, it was impossible that the perishing company should
have aided the perishing Stanton.   He was a hero of the
highest, noblest, grandest stamp.   No words can ever express a fitting tribute to his memory.   He gave his life for
strangers who had not the slightest claim to the sacrifice.
He left the valleys where friends, happiness, and abundance
prevailed, to perish amidst chilling snow-drifts—famished and
abandoned.   The act of returning to save the starving emigrants is as full of heroic grandeur as his death is replete with
mournful desolation.

In May, 1847, W. C. Graves, in company with a relief party,
found the remains of C. T. Stanton near the spot where he
had been left by his companions.   The wild animals had partially devoured his body, but the remains were easily identified by means of his clothing and pistols.

The following sketch of this hero is kindly furnished by
his brother, Sidney Stanton, of Cazenovia, New York:

"Charles Tyler Stanton was born at Pompey, Onondaga
County, New York, March 11, 1811.   He was five feet five
inches in height.   He had brown eyes and brown hair.   He
possessed a robust constitution, and although rather slender
during his youth, at the age of fifteen he became strong and
hearty, and could endure as great hardships as any of his
brothers.   He had five brothers and four sisters, and was the
seventh child.   His grandparents, on his father's side, were
well off at the close of the revolutionary war, but sold their

large farms, and took Continental money in payment. Soon afterward this money became worthless, and they lost all. They were at the time living in Berkshire, Massachusetts, but soon after removed west to the county where C. T. Stanton was born. There were in his father's family fourteen children—seven sons and seven daughters."

In his younger days Stanton was engaged as a clerk in a store. He was honest, industrious, and greatly beloved by those with whom he came in contact. His early education was limited, but during his employment as clerk he used every possible endeavor to improve his mind. During his journey across the plains, he was regarded as somewhat of a savant, on account of his knowledge of botany, geology, and other branches of natural science. His disposition was generous to a fault. He never was happier than when bestowing assistance upon needy friends. His widowed mother, for whom he entertained the most devoted affection, was kindly cared for by him until her death in 1835. After this sad event he removed to Chicago. At Chicago he made money rapidly for a time, and his hand was ever ready to give aid to those about him. Charity and heroic self-sacrifice appear to have been his predominant characteristics. They stand out in bold relief, not only in his early history, but during his connection with the Donner Party. While in the mountains he had no money to give, but instead he gave his strength, his energy, his love, his all, his very life, for his companions.

That he had a premonition of the gloomy fate which overtook him in the Sierra, or at least that he fully realized the perils to which he was exposing his life, is indicated by the following incident: When he set out from Sutter's Fort to return to the Donner train with provisions, he left a vest with Captain Sutter. In one of the pockets of this vest was subsequently found a package directed to the Captain with the following memorandum: "Captain Sutter will send the within, in the event of my death, to Sidney Stanton, Syracuse, New York." The package contained a diamond breastpin. Mr. Sidney Stanton writes as follows concerning this keepsake:

"I will give you a short history or account of the pin which was left for me at Sutter's Fort, which Mr. McKinstry forwarded to me. This was an event so peculiar at the time. He visited me here at Syracuse, while he was prospering in Chicago. He was on his way to New York, and wanted a sum of money, which I advanced. Before leaving he fastened this pin on the dress of my wife, remarking that she must consider it as a present from him. Nothing more was thought of this event until he again wanted money. Misfortune had overtaken him, and this event gave him much pain, not so much on his own account as because he could not relieve the distress of dear friends when asked for aid. I sent him a little more money; I had not much to spare, and in talking the matter over with my wife, she asked, 'Why not send him the pin? It is valuable, and in time of need he might dispose of it for his comfort.' In saying this she took the ground that it was left with her as a pledge, not as a gift. I therefore handed it to my sister to send to him for this purpose. But it appears by his keeping it and sending it back in the way he did, that he did consider it a gift, and hence he would not and did not dispose of it for necessary things for his own comfort. This pin was the only thing of value which he had at the time of his death."

Stanton was an excellent writer. His descriptions of his travels from Chicago to the South would make a good-sized and a very interesting book. His last composition is given below. It is an appropriate ending to this brief outline of the history of one who should be regarded as one of the noblest of California's pioneer heroes:

### "TO MY MOTHER IN HEAVEN.

"Oh, how that word my soul inspires
 With holy, fond, and pure desires!
  Maternal love, how bright the flame!
  For wealth of worlds I'd not profane
  Nor idly breathe thy sacred name,
   My mother.

"Thy sainted spirit dwells on high.
 How oft I weep, how oft I sigh
  Whene'er I think of bygone time,
  Thy smile of love, which once was mine,
  That look so heavenly and divine,
   My mother.

"Thy warning voice in prayers of love,
 Ascending to the throne above
  With tones of eloquence so rife,
  Hath turned my thoughts from wordly strife,
  And cheered me through my wayward life,
   My mother.

"When death shall close my sad career,
 And I before my God appear—
  There to receive His last decree—
  My only prayer there will be
  Forever to remain with thee,
   My mother."

# CHAPTER VII.

A Wife's Devotion—The Smoky Gorge—Caught in a Storm—Casting Lots to
See Who should Die—A Hidden River—The Delirium of Starvation—
Franklin Ward Graves—His Dying Advice—A Frontiersman's Plan—The
Camp of Death—A Dread Resort—A Sister's Agony—The Indians Refuse
to Eat—Lewis and Salvador Flee for Their Lives—Killing a Deer—Tracks
Marked by Blood—Nine Days without Food.

LET no one censure Stanton's companions for abandon-
ing their brave comrade. In less than twenty-four
hours all were without food, unless, indeed, it was
Mr. Eddy, who, in his narration published by Judge
Thornton, states that on the day of Stanton's death
he found half a pound of bear's meat which had been
secreted in a little bag by his wife. Attached to this meat
was a paper, upon which his wife had written in pencil a note
signed, "Your own dear Eleanor." Mr. Eddy had not discovered this meat until the sorest hour of need, and the hope
expressed in Mrs. Eddy's note, that it would be the means of
saving his life, was literally fulfilled. There is something extremely touching in the thought that this devoted wife, who,
as will presently be seen, was starving to death in the cabins,
saved her husband's life by clandestinely concealing about
his person a portion of the food which should have sustained
herself and her infant children.

MATTIE J. (PATTY) REED.

(Mrs. Frank Lewis )

1854.

In the account given by Mary Graves, is mentioned the following incident in the fourth day's travel: "Observing by the way a deep gorge at the right, having the appearance of being full of smoke, I wanted very much to go to it, but the Indians said no, that was not the way. I prevailed on the men to fire the gun, but there was no answer. Every time we neared the gorge I would halloo at the top of my voice, but we received no answer."

On this day the horror of the situation was increased by the commencement of a snow-storm. As the flakes fell thick and fast, the party sat down in the snow utterly discouraged and heartsick.

Mary Graves says: "What to do we did not know. We held a consultation, whether to go ahead without provisions, or go back to the cabins, where we must undoubtedly starve. Some of those who had children and families wished to go back, but the two Indians said they would go on to Captain Sutter's. I told them I would go too, for to go back and hear the cries of hunger from my little brothers and sisters was more than I could stand. I would go as far as I could, let the consequences be what they might."

There, in the deep, pitiless storm, surrounded on all sides by desolate wastes of snow, the idea was first advanced that life might be sustained if some one were to perish. Since leaving the cabins, they had at no time allowed themselves more than one ounce of meat per meal, and for two entire days they had not tasted food. The terrible pangs of hunger must be speedily allayed or death was inevitable. Some one proposed that lots be cast to see who should die. The terrible proposition met with opposition from Foster and others, but slips of paper were actually prepared by some of the men, and he who drew the longest—the fatal slip—was Patrick Dolan. Who should take Dolan's life? Who was to be the executioner of the man who had so generously given up the food which might have sustained his life, and joined the forlorn hope that others might live? With one accord they rose to their feet and staggered forward. As if to banish from their minds the horrid thought of taking Dolan's life, they attempted to pursue their journey.

With the greatest exertion and suffering they managed to crawl, and stagger, and flounder along until they attained a distance of two or three miles. Here they camped, and passed a most wretched, desolate night. The morning dawned; it was dreary, rainy, and discouraging. The little party set out as usual, but were too weak and lifeless to travel. The soft snow clung to their feet in heavy lumps like snow-balls. Instead of making a fire in a new place, Mary Graves says they crawled back to the camp-fire of the night previous. Here they remained until night came on—a night full of horrors. The wind howled through the shrieking forests like troops of demons. The rain had continued all day, but finally changed to snow and sleet, which cut their pinched faces, and made them shiver with cold. All the forces of nature seemed to combine for their destruction. At one time during the night, in attempting to kindle a fire, the ax or hatchet which they had carried was lost in the loose snow.

A huge fire was kindled at last, with the greatest difficulty, and in order to obtain more warmth, all assisted in piling fuel upon the flames. Along in the night, Mr. Foster thinks it was near midnight, the heat of the flames and the dropping coals and embers thawed the snow underneath the fire until a deep, well-like cavity was formed about the fire. Suddenly, as if to intensify the dreadful horrors of the situation, the bottom of this well gave way, and the fire disappeared! The camp and the fire had been built over a stream of water, and the fire had melted through the overlying snow until it had fallen into the stream!    Those who peered over the brink of the dark opening about which they were gathered, could hear, far down in the gloom, during the lull of the storm, the sound of running waters.

If there is anything lacking in this picture of despair, it is furnished in the groans and cries of the shivering, dying outcasts, and the demoniacal shrieks and ravings of Patrick Dolan, who was in the delirium which precedes death.    It was not necessary that life should be taken by the members of the company.    Death was busily at work, and before the wild winter night was ended, his ghastly victims were deaf to wind or storm.

When the fire disappeared, it became apparent that the entire forlorn hope would perish before morning if exposed to the cold and storm.    W. H. Eddy says the wind increased until it was a perfect tornado.    About midnight, Antoine, overcome by starvation, fatigue, and the bitter cold, ceased to breathe.    Mr. F. W. Graves was dying.    There was a point beyond which an iron nerve and a powerful constitution were unable to sustain a man.    This point had been reached, and Mr. Graves was fast passing away.    He was conscious, and calling his weeping, grief-stricken daughters to his side, exhorted them to use every means in their power to prolong their lives.    He reminded them of their mother, of their little brothers and sisters in the cabin at the lake. He reminded Mrs. Pike of her poor babies.    Unless these daughters succeeded in reaching Sutter's Fort, and were able to send back relief, all at the lake must certainly die.    Instances had been cited in history, where, under less provocation, human flesh had been eaten, yet Mr. Graves well knew that his daughters had said they would never touch the loathsome food.

Was there not something noble and grand in the dying

6

advice of this father? Was he not heroic when he counseled that all false delicacy be laid aside and that his body be sacrificed to support those that were to relieve his wife and children?

Earnestly pleading that these afflicted children rise superior to their prejudices and natural instincts—Franklin Ward Graves died. A sublimer death seldom is witnessed. In the solemn darkness, in the tempestuous storm, on the deep, frozen snow-drifts, overcome by pain and exposure, with the pangs of famine gnawing away his life, this unselfish father, with his latest breath urged that his flesh be used to prolong the lives of his companions. Truly, a soul that could prompt such utterances had no need, after death, for its mortal tenement—it had a better dwelling-place on high.

With two of their little number in the icy embraces of death, some plan to obtain warmth for the living was immediately necessary. W. H. Eddy proposed a frontiersman's method. It was for all to huddle closely together in a circle, lie down on a blanket with their heads outward, and be covered with a second blanket. Mr. Eddy arranged his companions, spread the blanket over them, and creeping under the coverlid, completed the circle. The wind swept the drifting snow in dense clouds over their heads. The chilling air, already white with falling snowflakes, became dense with the drifting masses. In a little while the devoted band were completely hidden from wind, or storm, or piercing cold, by a deep covering of snow. The warmth of their bodies, confined between the blankets, under the depth of snow, soon rendered them comfortably warm. Their only precaution now was to keep from being buried alive. Occasionally some member of the party would shake the rapidly accumulating snow from off their coverlid.

They no longer were in danger of freezing. But while the

elements were vainly waging fierce war above their heads, hunger was rapidly sapping the fountains of life, and claiming them for its victims. When, for a moment, sleep would steal away their reason, in famished dreams they would seize with their teeth the hand or arm of a companion. The delirium of death had attacked one or two, and the pitiful wails and cries of these death-stricken maniacs were heart-rending. The dead, the dying, the situation, were enough to drive one crazy.

The next day was ushered in by one of the most furious storms ever witnessed on the Sierra. All the day long, drifts and the fast-falling snow circled above them under the force of the fierce gale. The air was a frozen fog of swift-darting ice-lances. The fine particles of snow and sleet, hurled by maddened storm-fiends, would cut and sting so that one's eyes could not be opened in the storm, and the rushing gale would hurl one prostrate on the snow. Once or twice the demented Dolan escaped from his companions and disappeared in the blinding storm. Each time he returned or was caught and dragged 'neath the covering, but the fatal exposure chilled the little life remaining in his pulses. During the afternoon he ceased to shriek, or struggle, or moan. Patrick Dolan, the warm-hearted Irishman, was starved to death.

Mr. Eddy states, in Thornton's work, that they entered this Camp of Death, Friday, December 25, Christmas. According to his version they started from the cabins on the sixteenth day of December, with scanty rations for six days. On the twenty-second they consumed the last morsel of their provisions. Not until Sunday noon, December 27, did the storm break away. They had been over four days without food, and two days and a half without fire. They were almost dead.

Is there a mind so narrow, so uncharitable, that it can censure these poor dying people for the acts of this terrible day? With their loved ones perishing at Donner Lake, with the horror of a lingering death staring them in the face, can the most unfeeling heart condemn them?

Emerging from the dreary prison-house, they attempted to kindle a fire. Their matches were wet and useless. Their flint-lock gun would give forth a spark, but without some dry material that would readily ignite, it was of no avail.

On this morning of the twenty-seventh Eddy says that he blew up a powder-horn in an effort to strike fire under the blankets. His face and hands were much burned. Mrs. McCutchen and Mrs. Foster were also burned, but not seriously. For some time all efforts to obtain a fire proved fruitless. Their garments were drenched by the storm. Mrs. Pike had a mantle that was lined with cotton. The lining of this was cut open, and the driest portion of the cotton was exposed to the sun's rays, in the hope that it could be made to catch the spark from the flint. At last they were successful. A fire was kindled in a dead tree, and the flames soon leaped up to the loftiest branches. The famished, shivering wretches gathered round the burning tree. So weak and lifeless were they that when the great pine limbs burned off and fell crashing about them, neither man nor woman moved or attempted to escape the threatening danger. All felt that sudden death would be welcome. They were stunned and horrified by the dreadful alternative which it was evident they must accept.

The men finally mustered up courage to approach the dead. With averted eyes and trembling hand, pieces of flesh were severed from the inanimate forms and laid upon the coals. It was the very refinement of torture to taste such food, yet those who tasted lived. One could not eat.

Lemuel Murphy was past relief. A boy about thirteen years old, Lemuel was dearly loved by his sisters, and, full of courage, had endeavored to accompany them on the fearful journey. He was feeble when he started from the cabins, and the overwhelming sufferings of the fatal trip had destroyed his remaining strength. Starvation is agony during the first three days, apathy and inanition during the fourth and perhaps the fifth, and delirium from that time until the struggle ceases. When the delirium commences, hope ends. Lemuel was delirious Sunday morning, and when food was placed to his lips he either could not eat or was too near death to revive. All day Mrs. Foster held her brother's head in her lap, and by every means in her power sought to soothe his death agonies. The sunlight faded from the surrounding summits. Darkness slowly emerged from the canyons and enfolded forest and hill-slope in her silent embrace. The glittering stars appeared in the heavens, and the bright, full moon rose over the eastern mountain crests. The silence, the profound solitude, the ever-present wastes of snow, the weird moonlight, and above all the hollow moans of the dying boy in her lap, rendered this night the most impressive in the life of Mrs. Foster. She says she never beholds a bright moonlight without recurring with a shudder to this night on the Sierra. At two o'clock in the morning Lemuel Murphy ceased to breathe. The warm tears and kisses of the afflicted sisters were showered upon lips that would never more quiver with pain.

Until the twenty-ninth of December they remained at the "Camp of Death." Would you know more of the shuddering details? Does the truth require the narration of the sickening minutiæ of the terrible transactions of these days? Human beings were never called upon to undergo more trying ordeals. Dividing into groups, the members of each family were spared the pain of touching their own kindred.  Days and perhaps weeks of starvation were awaiting them in the future, and they dare not neglect to provide as best they might.  Each of the four bodies was divested of its flesh, and the flesh was dried. Although no person partook of kindred flesh, sights were often witnessed that were blood-curdling.  Mrs. Foster, as we have seen, fairly worshiped her brother Lemuel.  Has human pen power to express the shock of horror this sister received when she saw her brother's heart thrust through with a stick, and broiling upon the coals?  No man can record or read such an occurrence without a cry of agony!  What, then, did she endure who saw this cruel sight?

These are facts.  They are given just as they came from the lips of Mrs. Foster, a noble woman, who would have died of horror and a broken heart but for her starving babe, her mother, and her little brothers and sisters who were at Donner Lake.  Mary Graves corroborates Mrs. Foster, and W. H. Eddy gave a similar version to Judge Thornton.

The Indian guides, Lewis and Salvador, would not eat this revolting food.  They built a fire away from the company, and with true Indian stoicism endured the agonies of starvation without so much as beholding the occurrences at the other camp-fire.

Starved bodies possess little flesh, and starving people could carry but light burdens through such snow-drifts.  On these accounts, the provision which the Almighty seemed to have provided to save their lives, lasted only until the thirty-first. On New Year's morning they ate their moccasins and the strings of their snow-shoes.  On the night before, Lewis and Salvador caught the sound of ominous words, or perceived glances that were filled with dreadful import, and during the darkness they fled.

For several days past the party had been lost.  The Indians could not recognize the country when it was hidden from thirty to fifty feet in snow. Blindly struggling forward, they gradually separated into three parties. On the fourth, W. H. Eddy and Mary Graves were in advance with the gun. A starved deer crossed their path and providentially was slain. Drinking its warm blood and feasting upon its flesh, this couple waited for the arrival of Mr. and Mrs. Foster, Mrs. McCutchen, and Mrs. Pike, who were some distance behind. Night came and passed and they did not arrive. Indeed, Foster was dying for lack of nourishment. Behind this party were Mr. and Mrs. Jay Fosdick. During the night, Mr. Fosdick perishéd, and the faithful wife, after remaining with him until morning, struggled forward and met Mrs. Foster and a companion. Mrs. Fosdick related the death of her husband, and upon being informed of Foster's condition, consented that her husband's body be converted into food. It was done. This was the first time that women's hands had used the knife, but by the act a life was saved. Mrs. Fosdick, although dying, would not touch the food, and but for the venison would not have lived to see the setting of the sun. But what was one small deer among so many famished people? Hide, head, feet, entrails, all were eaten. On the sixth, the last morsel was consumed. They were now without hope. Their journey was apparently interminable. Wearied, foot-sore, freezing at night and tortured by hunger during the day, life could not last many hours. Some one must die; else none could live and reach the long-talked-of relief. Would it be Eddy, whose wife and two children were behind? Would it be Mrs. Pike, who left two babes? Mrs. McCutchen, who left one? Mr. or Mrs. Foster, whose baby boy was at the cabin? Or would it be Mary Graves or Mrs. Fosdick, who had left mother and family? On the night of the seventh, they lay down upon the snow without having tasted a mouthful of food during the day. Continued famine and exhaustion had so weakened their frames that they could not survive another day. Yet, on the morning of the seventh, they arose and staggered onward. Soon they halted and gathered about some freshly made tracks. Tracks marked by blood! Tracks that they knew had been made by Lewis and Salvador, whose bare feet were sore and bleeding from cuts and bruises inflicted by the cruel, jagged rocks, the frozen snow, and flinty ice. These Indians had eaten nothing for nine days, and had been without fire or blankets for four days. They could not be far ahead.

# CHAPTER VIII.

Starvation at Donner Lake—Preparing Rawhide for Food—Eating the Fire-rug—Shoveling Snow off the Beds—Playing they were Tea-cups of Custard—A Starving Baby—Pleading with Silent Eloquence—Patrick Breen's Diary—Jacob Donner's Death—A Child's Vow—A Christmas Dinner—Lost on the Summits—A Stump Twenty-two Feet High—Seven Nursing Babes at Donner Lake—A Devout Father—A Dying Boy—Sorrow and Suffering at the Cabins.

OW fared it with those left at Donner Lake? About the time the fifteen began their terrible journey, Baylis Williams starved to death. Such food as the rest had was freely given to him, but it did not satisfy the demands of his nature. Quietly, uncomplainingly, he had borne the pangs of famine, and when the company first realized his dreadful condition, he was in the delirium which preceded death. What words can portray the emotions of the starving emigrants, when they saw one of their number actually perish of hunger before their eyes! Williams died in the Graves cabin, and was buried near the house by W. C. Graves and John Denton.

All the Donner Party were starving. When the cattle were killed the hides had been spread over the cabins in lieu of shingles. These were now taken down and eaten. All the survivors describe the method of preparing this miserable

substitute for food.   The narration by Mrs. J. M. Murphy
(Virginia E. Reed), of San Jose, is among the most vivid.
She says the green rawhides were cut into strips and laid
upon the coals, or held in the flames until the hair was completely singed off.   Either side of the piece of hide was then
scraped with a knife until comparatively clean, and was
placed in a kettle and boiled until soft and pulpy.   There was
no salt, and only a little pepper, and yet this substance was
all that was between them and starvation.   When cold, the
boiled hides and the water in which they were cooked, became jellied and exactly resembled glue.   The tender
stomach of many of the little children revolted at this
disagreeable diet, and the loathing they acquired for the
sight of this substance still exists in the minds of some of
the survivors.   To this day, Thomas K. Reed, of San Jose,
who was then a tiny three-year-old, can not endure the sight
of calf's-foot jelly, or of similar dishes, because of its re-
semblance to the loathed food which was all his mother
could give him in the cabins at Donner Lake.

William G. Murphy describes how they gathered up the
old, castaway bones of the cattle—bones from which all the
flesh had been previously picked—and boiled, and boiled,
and boiled them until they actually would crumble between
the teeth, and were eaten.   The little children, playing upon
the fire-rug in his mother's cabin, used to cut off little pieces
of the rug, toast them crisp upon the coals, and then eat
them.   In this manner, before any one was fairly aware of
the fact, the fire-rug was entirely consumed.

The Donner families, at Prosser Creek, were, if possible,
in even a sadder condition.   In order to give a glimpse of
the suffering endured in these two tents, the following is
quoted from a letter written by Mrs. W. A. Babcock (Georgia
A. Donner), now residing at Mountain View, Santa Clara

County: "The families shared with one another as long as they had anything to share. Each one's portion was very small. The hides were boiled, and the bones were burned brown and eaten. We tried to eat a decayed buffalo robe, but it was too tough, and there was no nourishment in it. Some of the few mice that came into camp were caught and eaten. Some days we could not keep a fire, and many times, during both days and nights, snow was shoveled from off our tent, and from around it, that we might not be buried alive. Mother remarked one day that it had been two weeks that our beds and the clothing upon our bodies had been wet. Two of my sisters and myself spent some days at Keseberg's cabin. The first morning we were there they shoveled the snow from our bed before we could get up. Very few can believe it possible for human beings to live and suffer the exposure and hardships endured there."

Oh! how long and dreary the days were to the hungry children! Even their very plays and pastimes were pathetic, because of their piteous silent allusion to the pangs of starvation. Mrs. Frank Lewis (Patty Reed), of San Jose, relates that the poor, little, famishing girls used to fill the pretty porcelain tea-cups with freshly fallen snow, daintily dip it out with teaspoons and eat it, playing it was custard.

Dear Mrs. Murphy had the most sacred and pitiful charge. It was the wee nursing babe, Catherine Pike, whose mother had gone with the "Forlorn Hope," to try, if possible, to procure relief. All there was to give the tiny sufferer, was a little gruel made from snow water, containing a slight sprinkling of coarse flour. This flour was simply ground wheat, unbolted. Day after day the sweet little darling would lie helplessly upon its grandmother's lap, and seem with its large, sad eyes to be pleading for nourishment. Mrs. Murphy carefully kept the little handful of flour concealed—there was

only a handful at the very beginning—lest some of the starving children might get possession of the treasure.    Each day
she gave Catherine a few teaspoonfuls of the gruel.   Strangely
enough, this poor little martyr did not often cry with hunger,
but with tremulous, quivering mouth, and a low, subdued sob
or moan, would appear to be begging for something to eat.
The poor, dumb lips, if gifted with speech, could not have
uttered a prayer half so eloquent, so touching.   Could the
mother, Mrs. Pike, have been present, it would have broken
her heart to see her patient babe dying slowly, little by little.
Starvation had dried the maternal breasts long before Mrs.
Pike went away, so that no one can censure her for leaving
her baby.   She could only have done as Mrs. Murphy did,
give it the plain, coarse gruel, and watch it die, day by day,
upon her lap.

Up to this time, but little has been said of Patrick Breen.
He was an invalid during the winter of 1846 and '47.   A man
of more than ordinary intelligence, a devout Catholic, a faithful and devoted father, his life furnishes a rare type of the
pioneer Californian.   To Mr. Breen we are indebted for the
most faithful and authentic record of the days spent at the
cabins.   This record is in the form of a diary, in which the
events of the day were briefly noted in the order of their occurrence.   Lewis Keseberg kept a similar diary, but it was
subsequently accidentally destroyed.   Mrs. Tamsen Donner
kept a journal, but this, with her paintings and botanical collections, disappeared at the fatal tent on Alder Creek.   Mr.
Breen's diary alone was preserved.   He gave it into Col.
McKinstry's possession in the spring of 1847, and on the
fourth of September of that year it was published in the
Nashville (Tenn.) Whig.   A copy of the Whig of that date
is furnished by Wm. G. Murphy, of Marysville.   Other papers
have published garbled extracts from this diary, but none

have been reliable. The future history of the events which transpired at the cabins will be narrated in connection with this diary.

It must be remembered that the lake had always been known as "Truckee Lake," it having been named after an old Indian guide who had rendered much assistance to the Schallenberger party in 1844. The record appears without the slightest alteration. Even the orthography of the name of the lake is printed as it was written, "Truckey." (16)

The diary commences as follows:

"TRUCKEY'S LAKE, November 20, 1846.

"Came to this place on the thirty-first of last month; went into the pass; the snow so deep we were unable to find the road, and when within three miles from the summit, turned back to this shanty on Truckey's Lake; Stanton came up one day after we arrived here; we again took our teams and wagons, and made another unsuccessful attempt to cross in company with Stanton; we returned to this shanty; it continued to snow all the time. We now have killed most part of our cattle, having to remain here until next spring, and live on lean beef, without bread or salt. It snowed during the space of eight days, with little intermission, after our arrival, though now clear and pleasant, freezing at night; the snow nearly gone from the valleys.

"November 21. Fine morning; wind northwest; twenty-two of our company about starting to cross the mountains this day, including Stanton and his Indians.

"Nov. 22. Froze last night; fine and clear to-day; no account from those on the mountains.

"Nov. 23. Same weather; wind west; the expedition across the mountains returned after an unsuccessful attempt.

"Nov. 25. Cloudy; looks like the eve of a snow-storm;

our mountaineers are to make another trial to-morrow, if fair; froze hard last night.

"Nov. 26. Began to snow last **evening**; now rains or sleets; the party do not start to-day.

"Nov. 27. Still snowing; now about three feet deep; wind west; killed my last oxen to-day; gave another yoke to Foster; wood hard to be got.

"Nov. 30. Snowing fast; looks as likely to continue as when it commenced; no living thing without wings can get about.

"Dec. 1. Still snowing; wind west; snow about six or seven and a half feet deep; very difficult to get wood, and we are completely housed up; our cattle all killed but two or three, and these, with the horses and Stanton's mules, all supposed to be lost in the snow; no hopes of finding them alive.

"Dec. 3. Ceases snowing; cloudy all day; warm enough to thaw.

"Dec. 5. Beautiful sunshine; thawing a little; looks delightful after the long storm; snow seven or eight feet deep.

"Dec. 6. The morning fine and clear; Stanton and Graves manufacturing snow-shoes for another mountain scrabble; no account of mules.

"Dec. 8. Fine weather; froze hard last night; wind south-west; hard work to find wood sufficient to keep us warm or cook our beef.

"Dec. 9. Commenced snowing about eleven o'clock; wind northwest; took in Spitzer yesterday, so weak that he can not rise without help; caused by starvation. Some have a scanty supply of beef; Stanton trying to get some for himself and Indians; not likely to get much.

"Dec. 10. Snowed fast all night, with heavy squalls of wind; continues to snow; now about seven feet in depth.

"Dec. 14. Snows faster than any previous day; Stanton and Graves, with several others, making preparations to cross the mountains on snow-shoes; snow eight feet on a level.

"Dec. 16. Fair and pleasant; froze hard last night; the company started on snow-shoes to cross the mountains; wind southeast.

"Dec. 17. Pleasant; William Murphy returned from the mountain party last evening; Baylis Williams died night before last; Milton and Noah started for Donner's eight days ago; not returned yet; think they are lost in the snow.

"Dec. 19. Snowed last night; thawing to-day; wind northwest; a little singular for a thaw.

"Dec. 20. Clear and pleasant; Mrs. Reed here; no account from Milton yet. Charles Burger started for Donner's; turned back; unable to proceed; tough times, but not discouraged. Our hope is in God. Amen.

"Dec. 21. Milton got back last night from Donner's camp. Sad news; Jacob Donner, Samuel Shoemaker, Rhinehart, and Smith are dead; the rest of them in a low situation; snowed all night, with a strong southwest wind."

Jacob Donner was the first to die at Prosser Creek. He expired while sitting at the table in his tent, with his head bowed upon his hands, as if in deep meditation. The following terse account is from the gifted pen of Mrs. S. O. Houghton (Eliza P Donner), of San Jose: "Jacob Donner was a slight man, of delicate constitution, and was in poor health when we left Springfield, Illinois. The trials of the journey reduced his strength and exhausted his energy. When we reached the place of encampment in the mountains he was discouraged and gave up in despair. Not even the needs of his family could rouse him to action. He was utterly dejected and made no effort, but tranquilly awaited death."

"Dec. 23. Clear to-day; Milton took some of his meat away; all well at their camp. Began this day to read the 'Thirty Days' Prayers;' Almighty God, grant the requests of unworthy sinners!

"Dec. 24. Rained all night, and still continues; poor prospect for any kind of comfort, spiritual or temporal."

As will be seen by various references throughout this diary, Mr. Breen was a devout Catholic. During the darkest hour of trial the prayers were regularly read. That this might be done during the long weary evenings, as well as by day, pieces of pitch pine were split and laid carefully in one corner of the cabin, which would be lighted at the fire, and would serve as a substitute for candles. Those of the survivors who are living often speak of the times when they held these sticks while Mr. Breen read the prayers. So impressive were these religious observances that one girl, a bright, beautiful child, Virginia E. Reed, made a solemn vow that if God would hear these prayers, and deliver her family from the dangers surrounding them, she would become a Catholic. God did save her family, and she kept her vow. She is to-day a fervent Catholic.

"Dec. 25. Began to snow yesterday, snowed all night, and snows yet rapidly; extremely difficult to find wood; uttered our prayers to God this Christmas morning; the prospect is appalling, but we trust in Him."

What a desolate Christmas morning that was for the snow-bound victims! All were starving. Something to eat, something to satisfy the terrible cravings of appetite, was the constant wish of all. Sometimes the wishes were expressed aloud, but more frequently a gloomy silence prevailed. When anything was audibly wished for, it was invariably something whose size was proportional to their hunger.

They never wished for a meal, or a mouthful, but for a barrel full, a wagon load, a house full, or a storehouse full.

On Christmas eve the children spoke in low, subdued tones, of the visits Santa Claus used to make them in their beautiful homes, before they started across the plains. Now they knew that no Santa Claus could find them in the pathless depths of snow.

One family, the Reeds, were in a peculiarly distressing situation. They knew not whether the father was living or dead. No tidings had reached them since his letters ceased to be found by the wayside. The meat they had obtained from the Breen and Graves families was now gone, and on Christmas morning their breakfast was a "pot of glue," as the boiled rawhide was termed. But Mrs. Reed, the dear, tender-hearted mother, had a surprise in store for her children this day. When the last ox had been purchased, Mrs. Reed had placed the frozen meat in one corner of the cabin, so that pieces could be chipped off with a knife or hatchet. The tripe, however, she cleaned carefully and hung on the outside of the cabin, on the end of a log, close to the ground. She knew that the snow would soon conceal this from view. She also laid away secretly, one teacupful of white beans, about half that quantity of rice, the same measure of dried apples, and a piece of bacon two inches square. She knew that if Christmas found them alive, they would be in a terribly destitute condition. She therefore resolved to lay these articles away, and give them to her starving children for a Christmas dinner. This was done. The joy and gladness of these poor little children knew no bounds when they saw the treasures unearthed and cooking on the fire. They were, just this one meal, to have all they could eat! They laughed, and danced, and cried by turns. They eagerly watched the dinner as it boiled. The pork and tripe had been cut in dice-

7

like pieces. Occasionally one of these pieces would boil up to the surface of the water for an instant, then a bean would take a peep at them from the boiling kettle, then a piece of apple, or a grain of rice. The appearance of each tiny bit was hailed by the children with shouts of glee. The mother, whose eyes were brimming with tears, watched her famished darlings with emotions that can be imagined. It seemed too sad that innocent children should be brought to such destitution that the very sight of food should so affect them! When the dinner was prepared, the mother's constant injunction was, "Children, eat slowly, there is plenty for all." When they thought of the starvation of to-morrow, they could not repress a shade of sadness, and when the name of papa was mentioned all burst into tears. Dear, brave papa! Was he struggling to relieve his starving family, or lying stark and dead 'neath the snows of the Sierra? This question was constantly uppermost in the mother's mind.

"Dec. 27. Cleared off yesterday, and continues clear; snow nine feet deep; wood growing scarce; a tree, when felled, sinks into the snow, and is hard to be got at.

"Dec. 30. Fine clear morning; froze hard last night. Charles Burger died last evening about 10 o'clock.

"Dec. 31. Last of the year. May we, with the help of God, spend the coming year better than we have the past, which we propose to do if it is the will of the Almighty to deliver us from our present dreadful situation. Amen. Morning fair, but cloudy; wind east by south; looks like another snow-storm. Snow-storms are dreadful to us. The snow at present is very deep.

"Jan. 1, 1847. We pray the God of mercy to deliver us from our present calamity, if it be His holy will. Commenced snowing last night, and snows a little yet. Provisions getting very scanty; dug up a hide from under the snow yesterday; have not commenced on it yet.

"Jan. 3. Fair during the day, freezing at night. Mrs. Reed talks of crossing the mountains with her children.

"Jan. 4. Fine morning; looks like spring. Mrs. Reed and Virginia, Milton Elliott, and Eliza Williams started a short time ago with the hope of crossing the mountains; left the children here. It was difficult for Mrs. Reed to part with them."

This expedition was only one of many that the emigrants attempted. The suffering that was endured at these times was indescribable. The broken, volcanic nature of the summits rendered it extremely difficult to keep from getting lost. The white, snowy cliffs were everywhere the same. This party became bewildered and lost near the beautiful Lake Angeline, which is close to the present "Summit Station" of the Central Pacific. Had they attempted to proceed, all would undoubtedly have perished.

Within half a mile of the wagon road which now extends from Donner Lake to the Summit are places where rocks and cliffs are mingled in wildest confusion. Even in summer time it is difficult to find one's way among the broken, distorted mountain tops. In the mighty upheaval which produced the Sierra Nevada, these vast mounds or mountains of frowning granite were grouped into weird, fantastic labyrinths. Time has wrought little effect upon their bold precipitous sides, and made slight impress upon their lofty and almost inaccessible crests. Between these fragmentary mountains, in shapely, symmetrical bowls which have been delved by the fingers of the water nymphs and Undines, lie beautiful lakelets. Angeline is but one of a dozen which sparkle like a chain of gems between Donner Lake and the snowy, overhanging peaks of Mount Stanford. The clefts and fissures of

the towering granite cliffs are filled, in summer, with dainty
ferns, clinging mosses, and the loveliest of mountain wild
flowers, and the rims of the lakelets are bordered with grasses,
shrubbery, and a wealth of wild blossoms. But in winter this
region exhibits the very grandeur of desolation. No verdure
is visible save the dwarfed and shattered pines whose crushed
branches mark the path of the rushing avalanche. The furious winds in their wild sport toss and tumble the snow-drifts
here and there, baring the sterile peaks, and heaping the
white masses a hundred feet deep into chasm and gorge.
The pure, clear lakes, as if in very fear, hide their faces from
the turbulent elements in mantles of ice. The sun is darkened by dense clouds, and the icy, shivering, shrieking storm-
fiends hold undisturbed their ghastly revels. On every side
are lofty battlements of rock, whose trembling burden of
snow seems ever ready to slide from its glassy foundations of
ice, and entomb the bewildered traveler.

Into this interminable maze of rocks and cliffs and frozen
lakelets, the little party wandered. Elliott had a compass,
but it soon proved worthless, and only added to their per-
plexed and uncertain state of mind. They were out five days.
Virginia's feet became so badly frozen that she could not
walk. This occurrence saved the party. Reluctantly they
turned back toward the cabins, convinced that it was madness to attempt to go forward. They reached shelter just as
one of the most terrible storms of all that dreadful winter
broke over their heads. Had they delayed their return a few
hours, the path they made in ascending the mountains, and
by means of which they retraced their steps, would have been
concealed, and death would have been certain.

"Jan. 6. Eliza came back yesterday evening from the
mountains, unable to proceed; the others kept ahead.

"Jan. 8. Mrs. Reed and the others came back; could not

MARY A. GRAVES

(Mrs. J. T. Clark.)

1879.

find their way on the other side of the mountains. They have nothing but hides to live on.

"Jan. 10. Began to snow last night; still continues; wind west-north-west.

"Jan. 13. Snowing fast; snow higher than the shanty; it must be thirteen feet deep. Can not get wood this morning; it is a dreadful sight for us to look upon."

One of the stumps near the Graves-Reed cabin, cut while the snow was at its deepest, was found, by actual measurement, to be twenty-two feet in height. Part of this stump is (17) standing to-day.

"Jan. 14. Cleared off yesterday. The sun, shining brilliantly, renovates our spirits. Praise be to the God of heaven.

"Jan. 15. Clear to-day again. Mrs. Murphy blind; Landrum not able to get wood; has but one ax between him and Keseberg. It looks like another storm; expecting some account from Sutter's soon.

"Jan. 17. Eliza Williams came here this morning; Landrum crazy last night; provisions scarce; hides our main subsistence. May the Almighty send us help.

"Jan. 21. Fine morning; John Baptiste and Mr. Denton came this morning with Eliza; she will not eat hides. Mrs. —— sent her back to live or die on them."

The blanks which occasionally occur were in the original (18) diary. The delicacy which prompted Patrick Breen to omit these names can not fail to be appreciated. What if there was sometimes a shade of selfishness, or an act of harshness? What if some families had more than their destitute neighbors? The best provided had little. All were in reality strangely generous. All divided with their afflicted companions. The Reeds had almost nothing to eat when they arrived at the cabins, yet this family is the only one which reached the settlements without some one member having to partake of human flesh.

"Jan. 22. Began to snow after sunrise; likely to continue; wind north.

"Jan. 23. Blew hard and snowed all night; the most severe storm we have experienced this winter; wind west.

"Jan. 26. Cleared up yesterday; to-day fine and pleasant; wind south; in hopes we are done with snow-storms. Those who went to Sutter's not yet returned; provisions getting scant; people growing weak, living on a small allowance of hides.

"Jan. 27. Commenced snowing yesterday; still continues to-day. Lewis Keseberg, Jr., died three days ago; food growing scarce; don't have fire enough to cook our hides.

"Jan. 30. Fair and pleasant; wind west; thawing in the sun. John and Edward Breen went to Graves' this morning.
(19) Mrs. ⸺ seized on Mrs. ⸺'s goods until they would be paid; they also took the hides which herself and family subsisted upon. She regained two pieces only, the balance they have taken. You may judge from this what our fare is in camp. There is nothing to be had by hunting, yet perhaps there soon will be.

"Jan. 31. The sun does not shine out brilliant this morning; froze hard last night; wind north-west. Landrum Murphy died last night about ten o'clock; Mrs. Reed went to Graves' this morning to look after goods."

Landrum Murphy was a large and somewhat overgrown young man. The hides and burnt bones did not contain sufficient nourishment to keep him alive. For some hours before he died, he lay in a semi-delirious state, breathing heavily and seemingly in little or no pain. Mrs. Murphy went to the Breen camp, and asked Mrs. Breen for a piece of meat to save her starving boy.  Mrs. Breen gave her the meat, but it was too late, Landrum could not eat.  Finally he sank into a gentle slumber.  His breathing grew less and less distinct, and ere they were fairly aware of it life was extinct.

"Feb. 4.  Snowed hard until twelve o'clock last night; many uneasy for fear we shall all perish with hunger; we have but little meat left, and only three hides; Mrs. Reed has nothing but one hide, and that is on Graves' house; Milton lives there, and likely will keep that.  Eddy's child died last night.

"Feb. 5.  It snowed faster last night and to-day than it has done this winter before; still continues without intermission; wind south-west.  Murphy's folks and Keseberg say they can not eat hides.  I wish we had enough of them.  Mrs. Eddy is very weak.

"Feb. 7.  Ceased to snow at last; to-day it is quite pleasant.  McCutchen's child died on the second of this month."

This child died and was buried in the Graves cabin.  Mr. W. C. Graves helped dig the grave near one side of the cabin, and laid the little one to rest.  One of the most heart-rending features of this Donner tragedy is the number of infants that suffered.  Mrs. Breen, Pike, Foster, McCutchen, Eddy, Keseberg, and Graves each had nursing babes when the fatal camp was pitched at Donner Lake.

"Feb. 8.  Fine, clear morning.  Spitzer died last night, and we will bury him in the snow; Mrs. Eddy died on the night of the seventh.

"Feb. 9.  Mrs. Pike's child all but dead; Milton is at Murphy's, not able to get out of bed; Mrs. Eddy and child were buried to-day; wind south-east.

"Feb. 10.  Beautiful morning; thawing in the sun; Milton

Elliott died last night at Murphy's cabin, and Mrs. Reed went there this morning to see about his effects. John Denton trying to borrow meat for Graves; had none to give; they had nothing but hides; all are entirely out of meat, but a little we have; our hides are nearly all eat up, but with God's help spring will soon smile upon us.

"Feb. 12.   Warm, thawy morning.

"Feb. 14.   Fine morning, but cold.   Buried Milton in the snow; John Denton not well.

"Feb. 15.   Morning cloudy until nine o'clock, then cleared (20) off warm.   Mrs. —— refused to give Mrs. —— any hides. Put Sutter's pack hides on her shanty, and would not let her have them.

"Feb. 16.   Commenced to rain last evening, and turned to snow during the night, and continued until morning; weather changeable, sunshine and then light showers of hail, and wind at times.   We all feel unwell.   The snow is not getting much less at present."

# CHAPTER IX.

---

IT is recorded of Lewis and Salvador that they came willingly to the relief of the emigrants. Two of Sutter's best trained vaqueros, faithful, honest, reliable, they seemed rather proud when chosen to assist Stanton in driving the mules laden with provisions for the starving train. Now they were dying! Horrified at the sight of human beings eating the flesh of their comrades, they withdrew from the whites at the "Camp of Death." After that they always camped apart, but continued to act as guides until they became certain that their own lives were in danger. Then they fled. Starving, exhausted, with frozen and bleeding feet, the poor wretches dragged their weary bodies onward until they reached a little streamlet, and here they lay down to die. Nine days, with no other food than they could find in the snow, was too much even for their hardy natures. They were unable to move when the famished "Seven" passed. Yes, PASSED! for the starving emi-

grants went on by the poor fellows, unable to deprive them
of the l'ttle spark of life left in their wasted bodies.  Traveling was now slow work for the dying whites.  They only
went about two hundred yards.  In a few more hours, perhaps that very night, they would die of starvat'on.  Already
the terrible phantasies of delirium were beginning to dance
before their sunken eyes.  Ere the Indians would cease
breathing some of the Seven would be past relief.  There
were two men and five women.  William Foster could see
that his wife—the woman who was all the world to him—
was fast yielding to the deadly grasp of the fiends of starvation.  For the sake of his life she had stifled the most sacred
instincts of her womanly nature, and procured him food
from Fosdick's body.  Should he see her die the most terrible of deaths without attempting to rescue her?  Reader,
put yourself in this man's place.  Brave, generous, heroic,
full of lion-like nobility, William Foster could not stoop to a
base action.  Contemplate his position!  Lying there prostrate upon the snow was Mrs. Pike, the woman whom, accidentally, he had rendered a widow.  Her babes were dying
in the cabins.  His own boy was at the cabins.  His comrades, his wife, were in the last stages of starvation.  He,
also, was dying.  Eddy had not nerve enough, the women
could not, and William Foster must—what!  Was it murder?
No!  Every law book, every precept of that higher law, self-
preservation, every dictate of right, reason or humanity, de-
manded the deed.  The Indians were past all hope of aid.
They could not lift their heads from their pillow of snow.
It was not simply justifiable—it was duty; it was a necessity.

He told them, when he got back, that he was compelled
to take their lives.  They did not moan or struggle, or
appear to regret that their lingering pain was to cease.  The
five women and Eddy heard two reports of a gun.

The "Forlorn Hope" might yet save those who were dying at Donner Lake.

Even this relief was but temporary. Taking the wasted flesh from the bones, drying it, and staggering forward, the little band speedily realized that they were not yet saved. It was food for only a few days. Then they again felt their strength failing. Once more they endured the excruciating torments which precede starvation.

In the very complete account of this trip, which is kindly furnished by Mary Graves, are many interesting particulars concerning the suffering of these days. "Our only chance for camp-fire for the night," she says, "was to hunt a dead tree of some description, and set fire to it. The hemlock being the best and generally much the largest timber, it was our custom to select the driest we could find without leaving our course. When the fire would reach the top of the tree, the falling limbs would fall all around us and bury themselves in the snow, but we heeded them not. Sometimes the falling, blazing limbs would brush our clothes, but they never hit us; that would have been too lucky a hit. We would sit or lie on the snow, and rest our weary frames. We would sleep, only to dream of something nice to eat, and awake again to disappointment. Such was our sad fate! Even the reindeer's wretched lot was not worse! 'His dinner and his bed were snow, and supper he had not.' Our fare was the same! We would strike fire by means of the flint-lock gun which we had with us. This had to be carried by turns, as it was considered the only hope left in case we might find game which we could kill. We traveled over a ridge of mountains, and then descended a deep canyon, where one could scarcely see the bottom. Down, down we would go, or rather slide, for it is very slavish work going down hill, and in many cases we were compelled to slide on our shoes as sleds. On reaching the bottom we would plunge into the snow, so that it was difficult getting out, with the shoes tied to our feet, our packs lashed to our backs, and ourselves head and ears under the snow. But we managed to get out some way, and one by one reached the bottom of the canyon. When this was accomplished we had to ascend a hill as steep as the one we had descended. We would drive the toes of our shoes into the loose snow, to make a sort of step, and one by one, as if ascending stair-steps, we climbed up. It took us an entire day to reach the top of the mountain. Each time we attained the summit of a mountain, we hoped we should be able to see something like a valley, but each time came disappointment, for far ahead was always another and higher mountain. We found some springs, or, as we called them, wells, from five to twenty feet under ground, as you might say, for they were under the snow on which we walked. The water was so warm that it melted the snow, and from some of these springs were large streams of running water. We crossed numbers of these streams on bridges of snow, which would sometimes form upon a blade of grass hanging over the water; and from so small a foundation would grow a bridge from ten to twenty-five feet high, and from a foot and a half to three feet across the top. It would make you dizzy to look down at the water, and it was with much difficulty we could place our clumsy ox-bow snow-shoes one ahead of the other without falling. Our feet had been frozen and thawed so many times that they were bleeding and sore. When we stopped at night we would take off our shoes, which by this time were so badly rotted by constant wetting in snow, that there was very little left of them. In the morning we would push our shoes on, bruising and numbing the feet so badly that they would ache and ache with walking and the cold, until night

would come again. Oh! the pain! It seemed to make the
pangs of hunger more excruciating."

Thus the party traveled on day after day, until absolute
starvation again stared them in the face. The snow had
gradually grown less deep, until finally it disappeared or lay
only in patches. Their strength was well-nigh exhausted,
when one day Mary Graves says: "Some one called out,
'Here are tracks!' Some one asked, 'What kind of tracks—
human?' 'Yes, human!' Can any one imagine the joy
these footprints gave us? We ran as fast as our strength
would carry us."

Turning a chaparral point, they came in full view of an
Indian rancherie. The uncivilized savages were amazed.
Never had they seen such forlorn, wretched, pitiable human
beings, as the tattered, disheveled, skeleton creatures who
stood stretching out their arms for assistance. At first, they
all ran and hid, but soon they returned to the aid of these
dying wretches. It is said that the Indian women and children cried, and wailed with grief at the affecting spectacle of
starved men and women. Such food as they had was speedily
offered. It was bread made of acorns. This was eagerly
eaten. It was at least a substitute for food. Every person
in the rancherie, from the toddling papooses to the aged chief,
endeavored to aid them.

After what had recently happened, could anything be more
touching than these acts of kindness of the Indians?

After briefly resting, they pressed forward. The Indians
accompanied and even led them, and constantly supplied
them with food. With food? No, it was not such food as
their weakened, debilitated systems craved. The acorn bread
was not sufficient to sustain lives already so attenuated by
repeated starvations. All that the starved experience in the
way of pain and torture before they die, had been experi-

enced by these people at least four d'fferent times.   To their
horror, they now discovered that despite the acorn bread,
they must die of hunger and exhaustion a fifth and last time.
So sick and weak did they become, that they were compelled
to lie down and rest every hundred yards.   Finally, after being with the Indians seven days, they lay down, and felt that
they never should have strength to take another step.   Before them, in all its beauty and loveliness, spread the broad
valley of the Sacramento.   Behind them were the ever-plead-
ing faces of their starving dear ones.   Yet neither hope nor
affection could give them further strength.   They were dying
in full view of the long-desired haven of rest.

One of the number was hardly so near death's door as his
companions.   It was W. H. Eddy.   As a last resort, their
faithful allies, the Indians, took him upon either side, and
fairly carried him along.   His feet moved, but they were
frozen, and blistered, and cracked, and bleeding.   Left alone,
he would have fallen helplessly to the earth.   It was as terrible a journey as ever mortal man performed.   How far he
traveled, he knew not.   During the last six miles his path
was marked by blood-stains from his swollen feet.

By making abridgments from valuable manuscript contributed by George W. Tucker, of Calistoga, this narrative may
be appropriately continued.   Mr. Tucker's father and relatives had reached Johnson's Ranch on the twenty-fifth of
October, 1846.   They had been with the Donner Party until
Fort Bridger was reached, and then took the Fort Hall road.
Their journey had been full of dangers and difficulties, and
(21) reaching Johnson's Ranch, the first settlement on the west
side of the Sierra, they determined to remain during the
winter.

One evening, about the last of January, Mr. Tucker says a
man was seen coming down Bear River, accompanied by an

REASIN P. TUCKER.

1881.

Indian. His haggard, forlorn look showed he was in great distress. When he reached us, he said he was of the Donner Party. He told briefly how the train had been caught in the snow east of the mountains, and was unable to get back or forward. He told how the fifteen had started, and that six beside himself were still alive. That the six were back in the mountains, almost starved. R. P. Tucker and three other men started at once with provisions, the Indian acting as guide. They reached them, fifteen miles back, some time during the night, and brought them in the next day. The names of the seven were W. H. Eddy, William Foster, Mrs. S. A. C. Foster, Mrs. H. F. Pike, Mrs. William McCutchen, Mrs. Sarah Fosdick, and Mary Graves. It had been thirty-two days since they left Donner Lake!

At Johnson's Ranch there were only three or four families of poor emigrants. Nothing could be done toward relieving those at Donner Lake until help could arrive from Sutter's Fort. A rainy winter had flooded Bear River, and rendered the Sacramento plains a vast quagmire. Yet one man volunteered to go to Sacramento with the tale of horror, and get men and provisions. This man was John Rhodes. Lashing two pine logs together with rawhides, and forming a raft, John Rhodes was ferried over Bear River. Taking his shoes in his hands, and rolling his pants up above his knees, he started on foot through water that frequently was from one to three feet deep. Some time during the night he reached the Fort.

A train in the mountains! Men, women, and children starving! It was enough to make one's blood curdle to think of it! Captain Sutter, generous old soul, and Alcalde Sinclair, who lived at Norris' Ranch two and a half miles from the Fort, offered provisions, and five or six men volunteered to carry them over the mountains. In about a week, six men, fully provided with supplies, reached Johnson's Ranch. Meantime the Tuckers and their neighbors had slaughtered five or six fat cattle, and had dried or "jerked" the meat. The country was scoured for horses and mules, and for saddles and pack-saddles, but at last, in ten or twelve days, they were ready to start. Alcalde Sinclair had come up from the Fort, and when all were ready to begin their march, he made them a thrilling little address. They were, he said, starting out upon a hazardous journey. Nothing could justify them in attempting so perilous an undertaking except the obligations due to their suffering fellow-men. He urged them to do all in their power, without sacrificing their lives, to save the perishing emigrants from starvation and death. He then appointed Reasin P. Tucker, the father of our informant, captain of the company. With a pencil he carefully wrote down the name of each man in the relief party. The names were John (22) Rhodes, Daniel Rhodes, Aquilla Glover, R. S. Mootrey, Joseph Foster, Edward Coffeemire, M. D. Ritchie, James Curtis, William H. Eddy, William Coon, R. P. Tucker, George W. Tucker, and Adolph Brueheim. Thus the first relief party started.

# CHAPTER X.

CALIFORNIA, at this time, was sparsely settled, and it
was a fearful undertaking to cross the snowy mountains to the relief of the storm-bound emigrants. A
better idea of the difficulties to be encountered by the
various relief parties can not be presented than by
quoting from the manuscript of George W. Tucker. This
gentleman was sixteen years old at the time of the occurrences narrated, and his account is vouched for as perfectly
truthful and reliable. This sketch, like the remainder of this
book, treats of an epoch in California history which has
been almost forgotten. The scene of his adventures is laid
in a region familiar to thousands of miners and early Californians. Along the route over which he passed with so
much difficulty, scores of mining camps sprung up soon after
the discovery of gold, and every flat, ravine, and hill-slope
echoed to pick, and shovel, and pan, and to voices of legions

8

of men.   Truly, his narration relates to a lost, an almost un•
remembered era in the history of the famous mining counties, Placer and Nevada.   In speaking of the first relief party,
he says:

"We mounted our horses and started.   The ground was
very soft among the foothills, but we got along very well for
two or three miles after leaving Johnson's ranch.   Finally,
one of our pack-horses broke through the crust, and down
he went to his sides in the mud.   He floundered and plunged
until the pack turned underneath his body.   He then came
out of the mud, bucking and kicking; and he bucked and
kicked, and kicked and bucked, till he cleared himself of the
pack, pack-saddle and all, and away he went back to the
ranch.   We gathered up the pack, put it upon the horse
Eddy was riding, and the party traveled on.   Eddy and myself were to go back to the ranch, catch the horse, and returning, overtake them.   We failed to find the horse that day, but
the next morning an Indian got on my horse, and, about nine
o'clock, succeeded in finding the missing animal.   My horse,
however, was pretty well run down when he got back.   Eddy
and myself started about ten o'clock.   We had to travel in
one day what the company had traveled in two days.   About
the time we started it commenced clouding up, and we saw
we were going to have a storm.   We went on until about one
o'clock, when my horse gave out.   It commenced raining and
was very cold.   Eddy said he would ride on and overtake the
company, if possible, and have them stop.   He did not overtake them until about dark, after they had camped.

"My horse could only go in a slow walk, so I walked and
led him to keep from freezing.   The rain continued to in-
crease in volume, and by dark it was coming down in torrents.
It was very cold.   The little stream began to rise, but I waded
through, though sometimes it came up to my armpits.   It

was very dark, but I kept going on in hopes I would come in sight of the camp-fire. But the darkness increased, and it was very difficult to find the road. I would get down on my knees and feel for the road with my hands. Finally, about nine o'clock, it became so dark that I could not see a tree until I would run against it, and I was almost exhausted dragging my horse after me. I had lost the road several times, but found it by feeling for the wagon-ruts. At last I came to where the road made a short turn around the point of a hill, and I went straight ahead until I got forty or fifty yards from the road. I crawled around for some time on my knees, but could not find it. I knew if the storm was raging in the morning as it was then, if I got very far from the road, I could not tell which was east, west, north, or south, I might get lost and perish before the storm ceased, so I concluded to stay right there until morning. I had no blanket, and nothing on me but a very light coat and pair of pants. I tied my horse to a little pine tree, and sitting down, leaned against the tree. The rain came down in sheets. The wind blew, and the old pine trees clashed their limbs together. It seemed to me that a second deluge had come. I would get so cold that I would get up and walk around for a while. It seemed to me I should surely freeze. Toward morning I began to get numb, and felt more comfortable, but that was the longest and hardest night I ever experienced.

"In the morning, when it became light enough so that I could see two or three rods, I got up, but my legs were so numb that I could not walk. I rolled around until I got up a circulation, and could stand on my feet. Leaving my horse tied to the tree, I found the road, went about a hundred yards around the point of a hill, and saw the camp-fire up in a little flat about a quarter of a mile from where I had spent the night. Going up to camp, I found the men all standing

around a fire they had made, where two large pines had
fallen across each other.   They had laid down pine bark and
pieces of wood to keep them out of the water.   They had
stood up all night.   The water was running two or three
inches deep all through the camp.   When I got to the fire,
and began to get warm, my legs and arms began to swell so
that I could hardly move or get my hands to my face.

"It never ceased raining all that day nor the next night,
and we were obliged to stand around the fire.   Everything
we had was wet.   They had stacked up our dried beef and
flour in a pile, and put the saddles and pack saddles over it
as well as they could, but still it got more or less wet.   The
third morning it stopped raining about daylight, and the sun
came out clear and warm.   We made scaffolds and spread
our meat all out, hung up our blankets and clothing on lines,
and by keeping up fires and with the help of the sun, we
managed to get everything dry by night.   The next morning
we packed up and started on until we came to a little valley,
where we found some grass for our horses.   We stayed there
that night.   The next day we got to Steep Hollow Creek,
one of the branches of Bear River.   This stream was not
more than a hundred feet wide, but it was about twenty feet
deep, and the current was very swift.   We felled a large pine
tree across it, but the center swayed down so that the water
ran over it about a foot deep.   We tied ropes together and
stretched them across to make a kind of hand railing, and
succeeded in carrying over all our things.   We undertook to
make our horses swim the creek, and finally forced two of
them into the stream, but as soon as they struck the current
they were carried down faster than we could run.   One of
them at last reached the bank and got ashore, but the other
went down under the tree we had cut, and the first we saw of
him he came up about twenty yards below, heels upward.

He finally struck a drift about a hundred yards below, and we succeeded in getting him out almost drowned. We then tied ropes together, part of the men went over, and tying a rope to each horse, those on one side would force him into the water, and the others would draw him across. We lost a half day at this place. That night we climbed a high mountain, and came to snow. Camped that night without any feed for our horses. The next day, about noon, we reached Mule Springs. The snow was from three to four feet deep, and it was impossible to go any farther with the horses. Unpacking the animals, Joe Varro and Wm. Eddy started back with them to Johnson's Ranch. The rest of us went to work and built a brush tent in which to keep our provisions. We set forks into the ground, laid poles across, and covered them with cedar boughs. We finished them that evening, and the next morning ten of the men fixed up their packs, consisting of dried beef and flour, and started on foot, each one carrying about seventy-five pounds. They left Billy Coon and myself to watch the provisions until they returned. I have never been in that country since, but I think Mule Springs is on the opposite side of Bear River from (23) Dutch Flat.

"After the men had all gone, I amused myself the first day by getting wood and cutting cedar limbs to finish our camp with. My companion, Billy Coon, was partially insane, and was no company at all. He would get up in the morning, eat his food, and then lie down and sleep for two or three hours. He would only talk when he was spoken to; and all he knew was to sleep and eat. I got very lonesome, and would sit for hours thinking of our situation. Sixty miles from any human habitation! Surrounded with wild Indians and wild beasts! Then, when I would look away at the snow-capped peaks of the Sierra, and think that my father and the rest of the men where there, toiling under the heavy loads which they carried, I became still more gloomy. When night would come, the big gray wolves that had collected on the mountains facing to the south, where the snow had melted off, would set up their howlings. This, with the dismal sound of the wind roaring through the tall pine trees, was almost unendurable. To this day, when I am in pine timber, and hear the wind sighing through the tree-tops, I always think of the Donner Party and of those lonely days in the mountains.

"The third day after the men left I became so lonesome that I took the gun and went down in the direction in which I had heard the wolves howling. When I got down out of the snow, I found the deer had collected there by the hundreds. I killed two deer; went up and got Billy Coon, and we carried them up to camp. We hung one on each corner of our brush tent, not more than six feet from our bed, and not more than four feet from the fire. Next morning one of the deer was gone! I supposed the Indians had found us out and stolen it; but when I looked for tracks I found the thief had been a California lion. I tracked him two or three hundred yards, but he had walked off with the deer so easily, I thought he might keep it. That afternoon I went down to kill another deer, but when I reached a point from which I could see down to the river, I saw the smoke of an Indian camp. I was afraid to shoot for fear the Indians would hear the gun, and finding out we were there, would come up and give us trouble. I started back, and when in sight of camp I sat down on a log to rest. While sitting there I saw three Indians coming up the hill. I sat still to see what they would do. They came up to within sight of the camp, and all crawled up behind a large sugar-pine tree, and sat there watching the camp. I did not like their movements, so thought I would give them a scare. I leveled the old gun at the tree, about six feet above their heads, and fired away. They got away from there faster than they came, and I never saw them afterwards.

"On the fifth day after the men left, three of them came back to the camp. They informed me they had been three days in traveling from Mule Springs to Bear Valley, a distance of twelve miles. These three had found it impossible to stand the journey, but the other seven had started on from Bear Valley. It was thought they could never get over to Truckee Lake, for the snow was so soft it was impossible to carry their heavy loads through from ten to thirty feet of it."

M. D. Ritchie and R. P. Tucker kept a diary of the journey of the first relief party, which, thanks to Patty Reed, now Mrs. Frank Lewis, is before us. It is brief, concise, pointed, and completes the narration of Mr. George W. Tucker. Mr. Ritchie's diary reads:

"Feb. 5, 1847. First day traveled ten miles. Bad roads; often miring down horses and mules. On the sixth and seventh traveled fifteen miles. Road continued bad; commenced raining before we got to camp, and continued to rain all that day and night very severe. Lay by here on the eighth to dry our provisions and clothing.

"Feb. 9. Traveled fifteen miles. Swam the animals over one creek, and carried the provisions over on a log.

"Feb. 10. Traveled four miles; came to the snow; continued about four miles further. Animals floundering in snow, and camped at the Mule Springs.

"Feb. 11. Mr. Eddy started back with the animals; left William Coon and George Tucker to guard what provisions were left in camp; the other ten men, each taking about fifty pounds, except Mr. Curtis, who took about twenty-five pounds. Traveled on through the snow, having a very severe day's travel over mountains, making about six miles. Camped on Bear River, near a cluster of large pines.

"Feb. 12. Moved camp about two miles, and stopped to make snow-shoes; tried them on and found them of no benefit; cast them away.

"Feb. 13. Made Bear Valley. Upon digging for Curtis' wagon, found the snow ten feet deep, and the provisions destroyed by the bears. Rain and snow fell on us all night."

By Curtis' wagon is meant a cache made by Reed and McCutchen, which will be described in the next chapter.

"Feb. 14. Fine weather."

From this time forward, the journal was kept by Reasin P. Tucker.

"Feb. 15. Fine day. Three of our men decline going any further—W. D. Ritchie, A. Brueheim, and James Curtis. Only seven men being left, the party was somewhat discouraged. We consulted together, and under existing circumstances I took it upon myself to insure every man who persevered to the end, five dollars per day from the time they entered the snow. We determined to go ahead, and camped to-night on Yuba River, after traveling fifteen miles.

"Feb. 16. Traveling very bad, and snowing. Made but five miles, and camped in snow fifteen feet deep.

"Feb. 17. Traveled five miles.

"Feb. 18. Traveled eight miles, and camped on the head of the Yuba; on the pass we suppose the snow to be thirty feet deep."

The "pass" was the Summit. Relief was close at hand. Would it find the emigrants?

# CHAPTER XI.

JAMES F. REED encountered the most disheartening trials after leaving the Donner Party. He and Walter Herron were reduced to the utmost verge of starvation while on the Sierra Nevada. At one time they discovered five beans in the road, one after the other; and at another time they ate of the rancid tallow which was found in a tar bucket under an old wagon.

Mr. Reed has told the rest in an article contributed by him to the Rural Press. It explains so well the difficulties of getting relief to the emigrants, that it is copied:

"When I arrived at Captain Sutter's, making known my situation to him, asking if he would furnish me horses and saddles to bring the women and children out of the mountains (I expected to meet them at the head of Bear Valley by the time I could return there), he at once complied with the request, also saying that he would do everything possible for me and the company. On the evening of my arrival at the Captain's, I found Messrs. Bryant, Lippencott, Grayson, and Jacobs, some of the early voyagers in the Russel Company, they having left that company at Fort Laramie, most of them coming on horseback.

"During the evening a meeting was held, in which I participated, adopting a memorial to the commander of Sutter's Fort, to raise one or more companies of volunteers, to proceed to Los Angeles, we being at war with Mexico at this time. The companies were to be officered by the petitioners. Being requested to take command of one of the companies, I declined, stating that it would be necessary for the captain to stay with the company; also that I had to return to the mountains for the emigrants, but that I would take a lieutenancy. This was agreed to, and I was on my return to the emigrants to enlist all the men I could between there and Bear Valley. On my way up I enlisted twelve or thirteen.

"The second night after my arrival at Captain Sutter's, we had a light rain; next morning we could see snow on the mountains. The Captain stated that it was low down and heavy for the first fall of the season. The next day I started on my return with what horses and saddles Captain Sutter had to spare. He furnished us all the flour needed, and a hind quarter of beef, giving us an order for more horses and saddles at Mr. Cordway's, near where Marysville is located. In the mean time, Mr. McCutchen joined us, he being prevented from returning with Mr. Stanton on account of sickness. After leaving Mr. Johnson's ranch we had thirty horses, one mule, and two Indians to help drive.

"Nothing happened until the evening before reaching the head of Bear Valley, when there commenced a heavy rain and sleet, continuing all night. We drove on until a late hour before halting. We secured the flour and horses, the

C. T. STANTON.

(Photographed from an Oil Painting.)

1844.

rain preventing us from kindling a fire. Next morning, proceeding up the valley to where we were to take the mountain, we found a tent containing a Mr. Curtis and wife. They hailed us as angels sent for their delivery, stating that they would have perished had it not been for our arrival. Mrs. Curtis stated that they had killed their dog, and at the time of our arrival had the last piece in the Dutch oven baking. We told them not to be alarmed about anything to eat, for we had plenty, both of flour and beef, and that they were welcome to all they needed. Our appetites were rather keen, not having eaten anything from the morning previous. Mr. Curtis remarked that in the oven was a piece of the dog and we could have it. Raising the lid of the oven, we found the dog well baked, and having a fine savory smell. I cut out a rib, smelling and tasting, found it to be good, and handed it over to McCutchen, who, after smelling it some time, tasted it and pronounced it very good dog. We partook of Curtis' dog. Mrs. Curtis immediately commenced making bread, and in a short time had supper for all.

"At the lower end of the valley, where we entered, the snow was eighteen inches in depth, and when we arrived at the tent, it was two feet. Curtis stated that his oxen had taken the back track, and that he had followed them by the trail through the snow. In the morning, before leaving, Mrs. Curtis got us to promise to take them into the settlement when on our return with the women and children. Before leaving, we gave them flour and beef sufficient to keep them until our return, expecting to do so in a few days.

"We started, following the trail made by the oxen, and camped a number of miles up the mountain. In the night, hearing some of the horses going down the trail, we went to where the Indians had lain down, and found them gone. McCutchen mounted his horse and rode down to Curtis' camp, and found that the Indians had been there, stopped and warmed themselves, and then started down the valley. He returned to camp about the middle of the night.

"Next morning we started, still on the trail of the oxen, but unfortunately, the trail turned off to the left from our direction. We proceeded on, the snow deepening rapidly, our horses struggling to get through; we pushed them on until they would rear upon their hind feet to breast the snow, and when they would alight they would sink in it until nothing was seen of them but the nose and a portion of the head. Here we found that it was utterly impossible to proceed further with the horses. Leaving them, we proceeded further on foot, thinking that we could get in to the people, but found that impossible, the snow being soft and deep.

"I may here state that neither of us knew anything about snow-shoes, having always lived in a country where they never were used.

"With sorrowful hearts, we arrived that night at the camp of Mr. Curtis, telling them to make their arrangements for leaving with us in the morning. Securing our flour in the wagon of Mr. Curtis, so that we could get it on our return, we packed one horse with articles belonging to Mr. and Mrs. Curtis, and started down the valley to where the snow was light, and where there was considerable underbrush, so that our famished animals could browse, they not having eaten anything for several days.

"After packing Mr. Curtis' horse for him the next morning, we started; in a short time, Mr. and Mrs. Curtis proceeded ahead, leaving the pack-horse behind for us to drive, instead of his leading him; we having our hands full in driving the loose ones, they scattering in all directions. The pack turned on the horse. Mr. Curtis was requested to return and help repack and lead his horse, but he paid no attention to us. We stood this for some time; finally, McCutchen became angry, started after him, determined to bring him back; when he got with him he paid no attention to McCutchen's request to return; Mac becoming more exasperated, hit him several times over the shoulders with his riatta. This brought him to his senses. He said that if Mac would not kill him, he would come back and take care of the pack animal, and he did.

"As soon as we arrived at Captain Sutter's, I made a statement of all the circumstances attending our attempt to get into the mountains. He was no way surprised at our defeat. I also gave the Captain the number of head of cattle the company had when I left them. He made an estimate, and stated that if the emigrants would kill the cattle, and place the meat in the snow for preservation, there was no fear of starvation until relief could reach them. He further stated that there were no able-bodied men in that vicinity, all having gone down the country with and after Fremont to fight the Mexicans. He advised me to proceed to Yerba Buena, now San Francisco, and make my case known to the naval officer in command.

"I left Captain Sutter's, by the way of San Jose, for San Francisco, being unable to come by water. When I arrived at San Jose, I found the San Francisco side of the bay was occupied by the Mexicans. Here I remained, and was attached to a company of volunteers, commanded by Captain Webber, until after the fight at Santa Clara.

"The road now being clear, I proceeded to San Francisco with a petition from some of the prominent citizens of San Jose, asking the commander of the navy to grant aid to enable me to return to the mountains."

It is proper, perhaps, to interrupt the narrative in the Rural Press for the purpose of introducing the memorial referred to by Mr. Reed. The copy of the original document was recently found among his papers by his daughter, Patty Reed.

"To his Excellency, R. F. Stockton, Governor and Commander-in-Chief, by sea and land, of the United States Territory of California: We, the undersigned citizens and residents of the Territory of California, beg leave respectfully to present to your Excellency the following memorial, viz.: That, whereas, the last detachment of emigrants from the United States to California have been unable, from unavoidable causes, to reach the frontier settlements, and are now in the California mountains, seventy-five or one hundred miles east from the Sacramento Valley, surrounded by snow, most probably twenty feet deep, and being about eighty souls in number, a large proportion of whom are women and children, who must shortly be in a famishing condition from scarcity of provisions, therefore, the undersigned most earnestly beseech your Excellency to take into consideration the propriety of fitting out an expedition to proceed on snowshoes immediately to the relief of the sufferers. Your memorialists beg leave to subscribe themselves, very respectfully, yours, etc.

"January, 1847."

The article in the Rural Press continues: "Arriving at San Francisco, I presented my petition to Commodore Hull, also making a statement of the condition of the people in the mountains as far as I knew, the number of them, and what would be needed in provisions and help to get them out. He made an estimate of the expense, and said that he would do anything within reason to further the object, but was afraid that the department at Washington would not sustain him if he made the general outfit. His sympathy was that of a man and a gentleman.

"I also conferred with several of the citizens of Yerba Buena; their advice was not to trouble the Commodore further; that they would call a meeting of the citizens and see what could be done. At the meeting, the situation of the people was made known, and committees were appointed to collect money. Over a thousand dollars was raised in the town, and the sailors of the fleet gave over three hundred dollars. At the meeting, Midshipman Woodworth volunteered to go into the mountains. Commodore Hull gave me authority to raise as many men, with horses, as would be required. The citizens purchased all the supplies necessary for the outfit, and placed them on board the schooner ———, for Hardy's Ranch, mouth of Feather River. Midshipman Woodworth took charge of the schooner, and was the financial agent of the government.

"I left in a boat for Napa by way of Sonoma, to procure men and horses, and when I arrived at Mr. Gordon's, on Cache Creek, I had all the men and horses needed. From here I proceeded to the mouth of Feather River for the purpose of meeting Mr. Woodworth with the provisions. When we reached the river the boat had not arrived. The water was very high in the river, the tule lands being overflowed. From here I sent a man to a point on the Sacramento River opposite Sutter's Fort, to obtain information of the boat with our provisions; he returned and reported the arrival of the boat at the Fort.

"Before leaving Yerba Buena, news came of a party of fifteen persons having started from the emigrant encampment, and only seven getting to Johnson's. I was here placed in a quandary—no boat to take us across the river, and no provisions for our party to take into the mountains. We camped a short distance back from the river, where we killed a number of elk for the purpose of using the skins in covering a

skeleton boat.  Early next morning we started for the river,
and to our delight saw a small schooner, belonging to Perry
(24) McCan, which had arrived during the night.  We immediately crossed, McCutchen and myself, to the opposite bank
of the river.  I directed the men to cross and follow us to
Johnson's Ranch.  We arrived there early that day.  Making
known our situation, he drove his cattle up to the house, saying, 'There are the cattle, take as many as you need.'  We
shot down five head, staid up all night, and with the help of
Mr. Johnson and his Indians, by the time the men arrived the
next morning, we had the meat fire-dried and ready to be
placed in bags.  Mr. Johnson had a party of Indians making
flour by hand mills, they making, during the night, nearly
two hundred pounds.

"We packed up immediately and started.  After reaching
the snow, the meat and flour was divided into suitable packs
for us to carry, we leaving the horses here.  At Johnson's I
learned that a relief party had passed in a few days previous,
being sent by Captain Sutter and Mr. Sinclair."

This was the party commanded by Captain Reasin P.
Tucker, whose journey over the mountains as far as the summit was described in the last chapter.  Reed was faithful and
energetic in endeavoring to recross the mountains.  Mr. Mc-
Cutchen, also, did all in his power to reach the wife and baby
he left behind.  The snow belt is about four times as wide
on the west side of the summit as it is on the east side.  It
was almost impossible for relief parties to cross the mountains.  Captain Tucker's party was composed of men of great
nerve and hardihood, yet, as will be seen, the trip was almost
as much as their lives were worth.

On the morning of the nineteenth of February, 1847, the
relief party of Captain R. P. Tucker began the descent of the
gorge leading to Donner Lake.

Let us glance ahead at the picture soon to be unfolded to their gaze. The mid-winter snows had almost concealed the cabins. The inmates lived subterranean lives. Steps cut in the icy snow led up from the doorways to the surface. Deep despair had settled upon all hearts. The dead were lying all around, some even unburied, and nearly all with only a covering of snow. So weak and powerless had the emigrants become, that it was hardly possible for them to lift the dead bodies up the steps out of the cabins. All were reduced to mere skeletons. They had lived on pieces of rawhide, or on old, castaway bones, which were boiled or burned until capable of being eaten. They were so reduced that it seemed as if only a dry, shriveled skin covered their emaciated frames. The eyes were sunken deep in their sockets, and had a fierce, ghastly, demoniacal look. The faces were haggard, woebegone, and sepulchral. One seldom heard the sound of a voice, and when heard, it was weak, tremulous, pitiful. Sometimes a child would moan and sob for a mouthful of food, and the poor, helpless mothers, with breaking hearts, would have to soothe them, as best they could, with kind words and tender caresses. Food, there was none. Oh! what words can fitly frame a tribute for those noble mothers! When strong men gave up, and passively awaited the delirium of death, the mothers were actively administering to the wants of the dying, and striving to cheer and comfort the living. Marble monuments never bore more heroic names than those of Margaret W. Reed, Lavina Murphy, Elizabeth Graves, Margaret Breen, Tamsen Donner, and Elizabeth Donner. Their charity, fortitude, and self-sacrifice failed not in the darkest hour. Death came so often now, that little notice was taken of his approach, save by these mothers. A dreadful want of consciousness precedes starvation. The actual death is not so terrible. The delirious would rave of feasts,

9

and rich viands, and bountiful stores of food. As the shadows of death more closely enveloped the poor creatures, the mutterings grew unintelligible, and were interrupted, now and then, by startled cries of frenzy, which gradually grew fainter, until the victims finally slumbered. From this slumber there was no awakening. The breathing became feebler and more irregular, and finally ceased. It was not so terrible to the unconscious dying, as to the weeping mother who watched by the sufferer's side.

It was always dark and gloomy enough in the snow-covered cabins, but during the fierce, wild storms, the desolation became almost unendurable. The rushing gale, the furious storm, the lashing of storm-rent pine boughs, or the crash of giant trees overthrown by the hurricane, filled the souls of the imprisoned emigrants with nameless dread. Sometimes the silent darkness of the night would shudder with the howl of the great gray wolves which in those days infested the mountains. Too well did they know that these gaunt beasts were howling for the bodies of the living as well as of the dead.

Wood grew plentifully at short distances from the cabins, but for these weak, starving creatures to obtain it was a herculean task. To go out when the storms were raging, would be almost impossible for a well, strong man. To struggle through the deep, loose drifts, reaching frequently to the waist, required, at any time, fearful exertion. The numb, fleshless fingers could hardly guide, or even wield the ax. Near the site of the Breen cabin, to-day, stands a silent witness of the almost superhuman exertions that were made to procure fuel. On the side of a pine tree are old seams and gashes, which, by their irregular position, were evidently made by hands too weak to cut down a tree. Hundreds of blows, however, were struck, and the marks of

SUTTER'S FORT, 1847.

the ax-blade extend up and down the side of the tree for a
foot and a half.   Bark seared with age has partly covered
portions of the cuts, but in one place the incision is some
inches deep.   At the foot of this pine was found a short, decayed ax-handle, and a broad-bladed, old-fashioned ax-head.
The mute story of these witnesses is unmistakable.   The poor
starved being who undertook the task, never succeeded.

·Trees felled, frequently buried themselves out of sight in
the loose snow, or at best, only the uppermost branches
could be obtained.   Without fire, without food, without
proper shelter from the dampness occasioned by the melting
snows, in the bitter, biting wintry weather, the men, women,
and children were huddled together, the living and the dead.
When Milton Elliott died, there were no men to assist in re-
moving the body from the deep pit.   Mrs. Reed and her
daughter, Virginia, bravely undertook the task.   Tugging,
pushing, lifting as best they could, the corpse was raised up
the icy steps.   He died in the Murphy cabin by the rock.   A
few days before he died, he crawled over to the Breen cabin,
where were Mrs. Reed and her children.   For years he had
been one of the members of this family.   He worked for
Mr. Reed in the mill and furniture establishment owned by
the latter in Jamestown, Illinois.   He drove the same yoke
of oxen, "Bully" and "George," who were the wheel-oxen
of Reed's family team on the plains.   When Mr. Reed proposed crossing the plains, his wife and children refused to go,
unless Milt. could be induced to drive.   He was a kind, careful man, and after Mr. Reed had been driven away from the
company, Elliott always provided for them as best he was
able.   Now that he was going to die, he wanted to see "Ma"
and the children once more.   "Ma" was the term he always
used in addressing Mrs. Reed.   None realized better than he
the sorrowful position in which she was placed by having no

husband upon whom to lean in this time of great need.  Poor
Elliott! he knew that he was starving! starving!  "Ma, I am
not going to starve to death, I am going to eat of the bodies
of the dead."  This is what he told Mrs. Reed, yet when he
attempted to do so, his heart revolted at the thought.  Mrs.
Reed accompanied him a portion of the way back to the
Murphy cabin, and before leaving him, knelt on the snow
and prayed as only a mother can, that the Good Father
would help them in this hour of distress.  It was a starving
Christian mother praying that relief might come to her starving children, and especially to this, her starving boy.  From
the granite rocks, the solemn forests, and the snow-mantled
mountains of Donner Lake, a more fervent prayer never
ascended heavenward.  Could Elliott have heard, in his
dying moments, that this prayer was soon to be answered,
so far as Mrs. Reed and her little ones were concerned, he
would have welcomed death joyfully.

As time wore wearily on, another and more severe trial
awaited Mrs. Reed.  Her daughter Virginia was dying.  The
innutritious rawhide was not sufficient to sustain life in the
poor, famished body of the delicate child.  Indeed, toward
the last, her system became so debilitated that she found it
impossible to eat the loathsome, glue-like preparation which
formed their only food.  Silently she had endured her sufferings, until she was at the very portals of death.  This beautiful girl was a great favorite of Mrs. Breen's.  Oftentimes
during the days of horror and despair, this good Irish mother
had managed, unobserved, to slip an extra piece of meat or
morsel of food to Virginia.  Mrs. Breen was the first to discover that the mark of death was visible upon the girl's brow.
In order to break the news to Mrs. Reed, without giving those
in the cabin a shock which might prove fatal, Mrs. Breen
asked the mother up out of the cabin on the crisp, white snow.

It was the evening of the nineteenth of February, 1847. The sun was setting, and his rays, in long, lance-like lines, sifted through the darkening forests. Far to the eastward, the summits of the Washoe mountains lay bathed in golden sunlight, while the deep gorges at their feet were purpling into night. The gentle breeze which crept over the bosom of the ice-bound lake, softly wafted from the tree-tops a muffled dirge for the dying girl. Ere another day dawned over the expanse of snow, her spirit would pass to a haven of peace where the demons of famine could never enter.

In the desolate cabin, all was silence. Living under the snow, passing an underground life, as it were, seldom visiting each other, or leaving the cabins, these poor prisoners learned to listen rather than look for relief. During the first days they watched hour after hour the upper end of the lake where the "fifteen" had disappeared. With aching eyes and weary hearts, they always turned back to their subterranean abodes disappointed. Hope finally deserted the strongest hearts. The brave mothers had constantly encouraged the despondent by speaking of the promised relief, yet this was prompted more by the necessities of the situation than from any belief that help would arrive. It was human nature, however, to glance toward the towering summits whenever they ascended to the surface of the snow, and to listen at all times for an unfamiliar sound or footstep. So delicate became their sense of hearing, that every noise of the wind, every visitor's tread, every sound that ordinarily occurred above their heads, was known and instantly detected.

On this evening, as the two women were sobbing despairingly upon the snow, the silence of the twilight was broken by a shout from near Donner Lake! In an instant every person forgot weakness and infirmity, and clambered up the stairway! It was a strange voice, and in the distance they discovered strange forms approaching. The Reed and the Breen children thought, at first, that it was a band of Indians, but Patrick Breen, the good old father, soon declared that the strangers were white men. Captain Tucker and his men had found the wide expanse of snow covering forest and lake, and had shouted to attract attention, if any of the emigrants yet survived. Oh! what joy! There were tears in other eyes than those of the little children. The strong men of the relief party sat down on the snow and wept with the rest. It is related of one or two mothers, and can readily be believed, that their first act was to fall upon their knees, and with faces turned to God, to pour out their gratitude to Him for having brought assistance to their dying children. Virginia Reed did not die.

Captain Reasin P. Tucker, who had been acquainted with the Graves family on the plains before the Donner Party took the Hastings Cut-off, was anxious to meet them. They lived in the lower cabin, half a mile further down Donner Creek. When he came close enough to observe the smoke issuing from the hole in the snow which marked their abode, he shouted, as he had done at the upper cabins. The effect was as electrical as in the former instance. All came up to the surface, and the same unrestrained gladness was manifested by the famished prisoners. Famished they were. Mrs. Graves is especially praised by the survivors for her unstinted charity. Instead of selfishly hoarding her stores and feeding only her own children, she was generous to a fault, and no person ever asked at her door for food who did not receive as good as she and her little ones had to eat.

Dear Mrs. Graves! How earnestly she asked about her husband and daughters! Did all reach the valley? Captain Tucker felt his heart rise in his throat. How could he tell this weak, starved woman of the terrible fate which had be-

fallen her husband and her son-in-law! He could not! He
answered with assumed cheerfulness in the affirmative. So,
too, they deceived Mrs. Murphy regarding her dear boy
Lemuel. It was best. Had the dreadful truth been told,
not one of all this company would ever have had courage to
attempt the dangerous journey.

Little sleep was there in the Donner cabins that night.
The relief party were to start back in a couple of days, and
such as were strong enough were to accompany them. Mrs.
Graves had four little children, and told her son William C.
Graves that he must remain with her to cut wood to keep
the little ones from freezing. But William was anxious to
go and help send back provisions to his mother. So earnestly
did he work during the next two days, that he had two cords
of wood piled up near the cabin. This was to last until he
could return. His task was less difficult because this cabin
was built in a dense grove of tamarack.

Food had been given in small quantities to the sufferers.
Many of the snow-bound prisoners were so near death's door
that a hearty meal would have proven fatal. The remnant
of provisions brought by the relief party was carefully
guarded lest some of the famished wretches should obtain
more than was allotted them. This was rendered easier from
the fact that the members of the relief party were unable to
endure the scenes of misery and destitution in the cabins, and
so camped outside upon the snow. So hungry were the
poor people that some of them ate the strings of the snow-
shoes which part of the relief company had brought along.

On the twentieth of February, John Rhodes, R. S. Mootry,
and R. P. Tucker visited the Donner tents on Alder Creek,
seven miles from the cabins. Only one ox-hide remained to
these destitute beings. Here, as well as at the cabins, the
all-important question was, who should go with the relief

party and who remain. In each family there were little children who could not go unless carried. Few of the Donner Party had more than enough strength to travel unencumbered across the deep snows. Should a storm occur on the mountains, it was doubtful if even the members of the relief party could escape death. It was hopefully urged that other relief parties would soon arrive from California, and that these would bring over those who remained. In determining who should go and who stay, examples of heroism and devotion were furnished which were never surpassed in the history of man. Could their vision have penetrated the veil which interposed between them and the sad occurrences about to ensue, they would have known that almost every family, whose members separated, was bidding good-by to some member forever.

# CHAPTER XII.

A Wife's Devotion—Tamsen Donner's Early Life—The Early Settlers of Sangamon County—An Incident in School—Teaching and Knitting—School Discipline — Captain George Donner's Appearance — Parting Scenes at Alder Creek—Starting over the Mountains—A Baby's Death—A Mason's Vow—Crossing the Snow Barrier—More Precious than Gold or Diamonds —Elitha Donner's Kindness.

MRS. TAMSEN DONNER was well and comparatively strong, and could easily have crossed the mountains in safety with this party. Her husband, however, was suffering from a serious swelling on one of his hands. Some time before reaching the mountains he had accidentally hurt this hand while handling a wagon. After encamping at Alder Creek he was anxious to assist in the arrangements and preparations for winter, and while thus working the old wound reopened. Taking cold in the hand, it became greatly swollen and inflamed, and he was rendered entirely helpless. Mrs. Donner was urged to go with the relief party, but resolutely determined to heed the promptings of wifely devotion and remain by her husband.

No one will ever read the history of the Donner Party without greatly loving and reverencing the character of this

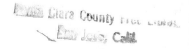

faithful wife. The saddest, most tear-stained page of the tragedy, relates to her life and death in the mountains. A better acquaintance with the Donner family, and especially with Mrs. Tamsen Donner, can not fail to be desirable in view of succeeding chapters. Thanks to Mr. Allen Francis, the present United States Consul at Victoria, British Columbia, very complete, authentic, and interesting information upon this subject has been furnished. Mr. Francis was publisher of the Springfield (Illinois) Journal in 1846, and a warm personal friend of the family.

The Donners were among the first settlers of Sangamon County, Ill. They were North Carolinians, immigrants to Kentucky in 1818, subsequently to the State of Indiana, and from thence to what was known as the Sangamon Country, in the year 1828.

George Donner, at the time of leaving Springfield, Ill., was a large, fine-looking man, fully six feet in height, with merry black eyes, and the blackest of hair, lined with an occasional silver thread. He possessed a cheerful disposition, an easy temperament, industrious habits, sound judgment, and much general information. By his associates and neighbors he was called "Uncle George." To him they went for instructions relating to the management of their farms, and usually they returned feeling they had been properly advised. Twice had death bequeathed him a group of motherless children, and Tamsen was his third wife.

Her parents, William and Tamsen Eustis, were respected and well to do residents of Newburyport, Mass., where she was born in November, 1801. Her love of books made her a student at an early age; almost as soon as the baby-dimples left her cheeks, she sought the school-room, which afforded her reat enjoyment. Her mother's death occurred before she attained her seventh year, and for a time her childish hopes and desires were overshadowed with sadness by this, her first real sorrow. But the sympathy of friends soothed her grief, and her thirst for knowledge led her back to the school-room, where she pursued her studies with greater eagerness than before.

Her father married again, and little Tamsen's life was rendered happier by this event; for in her step-mother she found a friend who tenderly directed her thoughts and encouraged her work. At fifteen years of age she finished the course of study, and her proficiency in mathematics, geometry, philosophy, etc., called forth the highest praise of her teachers and learned friends. She, like many daughters of New England, felt that talents are intrusted to be used, and that each life is created for some definite purpose. She therefore resolved to devote herself to the instruction of the young, and after teaching at Newburyport for a short time, she accepted a call to fill a vacancy in the academy at Elizabeth City, N. C., where she continued an earnest and appreciated teacher for a number of years. She became a fluent French scholar while at that institution, and her leisure hours were devoted to the fine arts. Her paintings and drawings were much admired for their correctness in outline, subdued coloring, and delicacy in shading.

In Elizabeth City she met Mr. Dozier, a young man of education and good family, and they were married. He was not a man of means, but her forethought enabled them to live comfortably. For a few brief years she enjoyed all the happiness which wedded bliss and maternal love could confer, then death came, and in a few short weeks her husband and two babes were snatched from her arms. In her desolation and bereavement she thought of her old home, and longed for the sympathy of her childhood's friends. She returned to Newburyport, where she spent three years in re-

tirement and rest. In 1836, she received a letter from her
brother in Illinois, urging her to come to his afflicted household, and teach his motherless children. She remained with
them one winter, but her field of action had been too wide to
permit her to settle quietly on a farm. Besides, she had
heard much of the manner in which country schools were
conducted, and became desirous of testing her ability in controlling and teaching such a school. She obtained one in
Auburn, and soon became the friend of her pupils. All
agreed that Mrs. Dozier was a faithful teacher until the following little incident occurred. The worthy Board of School
Trustees heard that Mrs. Dozier was in the habit of knitting
during school hours. "Surely, she could not knit and in-
struct her pupils properly; therefore, she must either give up
her knitting or her school." When Mrs. Dozier heard their
resolution, she smiled, and said: "Before those gentlemen
deny my ability to impart knowledge and work with my
fingers at the same time, I would like them to visit my
school, and judge me by the result of their observation."

A knock at the school-room door, a week later, startled
the children, and a committee of trustees entered. Mrs.
Dozier received them in the most ladylike manner, and after
they were seated, she called each class at its appointed time.
The recitations were heard, and lessons explained, yet no one
seemed disturbed by the faint, but regular, click of knitting
needles. For hours those gentlemen sat in silence, deeply interested in all that transpired. When the time for closing
school arrived, the teacher invited the trustees to address her
pupils, after which she dismissed school, thanked her visitors
for their kind attention, and went home without learning
their opinion.

The next morning she was informed that the Board of
Trustees had met the previous evening, and after hearing the

report of the visiting committee, had unanimously agreed that Mrs. Dozier might continue her school and her knitting also. This little triumph was much enjoyed by her friends.

The following year she was urged to take the school on Sugar Creek, where the children were older and further advanced than those at Auburn. Her connection with this school marked a new era for many of its attendants. Mr. J. Miller used to relate an incident which occurred a few days after she took charge of those unruly boys who had been in the habit of managing the teacher and school to suit themselves. "I will never forget," said Mr. Miller, "how Mrs. Dozier took her place at the table that morning, tapped for order, and in a kind, but firm, tone said: 'Young gentlemen and young ladies, as a teacher only, I can not criticise the propriety of your writing notes to each other when out of school; but as your teacher, with full authority in school, I desire and request you neither to write nor send notes to any one during school hours. I was surprised at your conduct yesterday, and should my wish be disregarded in the future, I will be obliged to chastise the offender.' She called the first class, and school began in earnest. I looked at her quiet face and diminutive form, and thought how easy it would be for me to pick up two or three such little bodies as she, and set them outside of the door! I wrote a note and threw it to the pupil in front of me, just to try Mrs. Dozier. When the recitation was finished, she stepped to the side of her table, and looked at me with such a grieved expression on her face, then said: 'Mr. Miller, I regret that my eldest scholar should be the first to violate my rule. Please step forward.' I quailed beneath her eye. I marched up to where she stood. The stillness of that room was oppressive. I held out my hand at the demand of that little woman, and took the punishment I deserved, and returned to my seat deeply humiliated, but

fully determined to behave myself in the future, and make
the other boys do likewise.   Well, she had no more trouble
while she was our teacher.   Her pluck had won our admira-
tion, and her quiet dignity held our respect, and we soon
ceased wondering at the ease with which she overturned our
plans and made us eager to adopt hers; for no teacher ever
taught on Sugar Creek who won the affections or ruled
pupils more easily or happily than she.   We were expected
to come right up to the mark; but if we got into trouble, she
was always ready to help us out, and could do it in the
quietest way imaginable."

She taught several young men the art of surveying, and had
a wonderful faculty of interesting her pupils in the study of
botany.   She sought by creek and over plain for specimens
with which to illustrate their lessons.   It was while engaged
in this place that Mrs. Dozier met George Donner, who at
that time resided about two and a half miles from Springfield.   Their acquaintance resulted in marriage.   Her pupils
always called her their "little teacher," for she was but five
feet in height, and her usual weight ninety-six pounds.   She
had grayish-blue eyes, brown hair, and a face full of character and intelligence.   She was gifted with fine conversa-
tional powers, and was an excellent reader.   Her voice would
hold in perfect silence, for hours, the circle of neighbors and
friends who would assemble during the long winter evenings
to hear her read.   Even those who did not fail to criticise her
ignorance of farm and dairy work, were often charmed by
her voice and absence of display; for while her dress was
always of rich material, it was remarkable for its Quaker
simplicity.

Mr. Francis says: "Mrs. George Donner was a perfect
type of an eastern lady, kind, sociable, and exemplary, ever
ready to assist neighbors, and even the stranger in distress.

Whenever she could spare time, she wielded a ready pen on
various topics.  She frequently contributed gems in prose
and poetry to the columns of the Journal, that awakened an
interest among its readers to know their author.  Herself
and husband were faithful members of the German Prairie
Christian Church, situated a little north of their residence.
Here they lived happily, and highly respected by all who
knew them, until the spring of 1846, when they started for
California."

Having said this much of the Donners, and especially of
the noble woman who refused to leave her suffering husband,
let us glance at the parting scenes at Alder Creek.  It had
been determined that the two eldest daughters of George
Donner should accompany Captain Tucker's party.  George
Donner, Jr., and William Hook, two of Jacob Donner's sons,
Mrs. Wolfinger, and Noah James were also to join the company.  This made six from the Donner tents.  Mrs. Elizabeth Donner was quite able to have crossed the mountains,
but preferred to remain with her two little children, Lewis
and Samuel, until another and larger relief party should
arrive.  These two boys were not large enough to walk, Mrs.
Donner was not strong enough to carry them, and the members of Captain Tucker's party had already agreed to take as
many little ones as they could carry.

Leanna C. Donner, now Mrs. John App, of Jamestown,
Tuolumne County, Cal., gives a vivid description of the trip
from George Donner's tent to the cabins at Donner Lake.
Miss Rebecca E. App, acting as her mother's amanuensis,
writes:

"Mother says: Never shall I forget the day when my
sister Elitha and myself left our tent.  Elitha was strong and
in good health, while I was so poor and emaciated that I
could scarcely walk.  All we took with us were the clothes

on our backs and one thin blanket, fastened with a string around our necks, answering the purpose of a shawl in the day-time, and which was all we had to cover us at night. We started early in the morning, and many a good cry I had before we reached the cabins, a distance of about eight miles. Many a time I sat down in the snow to die, and would have perished there if my sister had not urged me on, saying, 'The cabins are just over the hill.' Passing over the hill, and not seeing the cabins, I would give up, again sit down and have another cry, but my sister continued to help and encourage me until I saw the smoke rising from the cabins; then I took courage, and moved along as fast as I could. When we reached the Graves cabin it was all I could do to step down the snow-steps into the cabin. Such pain and misery as I endured that day is beyond description."

In Patrick Breen's diary are found the following entries, which allude to Captain Tucker's relief party:

"Feb. 19. Froze hard last night. Seven men arrived from California yesterday with provisions, but left the greater part on the way. To-day it is clear and warm for this region; some of the men have gone to Donner's camp; they will start back on Monday.

"Feb. 22. The Californians started this morning, twenty-three in number, some in a very weak state. Mrs. Keseberg started with them, and left Keseberg here, unable to go. Buried Pike's child this morning in the snow; died two days ago."

Poor little Catherine Pike lingered until this time! It will be remembered that this little nursing babe had nothing to eat except a little coarse flour mixed in snow water. Its mother crossed the mountains with the "Forlorn Hope," and from the sixteenth of December to the twentieth of February it lived upon the miserable gruel made from unbolted flour. How it makes the heart ache to think of this little sufferer, wasting away, moaning with hunger, and sobbing for something to eat. The teaspoonful of snow water would contain only a few particles of the flour, yet how eagerly the dying child would reach for the pitiful food. The tiny hands grew thinner, the sad, pleading eyes sank deeper in their fleshless sockets, the face became hollow, and the wee voice became fainter, yet, day after day, little Catherine Pike continued to breathe, up to the very arrival of the relief party.

Patrick Breen says twenty-three started across the mountains. Their names were: Mrs. Margaret W. Reed and her children—Virginia E. Reed, Patty Reed, Thomas Reed, and James F. Reed, Jr.; Elitha C. Donner, Leanna C. Donner, Wm. Hook, and George Donner, Jr.; Wm. G. Murphy, Mary M. Murphy, and Naomi L. Pike; Wm. C. Graves, Eleanor Graves, and Lovina Graves; Mrs. Phillipine Keseberg, and Ada Keseberg; Edward J. and Simon P. Breen, Eliza Williams, John Denton, Noah James, and Mrs. Wolfinger.

In starting from the camps at Donner Lake, Mrs. Keseberg's child and Naomi L. Pike were carried by the relief party. In a beautiful letter received from Naomi L. Pike (now Mrs. Schenck, of the Dalles, Oregon), she says: " I owe my life to the kind heart of John Rhodes, whose sympathies were aroused for my mother. He felt that she was deserving of some relic of all she had left behind when she started with the first party in search of relief, and he carried me to her in a blanket." We have before spoken of this noble man's bravery in bearing the news of the condition of the "Forlorn Hope" and of the Donner Party to Sutter's Fort. Here we find him again exhibiting the nobility of his nature by saving this little girl from starvation by carrying her on his back over forty miles of wintry snow.

10

Before the party had proceeded two miles, a most sad occurrence took place. It became evident that Patty and Thomas Reed were unable to stand the fatigue of the journey. Already they exhibited signs of great weakness and weariness, and it was not safe to allow them to proceed. Mr. Aquila Glover informed Mrs. Reed that it was necessary that these two children go back. Who can portray the emotions of this fond mother? What power of language can indicate the struggle which took place in the minds of this stricken family? Mr. Glover promised to return as soon as he arrived at Bear Valley, and himself bring Patty and Thomas over the mountains. This promise, however, was but a slight consolation for the agonized mother or weeping children, until finally a hopeful thought occurred to Mrs. Reed. She turned suddenly to Mr. Glover, and asked, "Are you a Mason?" He replied, "I am." "Do you promise me," she said, "upon the word of a Mason, that when you arrive at Bear Valley, you will come back and get my children?" Mr. Glover made the promise, and the children were by him taken back to the cabins. The mother had remembered, in this gloomiest moment of life, that the father of her little ones was a Mason, and that he deeply reverenced the order. If her children must be left behind in the terrible snows, she would trust the promise of this Mason to return and save them. It was a beautiful trust in a secret order by a Mason's wife in deep distress.

Rebecca E. App, writing for her mother, gives a vivid description of this journey across the summits, from which is taken the following brief extract:

"It was a bright Sunday morning when we left the cabins. Some were in good health, while others were so poor and emaciated that they could scarcely walk. I was one of the weakest in the party, and not one in the train thought I

JAMES F. REED.

would get to the top of the first hill. We were a sad spectacle to look upon as we left the cabins. We marched along in single file, the leader wearing snow-shoes, and the others following after, all stepping in the leader's tracks. I think my sister and myself were about the rear of the train, as the strongest were put in front. My sister Elitha and I were alone with strangers, as it were, having neither father, mother, nor brothers, to give us a helping hand or a word of courage to cheer us onward. We were placed on short allowance of food from the start, and each day this allowance was cut shorter and shorter, until we received each for our evening and morning meal two small pieces of jerked beef, about the size of the index finger of the hand. Finally, the last ration was issued in the evening. This was intended for that evening and the next morning, but I was so famished I could not resist the temptation to eat all I had—the two meals at one time. Next morning, of course, I had nothing for breakfast. Now occurred an incident which I shall never forget. While I sat looking at the others eating their morsels of meat, which were more precious than gold or diamonds, my sister saw my distress, and divided her piece with me. How long we went without food after that, I do not know. I think we were near the first station."

# CHAPTER XIII.

REASIN P. TUCKER'S relief party had twenty-one emigrants with them after Patty and Thomas Reed returned to the desolate cabins. On the evening of the first day, one of the twenty-one died. It was the baby child of Lewis Keseberg. The mother had fairly worshiped her girl. They buried the little one in the snow. It was all they could do for the pallid form of the starved little girl. Mrs. Keseberg was heart-broken over her baby's death. At the very outset she had offered everything she possessed—twenty-five dollars and a gold watch—to any one who would carry her child over the mountains. After the starved band resumed their weary march next morning, it is doubtful if many thought of the niche hollowed out of the white snow, or of the pulseless heart laid therein. Death had become fearfully common, and his victims were little heeded by the perishing company. The young German

mother, however, was inconsolable. Her only boy had
starved to death at the cabins, and now she was childless.

The next day the company reached Summit Valley. An
incident of this day's travel illustrates the exhausted condition of the members of the Donner Party. John Denton,
an Englishman, was missed when camp was pitched, and
John Rhodes returned and found him fast asleep upon the
snow. He had become so weary that he yielded to a slumber that would soon have proven fatal. With much labor
and exertion he was aroused and brought to camp. Denton
appreciated the kindness, but at the same time declared that
it would be impossible for him to travel another day. Sure
enough, after journeying a little way on the following morning, his strength utterly gave way. His companions built a
fire for him, gave him such food as they were able, and at
his earnest request continued their sorrowful march. If another relief came soon, he would, perhaps, be rescued.
Denton was well educated and of good family, was a gun-
smith by trade, and was skilled in metals. It is related, that
while in the Reed cabin, he discovered in the earth, ashes, and
burnt stones in the fireplace, some small pieces of yellowish
metal, which he declared to be gold. These he made into a
small lump, which he carefully preserved until he left the
lake, and it was doubtless lost on the mountains at his death.
This was in the spring of 1847, before the discovery of gold
in California. The strange little metallic lump was exhibited to several who are yet living, and who think there is reason for believing it was really gold. A few years before the
construction of the Central Pacific, Knoxville, about ten
miles south of Donner Lake, and Elizabethtown, some six
miles from Truckee, were famous mining camps. Gold (25)
never has been found on the very shore of Donner Lake,
but should the discovery be made, and especially should gold

be found in the rocks or earth near the Reed cabin, there
would be reason to believe that this poor unfortunate man
was in reality the first discoverer of the precious metal in
California.   Left alone in the snow-mantled forests of the
Sierra, what were this man's emotions?   In the California
Star of 1847, a bound volume of which is in the State Library in Sacramento, appears the following poem.   The second relief party found it written on the leaf of a memorandum
book by the side of Denton's lifeless body.   The pencil with
which it was written lay also by the side of the unfortunate
man.   Ere the lethargy of death stole away his senses, John
Denton's thoughts had been of his boyhood's beautiful home
in merry England.   These thoughts were woven into verse.
Are they not strangely pathetic and beautiful?   Judge Thornton, in 1849, published them with the following prefatory
words: "When the circumstances are considered in connection with the calamities in which the unhappy Denton was
involved, the whole compass of American and English poetry
may be challenged to furnish a more exquisitely beautiful, a
more touching and pathetic piece.   Simple and inornate to
the last degree, yet coming from the heart, it goes to the
heart.   Its lines are the last plaintive notes which wintry
winds have wakened from an Æolian harp, the strings of
which rude hands have sundered.   Bring before your mind
the picture of an amiable young man who has wandered far
from the paternal roof, is stricken by famine, and left by his
almost equally unhappy companions to perish among the
terrible snows of the great Sierra Nevada.   He knows that
his last, most solemn hour is near.   Reason still maintains
her empire, and memory, faithful to the last, performs her
functions.   On every side extends a boundless waste of trackless snow.   He reclines against a bank of it, to rise no more,
and busy memory brings before him a thousand images of

past beauty and pleasure, and of scenes he will never revisit. A mother's image presents itself to his mind, tender recollections crowd upon his heart, and the scenes of his boyhood and youth pass in review before him with an unwonted vividness. The hymns of praise and thanksgiving that in harmony swelled from the domestic circle around the family altar are remembered, and soothe the sorrows of the dying man, and finally, just before he expires, he writes: "

> "Oh! after many roving years,
>     How sweet it is to come
> Back to the dwelling-place of youth,
>     Our first and dearest home;
> To turn away our wearied eyes
>     From proud ambition's towers,
> And wander in those summer fields,
>     The scenes of boyhood's hours.
>
> "But I am changed since last I gazed
>     Upon that tranquil scene,
> And sat beneath the old witch elm
>     That shades the village green;
> And watched my boat upon the brook—
>     It was a regal galley—
> And sighed not for a joy on earth,
>     Beyond the happy valley.
>
> "I wish I could once more recall
>     That bright and blissful joy,
> And summon to my weary heart
>     The feelings of a boy.
> But now on scenes of past delight
>     I look, and feel no pleasure,
> As misers on the bed of death
>     Gaze coldly on their treasure."

When Captain Tucker's relief party were going to Donner Lake, they left a portion of their provisions in Summit Valley, tied up in a tree. They had found these provisions diffi-

cult to carry, and besides, it was best to have something
provided for their return, in case the famished emigrants ate
all they carried over the summit.   It was indeed true that all
was eaten which they carried over.   All the scanty allowances
were, one after another, consumed.   When the relief party,
and those they were rescuing, reached the place where the
provisions had been cached, they were in great need of the
reserve store which they expected to find.   To their horror
and dismay, they found that wild animals had gnawed the
ropes by which the cache had been suspended, and had destroyed every vestige of these provisions!   Death stared
them in the face, and the strongest men trembled at the prospect.

(26)    Here comes the sequel to the Reed-Snyder tragedy.   Had
it not been for Reed's banishment, there is every reason to
believe that these people would have died for want of food.
It will be remembered, however, that the relief party organized by Reed was only a few days behind Captain Tucker's.
On the twenty-seventh of February, just as the horror and
despair of their dreadful situation began to be realized,
Tucker, and those with him, were relieved by the second relief party.

In order to better understand these events, let us return
and follow the motions of Reed and the members of the second relief party.   In the article quoted in a former chapter
from the Rural Press, Reed traced their progress as far as
Johnson's ranch.   Patty Reed (Mrs. Frank Lewis) has in her
(27)  possession the original diary kept by her father during this
journey.   This diary shows that on the very morning Capt.
Tucker, and the company with him, left Donner Lake to return
to the valleys, Reed and the second relief party started from
Johnson's ranch to go to Donner Lake.   All that subsequently
occurred, is briefly and pointedly narrated in the diary.

"February 22, 1847. All last night I kept fire under the beef which I had drying on the scaffolds, and Johnson's Indians were grinding flour in a small hand-mill. By sunrise this morning I had about two hundred pounds of beef dried and placed in bags. We packed our horses and started with our supplies. Including the meat Greenwood had dried, we had seven hundred pounds of flour, and five beeves. Mr. Greenwood had three men, including himself. Traveled this day about ten miles.

"Feb. 23. Left camp early this morning, and pushed ahead, but camped early on account of grass. To-morrow we will reach the snow.

"Feb. 24. Encamped at Mule Springs this evening. Made arrangements to take to the snow in the morning, having left in camp our saddles, bridles, etc.

"Feb. 25. Started with eleven horses and mules lightly packed, each having about eighty pounds. Traveled two miles, and left one mule and his pack. Made to-day, with hard labor for the horses, in the snow, about six miles. Our start was late.

"Feb. 26. Left our encampment, Cady thinking the snow would bear the horses. Proceeded two hundred yards with difficulty, when we were compelled to unpack the horses and take the provisions on our backs. Usually the men had kept in the best of spirits, but here, for a few moments, there was silence. When the packs were ready to be strung upon their backs, however, the hilarity and good feeling again commenced. Made the head of Bear Valley, a distance of fifteen miles. We met in the valley, about three miles below the camp, Messrs. Glover and Rhodes, belonging to the party that went to the lake. They informed me they had started with twenty-one persons, two of whom had died, John Denton, of Springfield, Ill., and a child of Mr. and Mrs. Kese-

berg.   Mr. Glover sent two men back to the party with fresh
provisions.   They are in a starving condition, and all have
nearly given out.   I have lightened our packs with a sufficient
quantity of provisions to do the people when they shall arrive at this place.

"Feb. 27.   I sent back two men to our camp of night before
last, to bring forward provisions.   They will return to-morrow.
I also left one man to prepare for the people who were expected to-day.   Left camp on a fine, hard snow, and proceeded about four miles, when we met the poor, unfortunate,
starved people.   As I met them scattered along the snow-
trail, I distributed some bread that I had baked last night.   I
gave in small quantities to each.   Here I met my wife and
two of my little children.   Two of my children are still in
the mountains.   I can not describe the death-like look all
these people had.   'Bread!' 'Bread!' 'Bread!' 'Bread!' was
the begging cry of every child and grown person.   I gave all
I dared to them, and set out for the scene of desolation at
the lake.   I am now camped within twenty-five miles of the
place, which I hope to reach by traveling to-night and to-
morrow.   We had to camp early this evening, on account of
the softness of the snow, the men sinking in to their waists,
The party who passed us to-day were overjoyed when we
told them there was plenty of provision at camp.   I made a
cache, to-day, after we had traveled about twelve miles, and
encamped three miles further eastward, on the Yuba.   Snow
about fifteen feet deep."

The meeting between Reed and his family can better be
imagined than described.   For months they had been separated.   While the father was battling with fate in endeavoring
to reach California and return with assistance, the mother had
been using every exertion to obtain food for her starving
children.   Now they met in the mountains, in the deep

snows, amid pathless forests, at a time when the mother and children, and all with them, were out of provisions and ready to perish.

Meantime, the first relief, with their little company, now reduced to nineteen, passed forward toward the settlements. At Bear Valley, another cache of provisions had been made, and this was found unmolested. Camping at this place, the utmost precaution was taken to prevent the poor starved people from overeating. After a sufficient quantity of food had been distributed, the remainder of the provisions was hung up in a tree. Of course, the small portion distributed to each did not satisfy the cravings of hunger. Some time during the night, Wm. Hook quietly crept to the tree, climbed up to the food, and ate until his hunger was appeased. Poor boy, it was a fatal act. Toward morning it was discovered that he was dying. All that the company could do to relieve his sufferings was done, but it was of no avail. Finding that the poor boy was past relief, most of the emigrants moved on toward the settlements. Wm. G. Murphy's feet had been badly frozen, and he was suffering such excruciating agony that he could not travel and keep up with the others. At his request, his sister Mary had cut his shoes open, in order to get them off, and his feet thereupon swelled up as if they had been scalded. Because he could not walk, the company left him with William Hook. A camp-keeper also remained. This boy's death is thus described by Mr. Murphy, who writes:

"William Hook went out on the snow and rested on his knees and elbows. The camp-keeper called to him to come in. He then told me to make him come into camp. I went and put my hand on him, speaking his name, and he fell over, being already dead. He did not die in great agony, as is usually alleged. No groan, nor signs of dying, were manifested to us. The camp-keeper and myself took the biscuits and jerked beef from his pockets, and buried him just barely under the ground, near a tree which had been fired, and from around which the snow had melted." Those who were in the company thought Wm. G. Murphy could not possibly walk, but when all had gone, and Hook was dead, and no alternative remained but to walk or die, he did walk. It took him two days to go barefooted over the snow to Mule Springs, a journey which the others had made in one day. The agony which he endured during that trip can better be imagined than described. Nothing but an indomitable will could have sustained him during those two days.

All the members of this relief party suffered greatly, and several came near perishing. Little James F. Reed, Jr., was too small to step in the tracks made by the older members of the party. In order to travel with the rest he had to partly use his knees in walking. When one foot was in a track he would place the other knee on the untrodden snow, and was thus enabled to put his foot in the next track. John Denton was left with a good fire, and when last seen was reclining smoking, on a bed of freshly gathered pine boughs. He looked so comfortable that the little timid boy James begged hard to be allowed to remain with him. Mrs. Reed had hard work to coax him to come. Among other things, she promised that when he reached California he should have a horse "all for himself," and that he should never have to walk any more. This promise was literally fulfilled. James F. Reed, Jr., since reaching California, has always had a horse of his own. No matter what vicissitudes of fortune have overtaken him, he has always kept a saddle horse.

Sad scenes were occurring at the cabin at Donner Lake and the tents at Alder Creek. Starvation was fast claiming its victims. The poor sufferers tried to be brave and trust

God, but sometimes hope well-nigh disappeared.   The evening prayers were always read in Patrick Breen's cabin, and all the inmates knelt and joined in the responses.   Once when they were thus praying, they heard the cries of wild geese flying over the cabin.   With one accord all raised their heads and listened for a moment to the soul-inspiring sound. "Thank God, the spring is coming," was all Patrick Breen said, and again bowing their heads, the prayer was resumed.

Charles L. Cady, writing from Calistoga, says that Commodore Stockton employed Greenwood and Turner to guide the second relief party over the mountains to Donner Lake. Cady, Stone, and Clark, being young, vigorous men, left their companions, or were sent forward by Reed, and reached the cabins some hours in advance of the party.   At one time, near the present station of Summit Valley, Cady and Stone became bewildered, thought they were lost, and wanted to return. Mr. Clark, however, prevailed upon them to press forward, agreeing that if they did not catch some glimpse of Donner Lake when they reached a certain mountain top in the distance, he would give up and return with them.   Had they reached the mountain top they could not have seen the lake, and so would have turned back, but while they were ascending, they came to the lifeless body of C. T. Stanton sitting upright against a tree.   There was no longer room for doubting that they were going in the right direction to reach Donner Lake.   Poor Stanton! even in death he pointed out to the relief party the way to the starving emigrants, to save whom he had sacrificed his life.

Reed's diary continues:

"Feb. 28.   Left camp about twelve o'clock at night, but was compelled to camp about two o'clock, the snow still being soft.   Left again about four o'clock, all hands, and made this day fourteen miles.   Encamped early; snow very

soft.   The snow here is thirty feet deep.   Three of my men,
Cady, Clark, and Stone, kept on during the night to within
two miles of the cabins, where they halted, and remained
without fire during the night, on account of having seen ten
Indians.   The boys did not have any arms, and supposed
these Indians had taken the cabins and destroyed the people.
In the morning they started, and reached the cabins.   All
were alive in the houses.   They gave provisions to Keseberg,
Breen, Graves, and Mrs. Murphy, and the two then left for
Donner's, a distance of seven miles, which they made by the
middle of the day.

"March 1.   I came up with the remainder of my party,
and told the people that all who were able should start day
after to-morrow.   Made soup for the infirm, washed and
clothed afresh Eddy's and Foster's children, and rendered
every assistance in my power.   I left Mr. Stone with Keseberg's people to cook, and to watch the eating of Mrs. Murphy, Keseberg, and three children."

In Patrick Breen's diary is found the following:

"Feb. 23.   Froze hard last night.   To-day pleasant and
thawy; has the appearance of spring, all but the deep snow.
Wind south-south-east.   Shot a dog to-day and dressed his
flesh.

"Feb. 25.   To-day Mrs. Murphy says the wolves are about
to dig up the dead bodies around her shanty, and the nights
are too cold to watch them, but we hear them howl.

"Feb. 26.   Hungry times in camp; plenty of hides, but
the folks will not eat them; we eat them with tolerably good
appetite, thanks to the Almighty God.   Mrs. Murphy said
here yesterday that she thought she would commence on
Milton and eat him.   I do not think she has done so yet; it
is distressing.   The Donners told the California folks four
days ago that they would commence on the dead people if

they did not succeed that day or the next in finding their cattle, then ten or twelve feet under the snow, and they did not know the spot or near it; they have done it ere this.

"Feb. 28. One solitary Indian passed by yesterday; came from the lake; had a heavy pack on his back; gave me five or six roots resembling onions in shape; tasted some like a sweet potato; full of tough little fibers.

"March 1. Ten men arrived this morning from Bear Valley, with provisions. We are to start in two or three days, and cache our goods here. They say the snow will remain until June."

This closes Patrick Breen's diary. Its record has always been considered reliable. None of the statements made in this diary have ever been controverted.

The Indian spoken of refused to be interviewed. To quote the language of Mr. John Breen, "he did not seem to be at all curious as to how or why there was a white man alone (as it must have seemed to him) in the wilderness of snow." The Indian was trudging along with a heavy pack on his back. As soon as he saw Mr. Breen, he halted and warned him with a gesture not to approach. Taking from the pack a few of the fibrous roots, he laid them on the snow, still cautioning with his hand not to approach until he was well out of reach. As soon as the Indian was gone, Mr. Breen went out and got the roots, which were very palatable. It is probable that this was one of the band of Indians seen by Clark, Cady, and Stone.

When Patty and Thomas Reed had been returned to the cabins by Aquila Glover, they had been received by the Breen family, where they remained all the time until their father came. The Breen cabin was the first one at which Mr. Reed arrived. His meeting with his daughter is thus described by Mr. Eddy, in Thornton's work: "At this camp

Mr. Reed saw his daughter Patty sitting on the top of the snow with which the cabin was covered. Patty saw her father at some distance, and immediately started to run and meet him, but such was her weakness that she fell. Her father took her up, and the affectionate girl, bathed in tears, embraced and kissed him, exclaiming: 'Oh, papa! I never expected to see you again when the cruel people drove you out of camp. But I knew that God was good, and would do what was best. Is dear mamma living? Is Mr. Glover living? Did you know that he was a Mason? Oh, my dear papa, I am so happy to see you. Masons must be good men. Is Mr. Glover the same sort of Mason we had in Springfield? He promised mamma upon the word of a Mason that he would bring me and Tommy out of the mountains.' Mr. Reed told Patty that Masons were everywhere the same, and that he had met her mother and Mr. Glover, and had relieved him from his pledge, and that he himself had come to her and little Tommy to redeem that pledge and to take out all that were able to travel."

The greatest precaution was taken to keep the suffering emigrants from overeating. Cady, Stone, and Clark had distributed a small portion of food to each of the famished beings. Patty Reed was intrusted with the task of giving to each person a single biscuit. Taking the biscuits in her apron she went in turn to each member of the company. Who shall describe the rejoicings that were held over those biscuits? Several of the survivors, in speaking of the subject, say that to their hungry eyes these small pieces of bread assumed gigantic proportions. Never did the largest loaves of bread look half so large. Patty Reed says that some of the little girls cut their portions into thin slices, so as to eat them slowly and enjoy them more completely.

The names of the members of this second relief party were

MRS. MARGARET W. REED.

James F. Reed, Charles Cady, Charles Stone, Nicholas Clark, Joseph Jondro, Mathew Dofar, John Turner, Hiram Miller, (28) Wm. McCutchen, and Brit. Greenwood. A portion of the party went to the Donner tents, and the remainder assisted the emigrants in preparing to start over the mountains. The distress and suffering at each camp was extreme. Even after (29) the children had received as much food as was prudent, it is said they would stretch out their little arms and with cries and tears beg for something to eat. Mrs. Murphy informed Mr. Reed that some of the children had been confined to their beds for fourteen days. It was clearly to be seen that very few of the sufferers could cross the Sierra without being almost carried. They were too weak and helpless to walk. The threatening appearance of the weather and the short supply of provisions urged the party to hasten their depart- ure, and it was quickly decided who should go, and who remain. Those who started from Donner Lake on the third of March with Mr. Reed and his party were Patrick Breen, Mrs. Margaret Breen, John Breen, Patrick Breen, Jr., James F. Breen, Peter Breen, and Isabella M. Breen, Patty Reed and Thomas Reed, Isaac Donner and Mary M. Donner, Solomon Hook, Mrs. Elizabeth Graves, Nancy Graves, Jonathan Graves, Franklin Graves, and Elizabeth Graves, Jr. Many of the younger members of this party had to be carried. All were very much weakened and emaciated, and it was evident that the journey over the mountains would be slow and painful. In case a storm should occur on the summits, it was fearfully apparent that the trip would be exceedingly perilous.

Reed's party encamped the first night near the upper end of Donner Lake. They had scarcely traveled three miles. Upon starting from the Graves cabin, Mrs. Graves had taken with her a considerable sum of money. This money, Mr. McCutchen says, had been ingeniously concealed in auger-

11

holes bored in cleats nailed to the bed of the wagon. These cleats, as W. C. Graves informs us, were ostensibly placed in the wagon-bed to support a table carried in the back part of the wagon. On the under side of these cleats, however, were the auger-holes, carefully filled with coin. The sum is variously stated at from three to five hundred dollars. At the camping-ground, near the upper end of Donner Lake, one of the relief party jokingly proposed to another to play a game of euchre to see who should have Mrs. Graves' money. The next morning, Mrs. Graves remained behind when the party started, and concealed her money. All that (30) is known is, that she buried it behind a large rock on the north side of Donner Lake. So far as is known, this money has never been recovered, but still lies hidden where it was placed by Mrs. Graves.

# CHAPTER XIV.

Leaving Three Men in the Mountains—The Emigrants Quite Helpless—Bear
  Tracks in the Snow—The Clumps of Tamarack—Wounding a Bear—Blood-
  stains upon the Snow—A Weary Chase—A Momentous Day—Stone and
  Cady Leave the Sufferers—A Mother Offering Five Hundred Dollars—
  Mrs. Donner Parting from her Children—"God will Take Care of You"
  —Buried in the Snow, without Food or Fire—Pines Uprooted by the Storm
  —A Grave Cut in the Snow—The Cub's Cave—Firing at Random—A
  Desperate Undertaking—Preparing for a Hand-to-Hand Battle—Precipi-
  tated into the Cave—Seizing the Bear—Mrs. Elizabeth Donner's Death—
  Clark and Baptiste Attempt to Escape—A Death more Cruel than Starva-
  tion.

BEFORE Reed's party started to return, a consultation
was held, and it was decided that Clark, Cady, and
Stone should remain at the mountain camps. It was
intended that these men should attend to procuring
wood, and perform such other acts as would assist
the almost helpless sufferers. It was thought that a third relief party could be sent out in a few days to get all the emigrants who remained.

Nicholas Clark, who now resides in Honey Lake Valley,
Lassen County, California, says that as he and Cady were
going to the Donner tents, they saw the fresh tracks of a
bear and cub crossing the road. In those days, there were

several little clumps of tamarack along Alder Creek, just below the Donner tents, and as the tracks led towards these,
Mr. Clark procured a gun and started for an evening's hunt
among the tamaracks.   He found the bear and her cub
within sight of the tents, and succeeded in severely wounding
the old bear.   She was a black bear, of medium size.   For a
long distance, over the snow and through the forests, Clark
followed the wounded animal and her cub.   The approach
of darkness at last warned him to desist, and returning to the
tents, he passed the night.   Early next morning, Clark again
set out in pursuit of the bear, following her readily by the
blood-stains upon the snow.   It was another windy, cloudy,
threatening day, and there was every indication that a severe
storm was approaching.   Eagerly intent upon securing his
game, Mr. Clark gave little heed to weather, or time, or distance.   The endurance of the wounded animal was too great,
however, and late in the afternoon he realized that it was
necessary for him to give up the weary chase, and retrace
his steps.   He arrived at the tents hungry, tired, and foot-
sore, long after dark.

That day, however, had been a momentous one at the
Donner tents.   Stone had come over early in the morning,
and he and Cady concluded that it was sheer madness for
them to remain in the mountains.   That a terrible storm was
fast coming on, could not be doubted.   The provisions were
almost exhausted, and if they remained, it would only be to
perish with the poor emigrants.   They therefore concluded
to attempt to follow and overtake Reed and his companions.

Mrs. Tamsen Donner was able to have crossed the mountains with her children with either Tucker's or Reed's party.
On account of her husband's illness, however, she had firmly
refused all entreaties, and had resolutely determined to remain by his bedside.   She was extremely anxious, however,

that her children should reach California; and Hiram Miller relates that she offered five hundred dollars to any one in the second relief party, who would take them in safety across the mountains. When Cady and Stone decided to go, Mrs. Donner induced them to attempt the rescue of these children, Frances, Georgia, and Eliza. They took the children as far as the cabins at the lake, and left them. Probably they became aware of the impossibility of escaping the storm, and knew that it would be sure death, for both themselves and the children, should they take them any farther. In view of the terrible calamity which befell Reed's party on account of this storm, and the fact that Cady and Stone had a terrible struggle for life, every one must justify these men (31) in leaving the children at the cabins. The parting between the devoted mother and her little ones is thus briefly described by Georgia Donner, now Mrs. Babcock: "The men came. I listened to their talking as they made their agreement. Then they took us, three little girls, up the stone steps, and stood us on the bank. Mother came, put on our hoods and cloaks, saying, as if she was talking more to herself than to us: 'I may never see you again, but God will take care of you.' After traveling a few miles, they left us on the snow, went ahead a short distance, talked one to another, then came back, took us as far as Keseberg's cabin, and left us."

Mr. Cady recalls the incident of leaving the children on the snow, but says the party saw a coyote, and were attempting to get a shot at the animal.

When Nicholas Clark awoke on the morning of the third day, the tent was literally buried in freshly fallen snow. He was in what is known as Jacob Donner's tent. Its only occupants besides himself were Mrs. Elizabeth Donner, her son Lewis, and the Spanish boy, John Baptiste. George Donner

and wife were in their own tent, and with them was Mrs.
Elizabeth Donner's youngest child, Samuel.   Mr. Clark says
he can not remember how long the storm lasted, but it seems
as if it must have been at least a week.   The snow was so
deep that it was impossible to procure wood, and during all
those terrible days and nights there was no fire in either of
the tents.   The food gave out the first day, and the dreadful
cold was rendered more intense by the pangs of hunger.
Sometimes the wind would blow like a hurricane, and they
could plainly hear the great pines crashing on the mountain
side above them, as the wind uprooted them and hurled them
to the ground.   Sometimes the weather would seem to mod-
erate, and the snow would melt and trickle in under the sides
of the tent, wetting their clothes and bedding, and increasing
the misery of their situation.

When the storm cleared away, Clark found himself starving like the rest.   He had really become one of the Donner
Party, and was as certain to perish as were the unfortunates
about him.   It would necessarily be several days before relief
could possibly arrive, and utter despair seemed to surround
them.   Just as the storm was closing, Lewis Donner died,
and the poor mother was well-nigh frantic with grief.   As
soon as she could make her way to the other tent, she carried her dead babe over and laid it in Mrs. George Donner's
lap.   With Clark's assistance, they finally laid the child away
in a grave cut out of the solid snow.

In going to a tamarack grove to get some wood, Mr. Clark
was surprised to find the fresh track of the bear cub, which
had recrossed Alder Creek and ascended the mountain behind the tents.   It was doubtless the same one whose mother
he had wounded.   The mother had probably died, and after
the storm the cub had returned.   Mr. Clark at once followed
it, tracking it far up the mountain side to a cliff of rocks, and

losing the trail at the mouth of a small, dark cave. He says that all hope deserted him when he found that the cub had gone into the cave. He sat down upon the snow in utter despair. It was useless to return to the tents without food; he might as well perish upon the mountain side. After reflecting for some time upon the gloomy situation, he concluded to fire his gun into the cave, and see if the report might not frighten out the cub. He placed the muzzle of the gun as far down into the cave as he could, and fired. When the hollow reverberation died away among the cliffs, no sound disturbed the brooding silence. The experiment had failed. He seriously meditated whether he could not watch the cave day and night until the cub should be driven out by starvation. But suddenly a new idea occurred to him. Judging from the track, and from the size of the cub he had seen, Mr. Clark concluded that it was possible he might be able to enter the cave and kill the cub in a hand-to-hand fight. It was a desperate undertaking, but it was preferable to death from starvation. He approached the narrow opening, and tried again to peer into the cave and ascertain its depth. As he was thus engaged the snow suddenly gave way, and he was precipitated bodily into the cave. He partly fell, partly slid to the very bottom of the hole in the rocks. In endeavoring to regain an erect posture, his hand struck against some furry animal. Instinctively recoiling, he waited for a moment to see what it would do. Coming from the dazzling sunlight into the darkness, he could see nothing whatever. Presently he put out his foot and again touched the animal. Finding that it did not move, he seized hold of it and found that it was the cub—dead! His random shot had pierced its brain, and it had died without a struggle. The cave or opening in the rocks was not very deep, and after a long time he succeeded in dragging his prize to the surface.

There was food in the Donner tents from this time forward. It came too late, however, to save Mrs. Elizabeth Donner or her son Samuel. This mother was quite able to have crossed the mountains with either of the two relief parties; but, as Mrs. E. P. Houghton writes: "Her little boys were too young to walk through the deep snows, she was not able to carry them, and the relief parties were too small to meet such emergencies. She stayed with them, hoping some way would be provided for their rescue. Grief, hunger, and disappointed hopes crushed her spirit, and so debilitated her that death came before the required help reached her or her children. For some days before her death she was so weak that Mrs. George Donner and the others had to feed her as if she had been a child. At last, one evening, as the sun went down, she closed her eyes and awoke no more. Her life had been sacrificed for her children. Could words be framed to express a more fitting tribute to her memory! Does not the simple story of this mother's love wreathe a chaplet of glory about her brow far holier than could be fashioned by human hands!

Samuel Donner lingered but a few days longer. Despite the tenderest care and attention, he grew weaker day by day, until he slept by the side of his mother and brother in their snowy grave.

All this time Mrs. Tamsen Donner was tortured with fear and dread, lest her children had perished in the dreadful storm on the summits. At last Clark yielded to her importunities, and decided to visit the cabins at Donner Lake, and see if there was any news from beyond the Sierra. Clark found the children at Keseberg's cabin, and witnessed such scenes of horror and suffering that he determined at once to attempt to reach California. Returning to Alder Creek, he told Mrs. Donner of the situation of her children, and says he informed her that he believed their lives were in danger of a death more violent than starvation. He informed her of his resolution to leave the mountains, and taking a portion of the little meat that was left, he at once started upon his journey. John Baptiste accompanied him.

The cub would have weighed about seventy pounds when killed; and now that its flesh was nearly gone, there was really very little hope for any one unless relief came speedily. In attempting to make their way across the mountains, Clark and Baptiste did the wisest thing possible, yet they well knew that they would perish by the way unless they met relief.

Mrs. Tamsen Donner did not dare to leave her husband alone during the night, but told Clark and Baptiste that she should endeavor to make the journey to the cabins on the following day. It was a long, weary walk over the pitiless snow, but she had before her yearning eyes not only the picture of her starving children, but the fear that they were in danger of a more cruel death than starvation.

# CHAPTER XV.

A Mountain Storm—Provisions Exhausted—Battling the Storm-Fiends—Black Despair—Icy Coldness—A Picture of Desolation—The Sleep of Death—A Piteous Farewell—Falling into the Fire-well—Isaac Donner's Death—Living upon Snow-water—Excruciating Pain—A Vision of Angels—"Patty is Dying"—The Thumb of a Mitten—A Child's Treasures—The "Dolly" of the Donner Party.

ON the evening of the second day after leaving Donner Lake, Reed's party and the little band of famished emigrants found themselves in a cold, bleak, uncomfortable hollow, somewhere near the lower end of Summit Valley. Here the storm broke in all its fury upon the doomed company. In addition to the cold, sleet-like snow, a fierce, penetrating wind seemed to freeze the very marrow in their bones. The relief party had urged the tired, hungry, enfeebled emigrants forward at the greatest possible speed all day, in order to get as near the settlements as they could before the storm should burst upon them. Besides, their provisions were exhausted, and they were anxious to reach certain caches of supplies which they had made while going to the cabins. Fearing that the storm would prevent the party from reaching these caches, Mr. Reed sent Joseph Jondro, Matthew Dofar, and Hiram Turner forward to the first cache, with instructions to get the provisions and return to the suffering emigrants. That very night the storm came, and the three men had not been heard from.

The camp was in a most inhospitable spot. Exposed to the fury of the wind and storm, shelterless, supperless, overwhelmed with discouragements, the entire party sank down exhausted upon the snow. The entire party? No! There was one man who never ceased to work. When a fire had been kindled, and nearly every one had given up, this one man, unaided, continued to strive to erect some sort of shelter to protect the defenseless women and children. Planting large pine boughs in the snow, he banked up the snow on either side of them so as to form a wall. Hour after hour, in the darkness and raging storm, he toiled on alone, building the sheltering breastwork which was to ward off death from the party who by this time had crept shiveringly under its protection. But for this shelter, all would have perished before morning. At midnight the man was still at work. The darting snow particles seemed to cut his eye-balls, and the glare of the fire and the great physical exhaustion under which he was laboring, gradually rendered him blind. Like his companions, he had borne a child in his arms all day over the soft, yielding snow. Like them, he was drenched to the skin, and his clothing was frozen stiff and hard with ice. Yet he kept up the fire, built a great sheltering wall about the sufferers, and went here and there amongst the wailing and dying. With unabated violence the storm continued its relentless fury. The survivors say it was the coldest night they ever experienced. There is a limit to human endurance. The man was getting stone-blind. Had he attempted to speak, his tongue would have cloven to the roof of his mouth. His senses were chilled, blunted, dead. Sleep had stilled the plaintive cries of those about him. All was silent save the storm.  Without knowing it, this heroic man was yielding to a sleep more powerful than that which had overcome his companions.  While trying to save those who were weaker than himself, he had been literally freezing.  Sightless, benumbed, moving half unconsciously about his work, he staggered, staggered, staggered, and finally sank in the snow. All slept!  As he put no more fuel upon the fire, the flames died down   The logs upon which the fire had rested gave way, and most of the coals fell upon the snow.  They were in almost total darkness.

Presently some one awoke.  It was Mrs. Breen, whose motherly watchfulness prevented more than a few consecutive moments' sleep.  The camp was quickly aroused.  All were nearly frozen.  Hiram Miller's hands were so cold and frosted that the skin on the fingers cracked open when he tried to split some kindlings.  At last the fire was somehow renewed.  Meantime they had discovered their leader—he who had been working throughout the night—lying cold, speechless, and apparently dead upon the snow.  Hiram Miller and Wm. McCutchen carried the man to the fire, chafed his hands and limbs, rubbed his body vigorously, and worked with him as hard as they could for two hours before he showed signs of returning consciousness.  Redoubling their exertions, they kept at work until the cold, gray morning dawned, ere the man was fully restored.  Would you know the name of this man, this hero?  It was James Frazier Reed.

From this time forward, all the toil, all the responsibility devolved upon Wm. McCutchen and Hiram Miller.  Jondro, Dofar, and Turner were caught in the drifts ahead.  The fishers or other wild animals had almost completely devoured the first cache of provisions, and while these men were trying to reach the second cache, the storm imprisoned them. They could neither go forward nor return. Cady and Stone were between Donner Lake and Starved Camp, and were in a like helpless condition. McCutchen and Miller were the only ones able to do anything toward saving the poor creatures who were huddled together at the miserable camp. All the other men were completely disheartened by the fearful calamity which had overtaken them. But for the untiring exertions of these two men, death to all would have been certain. McCutchen had on four shirts, and yet he became so chilled while trying to kindle the fire, that in getting warm he burned the back out of his shirts. He only discovered the mishap by the scorching and burning of his flesh.

What a picture of desolation was presented to the inmates of Starved Camp during the next three days! It stormed incessantly. One who has not witnessed a storm on the Sierra can not imagine the situation. A quotation from Bret Harte's "Gabriel Conroy" will afford the best idea of the situation:

"Snow. Everywhere. As far as the eye could reach— fifty miles, looking southward from the highest white peak. Filling ravines and gulches, and dropping from the walls of canyons in white shroud-like drifts, fashioning the dividing ridge into the likeness of a monstrous grave, hiding the bases of giant pines, and completely covering young trees and larches, rimming with porcelain the bowl-like edges of still, cold lakes, and undulating in motionless white billows to the edge of the distant horizon. Snow lying everywhere on the California Sierra, and still falling. It had been snowing in finely granulated powder, in damp, spongy flakes, in thin, feathery plumes; snowing from a leaden sky steadily, snowing fiercely, shaken out of purple-black clouds in white flocculent masses, or dropping in long level lines like white lances from the tumbled and broken heavens. But always

silently! The woods were so choked with it, it had so cush-
ioned and muffled the ringing rocks and echoing hills, that
all sound was deadened. The strongest gust, the fiercest
blast, awoke no sigh or complaint from the snow-packed,
rigid files of forest. There was no cracking of bough nor
crackle of underbrush; the overladen branches of pine and
fir yielded and gave away without a sound. The silence was
vast, measureless, complete!"

In alluding to these terrible days, in his diary, Mr. Reed
says, under date of March 6:

"With the snow there is a perfect hurricane. In the night
there is a great crying among the children, and even with the
parents there is praying, crying, and lamentation on account
of the cold and the dread of death from hunger and the
howling storm. The men up nearly all night making fires.
Some of the men began praying. Several of them became
blind. I could not see the light of the fire blazing before me,
nor tell when it was burning. The light of heaven is, as it
were, shut out from us. The snow blows so thick and fast
that we can not see twenty feet looking against the wind. I
dread the coming night. Three of my men only, able to get
wood. The rest have given out for the present. It is still
snowing, and very cold. So cold that the few men employed
in cutting the dry trees down, have to come and warm about
every ten minutes. 'Hungry!' 'Hungry!' is the cry with
the children, and nothing to give them. 'Freezing!' is the
cry of the mothers who have nothing for their little, starving,
freezing children. Night closing fast, and with it the hurricane increases.

"Mar. 7. Thank God day has once more appeared, although darkened by the storm. Snowing as fast as ever,
and the hurricane has never ceased for ten minutes at a time
during one of the most dismal nights I have ever witnessed.

I hope I shall never witness another such in a similar situation. Of all the praying and crying I ever heard, nothing ever equaled it. Several times I expected to see the people perish of the extreme cold. At one time our fire was nearly gone, and had it not been for McCutchen's exertions it would have entirely disappeared. If the fire had been lost, two thirds of the camp would have been out of their misery before morning; but, as God would have it, we soon had it blazing comfortably, and the sufferings of the people became less for a time. Hope began to animate the bosoms of many, young and old, when the cheering blaze rose through the dry pine logs we had piled together. One would say, 'Thank God for the fire!' Another, 'How good it is!' The poor, little, half-starved, half-frozen children would say, 'I'm glad, I'm glad we have got some fire! Oh, how good it feels! It is good our fire didn't go out!' At times the storm would burst forth with such fury that I felt alarmed for the safety of the people on account of the tall timber that surrounded us."

Death entered the camp on the first night. He came to claim one who was a true, faithful mother. One who merits greater praise than language can convey. Though comparatively little has been told concerning her life by the survivors, doubt not that Mrs. Elizabeth Graves was one of the noblest of the mothers of the Donner Party. Her charity is kindly remembered by all who have spoken her name. To her companions in misfortune she always gave such food as she possessed; for her children she now gave her life. The last morsels of food, the last grain of flour, she had placed in the mouths of her babes, though she was dying of starvation.

Mrs. Farnham, who talked personally with Mrs. Breen, gives the following description of that terrible night:

(32)

"Mrs. Breen told me that she had her husband and five children together, lying with their feet to the fire, and their heads under shelter of the snow breast-work. She sat by them, with only moccasins on her feet, and a blanket drawn over her shoulders and head, within which, and a shawl she constantly wore, she nursed her poor baby on her knees. Her milk had been gone several days, and the child was so emaciated and lifeless that she scarcely expected at any time on opening the covering to find it alive. Mrs. Graves lay with her babe and three or four older children at the other side of the fire. The storm was very violent all night, and she watched through it, dozing occasionally for a few minutes, and then rousing herself to brush the snow and flying sparks from the covering of the sleepers. Toward morning she heard one of the young girls opposite call to her mother to cover her. The call was repeated several times impatiently, when she spoke to the child, reminding her of the exhaustion and fatigue her mother suffered in nursing and carrying the baby, and bidding her cover herself, and let her mother rest. Presently she heard the mother speak, in a quiet, unnatural tone, and she called to one of the men near her to go and speak to her. He arose after a few minutes and found the poor sufferer almost past speaking. He took her infant, and after shaking the snow from her blanket, covered her as well as might be. Shortly after, Mrs. Breen observed her to turn herself slightly, and throw one arm feebly up, as if to go to sleep. She waited a little while, and seeing her remain quite still, she walked around to her. She was already cold in death. Her poor starving child wailed and moaned piteously in the arms of its young sister, but the mother's heart could no more warm or nourish it."

The members of the second relief party realized that they

were themselves in imminent danger of death. They were powerless to carry the starving children over the deep, soft, treacherous snow, and it was doubtful if they would be able to reach the settlements unincumbered. Isaac Donner, one of the sons of Jacob and Elizabeth Donner, perished during one of the stormy nights. He was lying on the bed of pine boughs between his sister Mary and Patty Reed, and died so quietly that neither of the sleeping girls awoke.

The relief party determined to set out over the snow, hasten to the settlements, and send back relief. Solomon Hook, Jacob Donner's oldest boy, insisted that he was able to walk, and therefore joined the party. Hiram Miller, an old friend of the Reed family, took little Thomas Reed in his arms, and set out with the others. Patty Reed, full of hope and courage, refused to be carried by her father, and started on foot.

With what emotions did the poor sufferers in Starved Camp watch the party as it disappeared among the pines! There was no food in camp, and death had already selected two of their number. What a pitiable group it was! Could a situation more desolate or deplorable be imagined? Mr. Breen, as has been heretofore mentioned, was feeble, sickly, and almost as helpless as the children. Upon Mrs. Breen devolved the care, not only of her husband, but of all who remained in the fatal camp, for all others were children. John Breen, their eldest son, was the strongest and most vigorous in the family, yet the following incident shows how near he was to death's door. It must have occurred the morning the relief party left. The heat of the fire had melted a deep, round hole in the snow. At the bottom of the pit was the fire. The men were able to descend the sides of this cavity, and frequently did so to attend to the fire. At one time, while William McCutchen was down by the fire, John Breen

12

was sitting on the end of one of the logs on which the fire had originally been kindled.   Several logs had been laid side by side, and the fire had been built in the middle of the floor thus constructed.   While the central logs had burned out and let the fire descend, the outer logs remained with their ends on the firm snow.   On one of these logs John Breen was sitting.   Suddenly overcome by fatigue and hunger, he fainted and dropped headlong into the fire-pit.   Fortunately, Mr. McCutchen caught the falling boy, and thus saved him from a horrible death.   It was some time before the boy was fully restored to consciousness.   Mrs. Breen had a small quantity of sugar, and a little was placed between his clenched teeth.   This seemed to revive him, and he not only survived, but is living to-day, the head of a large family, in San Benito County.

Mrs. Breen's younger children, Patrick, James, Peter, and the nursing babe, Isabella, were completely helpless and dependent.   Not less helpless were the orphan children of Mr. and Mrs. Graves.   Nancy was only about nine years old, and upon her devolved the task of caring for the babe, Elizabeth.   Nancy Graves is now the wife of the earnest and eloquent divine, Rev. R. W. Williamson, of Los Gatos, Santa Clara County.   To her lasting honor be it said, that although she was dying of hunger in Starved Camp, yet she faithfully tended, cared for, and saved her baby sister.   Aside from occasional bits of sugar, this baby and Mrs. Breen's had nothing for an entire week, save snow-water.   Besides Nancy and Elizabeth, there were of the Graves children, Jonathan, aged seven, and Franklin, aged five years.   Franklin soon perished.   Starvation and exposure had so reduced his tiny frame, that he could not endure these days of continual fasting.

Mary M. Donner, whom all mention as one of the most

lovely girls in the Donner Party, met with a cruel accident the night before the relief party left Starved Camp. Her feet had become frozen and insensible to pain. Happening to lie too near the fire, one of her feet became dreadfully burned. She suffered excruciating agony, yet evinced remarkable fortitude. She ultimately lost four toes from her left foot, on account of this sad occurrence.

Seven of the Breens, Mary Donner, and the three children of Mr. and Mrs. Graves, made the eleven now waiting for relief at Starved Camp. Mrs. Graves, her child Franklin, and the boy, Isaac Donner, who lay stark in death upon the snow, completed the fourteen who were left by the relief party.

Meantime, how fared it with those who were pressing forward toward the settlements? At each step they sank two or three feet into the snow. Of course those who were ahead broke the path, and the others, as far as possible, stepped in their tracks. This, Patty Reed could not do, because she was too small. So determined was she, however, that despite the extra exertion she was compelled to undergo, she would not admit being either cold or fatigued. Patty Reed has been mentioned as only eight years old. Many of the survivors speak of her, however, in much the same terms as John Breen, who says: "I was under the impression that she was older. She had a wonderful mind for one of her age. She had, I have often thought, as much sense as a grown person." Over Patty's large, dark eyes, on this morning, gradually crept a film. Previous starvation had greatly attenuated her system, and she was far too weak to endure the hardship she had undertaken. Gradually the snow-mantled forests, the forbidding mountains, the deep, dark canyon of Bear River, and even the forms of her companions, faded from view. In their stead came a picture of such glory and brightness as seldom comes to human eyes. It was a vision of angels and of brilliant stars. She commenced calling her father, and those with him, and began talking about the radiant forms that hovered over her. Her wan, pale face was illumined with smiles, and with an ecstasy of joy she talked of the angels and stars, and of the happiness she experienced. "Why, Reed," exclaimed McCutchen, "Patty is dying!" And it was too true.

For a few moments the party forgot their own sufferings and trials, and ministered to the wants of the spirituelle child, whose entrance into the dark valley had been heralded by troops of white-winged angels. At Starved Camp, Reed had taken the hard, frozen sacks in which the provisions had been carried, and by holding them to the fire had thawed out the seams, and scraped therefrom about a teaspoonful of crumbs. These he had placed in the thumb of his woolen mitten to be used in case of emergency. Little did he suppose that the emergency would come so soon. Warming and moistening these crumbs between his own lips, the father placed them in his child's mouth. Meantime they had wrapped a blanket around her chilled form, and were busily chafing her hands and feet. Her first return to consciousness was signaled by the regrets she expressed at having been awakened from her beautiful dream. To this day she cherishes the memory of that vision as the dearest, most enchanting of all her life. After this, some of the kind-hearted Frenchmen in the party took turns with Reed in carrying Patty upon their backs.

Past-midshipman S. E. Woodworth is a name that in most published accounts figures conspicuously among the relief parties organized to rescue the Donner Party. At the time Reed and his companions were suffering untold horrors on the mountains, and those left at Starved Camp were perishing of starvation, Woodworth, with an abundance of supplies, was lying idle in camp at Bear Valley. This was the part that Selim E. Woodworth took in the relief of the sufferers.

The three men who had been sent forward to the caches, left the remnant of the provisions which had not been destroyed, where it could easily be seen by Reed and his companions. Hurrying forward, they reached Woodworth's camp, and two men, John Stark and Howard Oakley, returned and met Reed's party. It was quite time. With frozen feet and exhausted bodies, the members of the second relief were in a sad plight. They left the settlements strong, hearty men. They returned in a half-dead condition. Several lost some of their toes on account of having them frozen, and one or two were crippled for life. They had been three days on the way from Starved Camp to Woodworth's. Cady and Stone overtook Reed and his companions on the second day after leaving Starved Camp. On the night of the third day, they arrived at Woodworth's.

When Patty Reed reached Woodworth's and had been provided with suitable food, an incident occurred which fully illustrates the tenderness and womanliness of her nature. Knowing that her mother and dear ones were safe, knowing that relief would speedily return to those on the mountains, realizing that for her there was to be no more hunger, or snow, and that she would no longer be separated from her father, her feelings may well be imagined. In her quiet joy she was not wholly alone. Hidden away in her bosom, during all the suffering and agony of the journey over the mountains, were a number of childish treasures. First, there was a lock of silvery gray hair which her own hand had cut from the head of her Grandmother Keyes way back on the Big Blue River. Patty had always been a favorite with her grandma, and when the latter died, Patty secured this lock of hair. She tied it up in a little piece of old-fashioned lawn, dotted with wee blue flowers, and always carried it in her bosom. But this was not all. She had a dainty little glass salt-cellar, scarcely larger than the inside of a humming-bird's nest, and, what was more precious than this, a tiny, wooden doll. This doll had been her constant companion. It had black eyes and hair, and was indeed very pretty. At Woodworth's camp, Patty told "Dolly" all her joy and gladness, and who can not pardon the little girl for thinking her dolly looked happy as she listened?

Patty Reed is now Mrs. Frank Lewis, of San Jose, Cal. She has a pleasant home and a beautiful family of children. Yet oftentimes the mother, the grown-up daughters, and the younger members of the family, gather with tear-dimmed eyes about a little sacred box. In this box is the lock of hair in the piece of lawn, the tiny salt-cellar, the much loved "Dolly," and an old woolen mitten, in the thumb of which are yet the traces of fine crumbs.

# CHAPTER XVI.

VERY noble was the part which Mrs. Margaret Breen performed in this Donner tragedy, and very beautifully has that part been recorded by a woman's hand. It is written so tenderly, so delicately, and with so much reverence for the maternal love which alone sustained Mrs. Breen, that it can hardly be improved. This account was published by its author, Mrs. Farnham, in 1849, and is made the basis of the following sketch. With alterations here and there, made for the sake of brevity, the article is as it was written:

There was no food in Starved Camp. There was nothing to eat save a few seeds, tied in bits of cloth, that had been brought along by some one, and the precious lump of sugar. There were also a few teaspoonfuls of tea. They sat and lay by the fire most of the day, with what heavy hearts, who shall know! They were upon about thirty feet of snow. The dead lay before them, a ghastlier sight in the sunshine that succeeded the storm, than when the dark clouds over-hung them. They had no words of cheer to speak to each other, no courage or hope to share, but those which pointed to a life where hunger and cold could never come, and their benumbed faculties were scarcely able to seize upon a con-solation so remote from the thoughts and wants that ab-sorbed their whole being.

A situation like this will not awaken in common natures religious trust. Under such protracted suffering, the animal outgrows the spiritual in frightful disproportion. Yet the mother's sublime faith, which had brought her thus far through her agonies, with a heart still warm toward those who shared them, did not fail her now. She spoke gently to one and another; asked her husband to repeat the litany, and the children to join her in the responses; and endeavored to fix their minds upon the time when the relief would prob-ably come. Nature, as unerringly as philosophy could have done, taught her that the only hope of sustaining those about her, was to set before them a termination to their sufferings.

What days and nights were those that went by while they waited! Life waning visibly in those about her; not a morsel of food to offer them; her own infant—and the little one that had been cherished and saved through all by the mother now dead—wasting hourly into the more perfect image of death; her husband worn to a skeleton; it needed the fullest measure of exalted faith, of womanly tenderness and self-sacrifice, to sustain her through such a season. She watched by night as well as by day. She gathered wood to keep them warm. She boiled the handful of tea and dispensed it to them, and when she found one sunken and speechless, she broke with her teeth a morsel of the precious sugar, and put it in his lips. She fed her babe freely on snow-water, and

NICHOLAS CLARK

1879.

scanty as was the wardrobe she had, she managed to get fresh clothing next to its skin two or three times a week. Where, one asks in wonder and reverence, did she get the strength and courage for all this? She sat all night by her family, her elbows on her knees, brooding over the meek little victim that lay there, watching those who slept, and occasionally dozing with a fearful consciousness of their terrible condition always upon her. The sense of peril never slumbered. Many times during the night she went to the sleepers to ascertain if they all still breathed. She put her hand under their blankets, and held it before the mouth. In this way she assured herself that they were yet alive. But once her blood curdled to find, on approaching her hand to the lips of one of her own children, there was no warm breath upon it. She tried to open his mouth, and found the jaws set. She roused her husband, "Oh! Patrick, man! arise and help me! James is dying!" "Let him die!" said the miserable father, "he will be better off than any of us." She was terribly shocked by this reply. In her own expressive language, her heart stood still when she heard it. She was bewildered, and knew not where to set her weary hands to work, but she recovered in a few moments and began to chafe the breast and hands of the perishing boy. She broke a bit of sugar, and with considerable effort forced it between his teeth with a few drops of snow-water. She saw him swallow, then a slight convulsive motion stirred his features, he stretched his limbs feebly, and in a moment more opened his eyes and looked upon her. How fervent were her thanks to the Great Father, whom she forgot not day or night.

Thus she went on. The tea leaves were eaten, the seeds chewed, the sugar all dispensed. The days were bright, and compared with the nights, comfortable. Occasionally, when the sun shone, their voices were heard, though generally they

sat or lay in a kind of stupor from which she often found it
alarmingly difficult to arouse them.   When the gray evening
twilight drew its deepening curtain over the cold glittering
heavens and the icy waste, and when the famishing bodies
had been covered from the frost that pinched them with but
little less keenness than the unrelenting hunger, the solitude
seemed to rend her very brain.   Her own powers faltered.
But she said her prayers over many times in the darkness
as well as the light, and always with renewed trust in Him
who had not yet forsaken her, and thus she sat out her
weary watch.   After the turning of the night she always sat
watching for the morning star, which seemed every time she
saw it rise clear in the cold eastern sky, to renew the promise,
"As thy day is, so shall thy strength be."

Their fire had melted the snow to a considerable depth,
and they were lying on the bank above.   Thus they had less
of its heat than they needed, and found some difficulty in
getting the fuel she gathered placed so it would burn.   One
morning after she had hailed her messenger of promise, and
the light had increased so as to render objects visible in the
distance, she looked as usual over the white expanse that lay
to the south-west, to see if any dark moving specks were
visible upon its surface.   Only the tree-tops, which she had
scanned so often as to be quite familiar with their appearance, were to be seen.   With a heavy heart she brought
herself back from that distant hope to consider what was
immediately about her.   The fire had sunk so far away that
they had felt but little of its warmth the last two nights, and
casting her eyes down into the snow-pit, whence it sent forth
only a dull glow, she thought she saw the welcome face of
beloved mother Earth.   It was such a renewing sight after
their long, freezing separation from it !   She immediately
aroused her eldest son, John, and with a great deal of diffi-

culty, and repeating words of cheer and encouragement, brought him to understand that she wished him to descend by one of the tree-tops which had fallen in so as to make a sort of ladder, and see if they could reach the naked earth, and if it were possible for them all to go down. She trembled with fear at the vacant silence in which he at first gazed at her, but at length, after she had told him a great many times, he said "Yes, mother," and went.

He reached the bottom safely, and presently spoke to her. There was naked, dry earth under his feet; it was warm, and he wished her to come down. She laid her baby beside some of the sleepers, and descended. Immediately she determined upon taking them all down. How good, she thought, as she descended the boughs, was the God whom she trusted. By perseverence, by entreaty, by encouragement, and with her own aid, she got them into this snug shelter.

Relief came not, and as starvation crept closer and closer to himself and those about him, Patrick Breen determined that it was his duty to employ the means of sustaining life which God seemed to have placed before them. The lives of all might be saved by resorting to such food as others, in like circumstances, had subsisted upon. Mrs. Breen, however, declared that she would die, and see her children die, before her life or theirs should be preserved by such means. If ever the father gave to the dying children, it was without her consent or knowledge. She never tasted, nor knew of her children partaking. Mrs. Farnham says that when Patrick Breen ascended to obtain the dreadful repast, his wife, frozen with horror, hid her face in her hands, and could not look up. She was conscious of his return, and of something going on about the fire, but she could not bring herself to uncover her eyes till all had subsided again into silence.

Her husband remarked that perhaps they were wrong in rejecting a means of sustaining life of which others had availed themselves, but she put away the suggestion so fearfully that it was never renewed, nor acted upon by any of her family. She and her children were now, indeed, reaching the utmost verge of life. A little more battle with the grim enemies that had pursued them so relentlessly, twenty-four, or at most forty-eight hours of such warfare, and all would be ended. The infants still breathed, but were so wasted they could only be moved by raising them bodily with the hands. It seemed as if even their light weight would have dragged the limbs from their bodies. Occasionally, through the day, she ascended the tree to look out. It was an incident now, and seemed to kindle more life than when it only required a turn of the head or a glance of the eye to tell that there was no living thing near them. She could no longer walk on the snow, but she had still strength enough to crawl from tree to tree to gather a few boughs, which she threw along before her to the pit, and piled them in to renew the fire. The eighth day was passed. On the ninth morning she ascended to watch for her star of mercy. Clear and bright it stood over against her beseeching gaze, set in the light liquid blue that overflows the pathway of the opening day. She prayed earnestly as she gazed, for she knew that there were but few hours of life in those dearest to her. If human aid came not that day, some eyes, that would soon look imploringly into hers, would be closed in death before that star would rise again. Would she herself, with all her endurance and resisting love, live to see it? Were they at length to perish? Great God! should it be permitted that they, who had been preserved through so much, should die at last so miserably?

Her eyes were dim, and her sight wavering. She could not

distinguish trees from men on the snow, but had they been near, she could have heard them, for her ear had grown so sensitive that the slightest unaccustomed noise arrested her attention. She went below with a heavier heart than ever before. She had not a word of hope to answer the languid, inquiring countenances that were turned to her face, and she was conscious that it told the story of her despair. Yet she strove with some half-insane words to suggest that somebody would surely come to them that day. Another would be too late, and the pity of men's hearts and the mercy of God would surely bring them. The pallor of death seemed already to be stealing over the sunken countenances that surrounded her, and, weak as she was, she could remain below but a few minutes together. She felt she could have died had she let go her resolution at any time within the last forty-eight hours. They repeated the Litany. The responses came so feebly that they were scarcely audible, and the protracted utterances seemed wearisome. At last it was over, and they rested in silence.

The sun mounted high and higher in the heavens, and when the day was three or four hours old she placed her trembling feet again upon the ladder to look out once more. The corpses of the dead lay always before her as she reached the top—the mother and her son, and the little boy, whose remains she could not even glance at since they had been mutilated. The blanket that covered them could not shut out the horror of the sight.

The rays of the sun fell on her with a friendly warmth, but she could not look into the light that flooded the white expanse. Her eyes lacked strength and steadiness, and she rested herself against a tree and endeavored to gather her wandering faculties in vain. The enfeebled will could no longer hold rule over them. She had broken perceptions, fragments of visions, contradictory and mixed—former mingled with latter times. Recollections of plenty and rural peace came up from her clear, tranquil childhood, which seemed to have been another state of existence; flashes of her latter life—its comfort and abundance—gleams of maternal pride in her children who had been growing up about her to ease and independence.

She lived through all the phases which her simple life had ever worn, in the few moments of repose after the dizzy effort of ascending; as the thin blood left her whirling brain and returned to its shrunken channels, she grew more clearly conscious of the terrible present, and remembered the weary quest upon which she came. It was not the memory of thought, it was that of love, the old tugging at the heart that had never relaxed long enough to say, "Now I am done; I can bear no more!" The miserable ones down there—for them her wavering life came back; at thought of them she turned her face listlessly the way it had so often gazed. But this time something caused it to flush as if the blood, thin and cold as it was, would burst its vessels! What was it? Nothing that she saw, for her eyes were quite dimmed by the sudden access of excitement! It was the sound of voices! By a superhuman effort she kept herself from falling! Was it reality or delusion? She must at least live to know the truth. It came again and again. She grew calmer as she became more assured, and the first distinct words she heard uttered were, "There is Mrs. Breen alive yet, anyhow!" Three men were advancing toward her. She knew that now there would be no more starving. Death was repelled for this time from the precious little flock he had so long threatened, and she might offer up thanksgiving unchecked by the dreads and fears that had so long frozen her.

# CHAPTER XVII.

The Rescue—California Aroused—A Yerba Buena Newspaper—Tidings of Woe
—A Cry of Distress—Noble Generosity—Subscriptions for the Donner
Party—The First and Second Reliefs—Organization of the Third—The
Dilemma—Voting to Abandon a Family—The Fatal Ayes—John Stark's
Bravery—Carrying the Starved Children—A Plea for the Relief Party.

OSTER and Eddy, it will be remembered, were of the
fifteen who composed the "Forlorn Hope." Foster
was a man of strong, generous impulses, and great
determination. His boy was at Donner Lake, and
his wife's mother and brother. He hardly took time
to rest and recruit his wasted strength before he began or-
ganizing a party to go to their rescue. His efforts were
ably seconded by W. H. Eddy, whose wife and daughter had
perished, but whose boy was still alive at the cabins.

California was thoroughly aroused over tidings which had
come from the mountains. It was difficult to get volunteers
to undertake the journey over the Sierra, but horses, mules,
provisions, and good wages were allowed all who would venture the perilous trip. The trouble with Mexico had caused
many of the able-bodied citizens of California to enlist in the
service. Hence it was that it was so difficult to organize relief parties.

The following extracts are made from the California Star, a newspaper published at "Yerba Buena," as San Francisco was then called. They do justice to the sentiment of the people of California, and indicate something of the willingness of the pioneers to aid the Donner Party. From the Star of January 16, 1847, is taken the following article, which appeared as an editorial:

### "EMIGRANTS ON THE MOUNTAINS.

" It is probably not generally known to the people that there is now in the California mountains, in a most distressing situation, a party of emigrants from the United States, who were prevented from crossing the mountains by an early, heavy fall of snow. The party consists of about sixty persons—men, women, and children. They were almost entirely out of provisions when they reached the foot of the mountains, and but for the timely succor afforded them by Capt. J. A. Sutter, one of the most humane and liberal men in California, they must have all perished in a few days. Capt. Sutter, as soon as he ascertained their situation, sent five mules loaded with provisions to them. A second party was dispatched with provisions for them, but they found the mountains impassable in consequence of the snow. We hope that our citizens will do something for the relief of these unfortunate people."

From the same source, under date of February 6, 1847, is taken the following:

### "PUBLIC MEETING.

" It will be recollected that in a previous number of our paper, we called the attention of our citizens to the situation of a company of unfortunate emigrants now in the California mountains. For the purpose of making their situation more fully known to the people, and of adopting measures for their relief, a public meeting was called by the Honorable Washington A. Bartlett, alcalde of the town, on Wednesday evening last. The citizens generally attended, and in a very short time the sum of $800 was subscribed to purchase provisions, clothing, horses, and mules to bring the emigrants in. Committees were appointed to call on those who could not attend the meeting, and there is no doubt but that $500 or $600 more will be raised. This speaks well for Yerba Buena."

One other extract is quoted from the Star of February 13, 1847:

## "COMPANY LEFT.

"A company of twenty men left here on Sunday last for the California mountains, with provisions, clothing, etc., for the suffering emigrants now there. The citizens of this place subscribed about $1,500 for their relief, which was expended for such articles as the emigrants would be most likely to need. Mr. Greenwood, an old mountaineer, went with the company as pilot. If it is possible to cross the mountains, they will get to the emigrants in time to save them."

These three articles may aid the reader in better understanding what has heretofore been said about the organization of the relief parties. It will be remembered that James F. Reed and William McCutchen first procured animals and provisions from Capt. Sutter, attempted to cross the mountains, found the snow impassable, cached their provisions, and returned to the valleys. Reed, as described in his letter to the Rural Press, went to San Jose, Cal., and thence to Yerba Buena. McCutchen went to Napa and Sonoma, and awakened such an interest that a subscription of over $500 was subscribed for the emigrants, besides a number of horses and mules. Lieut. W. L. Maury and M. G. Vallejo headed this

13

subscription, and $500 was promised to Greenwood if he suc-
ceeded in raising a company, and in piloting them over the
mountains. In order to get men, Greenwood and McCutchen
went to Yerba Buena, arriving there almost at the same time
with Reed. The above notices chronicle the events which
succeeded the announcement of their mission. The funds
and supplies contributed were placed in charge of Lieut.
Woodworth. This party set out immediately, and their
journey has been described. They form the second relief
party, because immediately upon the arrival of the seven
who survived of the "Forlorn Hope," Capt. Tucker's party
had been organized at Johnson's and Sutter's, and had
reached Donner Lake first.

When Foster and Eddy attempted to form a relief party,
they found the same difficulty in securing volunteers which
others had encountered. It was such a terrible undertaking,
that no man cared to risk his life in the expedition.

Captain J. B. Hull, of the United States navy, and Commander of the Northern District of California, furnished
Foster and Eddy with horses and provisions. Setting out
from Johnson's ranch, they arrived at Woodworth's camp in
the afternoon. During that very night two of Reed's men
came to the camp, and brought news that Reed and a portion of his party were a short distance back in the mountains. When Reed and his companions were brought into
camp, and it was ascertained that fourteen people had been
left in the snow, without food, the third relief party was at
once organized. The great danger and suffering endured by
those who had composed the first and second relief parties,
prevented men from volunteering. On this account greater
honor is due those who determined to peril their lives to save
the emigrants. Hiram Miller, although weak and exhausted
with the fatigues and starvation he had just undergone in the

second relief party, joined Messrs. Foster and Eddy. These three, with Wm. Thompson, John Stark, Howard Oakley, and Charles Stone, set out from Woodworth's camp the next morning after Reed's arrival. It was agreed that Stark, Oakley, and Stone were to remain with the sufferers at Starved Camp, supply them with food, and conduct them to Woodworth's camp. Foster, Eddy, Thompson, and Miller were to press forward to the relief of those at Donner Lake. The three men, therefore, whose voices reached Mrs. Breen, were Stark, Oakley, and Stone.

When these members of the third relief party reached the deep, well-like cavity in which were the seven Breens, the three Graves children, and Mary Donner, a serious question arose. None of the eleven, except Mrs. Breen and John Breen, were able to walk. A storm appeared to be gathering upon the mountains, and the supply of provisions was very limited. The lonely situation, the weird, desolate surroundings, the appalling scenes at the camp, and above all, the danger of being overtaken by a snow-storm, filled the minds of Oakley and Stone with terror. When it was found that nine out of the eleven people must be carried over the snow, it is hardly to be wondered at that a proposition was made to leave a portion of the sufferers. It was proposed to take the three Graves children and Mary Donner. These four children would be quite a sufficient burden for the three men, considering the snow over which they must travel. The Breens, or at least such of them as could not walk, were to be abandoned. This was equivalent to leaving the father, mother, and five children, because the mother would not abandon any member of her family, and John, who alone could travel, was in a semi-lifeless condition. The members of the third relief party are said to have taken a vote upon the question. This scene is described in the manuscript of

Hon. James F. Breen: "Those who were in favor of returning to the settlements, and leaving the Breens for a future relief party (which, under the circumstances, was equivalent to
the death penalty), were to answer 'aye.' The question was
put to each man by name, and as the names were called, the
dreadful 'aye' responded. John Stark's name was the last
one called, because he had, during the discussion of the question, strongly opposed the proposition for abandonment, and
it was naturally supposed that when he found himself in so
hopeless a minority he would surrender. When his name
was called, he made no answer until some one said to him:
'Stark, won't you vote?' Stark, during all this proceeding of
calling the roll, had stood apart from his companions with
bowed head and folded arms. When he was thus directly
appealed to, he answered quickly and decidedly: "No, gentlemen, I will not abandon these people. I am here on a mission of mercy, and I will not half do the work. You can all
go if you want to, but I shall stay by these people while they
and I live.'"

It was nobly said. If the Breens had been left at Starved
Camp, even until the return of Foster, Eddy, Miller, and
Thompson from the lake, none would have ever reached the
settlements. In continuation of the above narration, the following is taken from the manuscript of John Breen: "Stark
was finally left alone. To his great bodily strength, and un-
excelled courage, myself and others owe our lives. There
was probably no other man in California at that time, who
had the intelligence, determination, and what was absolutely
necessary in that emergency, the immense physical powers
of John Stark. He was as strong as two ordinary men. On
his broad shoulders, he carried the provisions, most of the
blankets, and most of the time some of the weaker children.
In regard to this, he would laughingly say that he could

carry them all, if there was room on his back, because they were so light from starvation."

By every means in his power, Stark would cheer and encourage the poor sufferers. Frequently he would carry one or two ahead a little way, put them down, and return for the others. James F. Breen says: "I distinctly remember that myself and Jonathan Graves were both carried by Stark, on his back, the greater part of the journey." Others speak similarly.

Regarding this brave man, Dr. J. C. Leonard has contributed much valuable information, from which is selected the following:

"John Stark was born in 1817, in Wayne County, Indiana. His father, William Stark, came from Virginia, and was one of the first settlers of Kentucky, arriving there about the same time as Daniel Boone. He married a cousin of Daniel Boone, and they had a family of eight children. T. J. Stark, the oldest son, now lives at French Corral, Nevada County, California. John Stark, the younger brother, started from Monmouth County, Illinois, in the spring of 1846, but taking the Fort Hall road, reached California in safety. He was a powerfully built man, weighing two hundred and twenty pounds. He was sheriff of Napa County for six years, and in 1852 represented that county in the State Legislature. He died near Calistoga, in 1875, of heart disease. His death was instantaneous, and occurred while pitching hay from a wagon. He was the father of eleven children, six of whom, with his wife, are now living."

Each one of the persons who were taken from Starved Camp by this man and his two companions, reached Sutter's Fort in safety. James F. Breen had his feet badly frozen, and afterwards burned while at the camp. No one had any hope that they could be saved, and when the party reached the fort, a doctor was sought to amputate them. None could be found, and kind nature effected a cure which a physician would have pronounced impossible.

In concluding this chapter, it is quite appropriate to quote the following, written by J. F. Breen: "No one can attach blame to those who voted to leave part of the emigrants. It was a desperate case. Their idea was to save as many as possible, and they honestly believed that by attempting to save all, all would be lost. But this consideration—and the further one that Stark was an entire stranger to every one in the camps, not bound to them by any tie of blood or kindred, nor having any hope of reward, except the grand consciousness of doing a noble act—makes his conduct shine more lustrously in the eyes of every person who admires nature's true and only nobility."

# CHAPTER XVIII.

Arrival of the Third Relief—The Living and the Dead—Captain George Don-
ner Dying—Mrs. Murphy's Words—Foster and Eddy at the Lake—Tamsen
Donner and her Children—A Fearful Struggle—The Husband's Wishes—
Walking Fourteen Miles—Wifely Devotion—Choosing Death—The Night
Journey—An Unparalleled Ordeal—An Honored Name—Three Little
Waifs—"And Our Parents are Dead."

DDY, Foster, Thompson, and Miller passed Nicholas
Clark and John Baptiste near the head of Donner
Lake. These starving fugitives had journeyed thus
far in their desperate effort to cross the mountains.
Of all those encamped at Alder Creek the sole sur-
vivors now were George Donner, the captain of the Donner
Party, and his faithful wife, Tamsen Donner. Under the
snow-drifts which covered the valley, lay Jacob Donner,
Elizabeth Donner, Lewis Donner, Samuel Donner, Samuel (33)
Shoemaker, Joseph Rhinehart, and James Smith. One more
was soon to be added to the number. It was the man whose
name had been given to the company; the only one who
died of a lingering, painful disease. The injury of George
Donner's hand had grown into a feverish, virulent ulceration,
which must have partaken of the nature of erysipelas. At
all events, mortification had set in, and when the third relief

party arrived it had reached his shoulder.   In a few hours at most he must die.

Foster's party found that much suffering had occurred at Donner Lake during the tearful days which elapsed between Reed's departure and their own arrival.   Mrs. Lavina Murphy had charge of her son, Simon Murphy, her grandchild, George Foster, of the child James Eddy, and of the three little Donner girls, Frances, Georgia, and Eliza.   All dwelt in the same cabin, and with them was Lewis Keseberg.   Foster and Eddy found all there, save their own children.   They were both dead.   Keseberg has generally been accused of the murder of little George Foster.   Except Mrs. Murphy, the oldest of those who were with Keseberg was only nine years of age.   All that the children know is that Keseberg took the child to bed with him one night, and that it was dead next morning.   One of the little ones who survived—one whose memory has proven exceedingly truthful upon all points wherein her evidence could be possibly substantiated —and who is now Mrs. Georgia A. Babcock—gives the mildest version of this sad affair which has ever appeared in print.   She denies the story, so often reiterated, that Keseberg took the child to bed with him and ate it up before morning; but writes the following: "In the morning the child was dead.   Mrs. Murphy took it, sat down near the bed where my sister and myself were lying, laid the little one on her lap, and made remarks to other persons, accusing Keseberg of killing it.   After a while he came, took it from her, and hung it up in sight, inside the cabin, on the wall."

Foster, Eddy, Thompson, and Miller remained but a little while at the mountain camp.   During this time Mr. Foster had no opportunity to talk with Mrs. Murphy save in Keseberg's presence.   Afterwards, when the children told him of the suspicions expressed in their presence by Mrs. Murphy,

Foster deeply regretted that he had not sought a private interview with her, for the purpose of learning the reasons for her belief.

In the morning the relief party was to start back to the settlements. Eddy was to carry Georgia Donner; Thompson, Frances Donner; Miller, Eliza Donner; and Foster was to carry Simon Murphy. John Baptiste and Nicholas Clark remained at the head of Donner Lake, and were to accompany the party. This left Mr. and Mrs. Donner at Alder Creek, and Keseberg and Mrs. Murphy at the cabins. Mrs. Murphy had cared for her children and her grandchildren, and ministered to the wants of those around her, until she was sick, exhausted, and utterly helpless. She could not walk. She could scarcely rise from her bed. With all the tenderness of a son, Mr. Foster gave her such provisions as he could leave, procured her wood, and did whatever he was able to do to render her comfortable. He also promised to return speedily, and with such assistance that he could carry her over the summits to her children.

The very afternoon that the third relief party reached the cabins, Simon Murphy discovered a woman wandering about in the snow as if lost. It proved to be Mrs. Tamsen Donner. She had wearily traveled over the deep snows from Alder Creek, as narrated in a previous chapter, to see her children, and, if necessary, to protect their lives. Oh! the joy and the pain of the meeting of those little ones and their mother. As they wound their arms about her neck, kissed her lips, laughed in her eyes, and twined their fingers in her hair, what a struggle must have been taking place in her soul. As the pleading, upturned faces of her babies begged her not to leave them, her very heart-strings must have been rent with agony. Well may the voice quiver or the hand tremble that attempts to portray the anguish of this mother during that

farewell interview.   From the very first moment, her resolution to return to her husband remained unshaken.   The
members of the relief party entreated her to go with her
children and save her own life.   They urged that there could
only be a few hours of life left in George Donner.   This was
so true that she once ventured the request that they remain
until she could return to Alder Creek, and see if he were yet
alive.   The gathering storm-clouds, which had hovered over
the summit for days, compelled them to refuse this request.
An hour's delay might be fatal to all.

George Donner knew that he was dying, and had frequently urged his wife to leave him, cross the mountains,
and take care of her children.   As she held her darlings in
her arms, it required no prophetic vision to disclose pictures
of sadness, of lonely childhood, of longing girlhood, of pil-
lows wet with tears, if these three little waifs were left to
wander friendless in California.   She never expressed a belief
that she would see that land of promise beyond the Sierra.
Often had her calm, earnest voice told them of the future
which awaited them, and so far as possible had she prepared
them to meet thatf uture without the counsel or sympathy of
father or mother.

The night-shadows, creeping through the shivering pines,
warned her of the long, dreary way over which her tired feet
must pass ere she reached her dying husband's side.   She is
said to have appeared strangely composed.   The struggle
was silent.   The poor, bleeding heart brought not a single
moan to the lips.   It was a choice between life, hope, and
her clinging babes, or a lonely vigil by a dying husband, and
an unknown, shroudless death in the wintry mountains.   Her
husband was sixty-three; he was well stricken in years, and
his life was fast ebbing away.   If she returned through the
frosty night-winds, over the crisp, freezing snow, she would

W. C. GRAVES.
1879.

travel fourteen miles that day. The strong, healthy men composing the relief parties frequently could travel but five or six miles in a day. If she made the journey, and found her husband was dead, she could have no hope of returning on the morrow. She had suffered too long from hunger and privation to hope to be able to return and overtake the relief party. It was certain life or certain death. On the side of the former was maternal love; on the side of the latter, wifely devotion. The whole wide range of history can not produce a parallel example of adherence to duty, and to the dictates of conjugal fidelity. With quick, convulsive pressure of her little ones to her heart; with a hasty, soul-throbbing kiss upon the lips of each; with a prayer that was stifled with a sob of agony, Tamsen Donner hurried away to her husband. Through the gathering darkness, past the shadowy sentinels of the forest, they watched with tearful eyes her retreating form. As if she dared not trust another sight of the little faces—as if to escape the pitiful wail of her darlings—she ran straight forward until out of sight and hearing. She never once looked back.

There are mental struggles which so absorb the being and soul that physical terrors or tortures are unnoticed. Tamsen Donner's mind was passing through such an ordeal. The fires of Moloch, the dreadful suttee, were sacrifices which long religious education sanctioned, and in which the devotees perished amidst the plaudits of admiring multitudes. This woman had chosen a death of solitude, of hunger, of bitter cold, of pain-racked exhaustion, and was actuated by only the pure principles of wifely love. Already the death-damp was gathering on George Donner's brow. At the utmost, she could hope to do no more than smooth the pillow of the dying, tenderly clasp the fast-chilling hand, press farewell kisses upon the whitening lips, and finally close the dear, tired eyes. For this, only this, she was yielding life, the world, and her darling babes. Fitted by culture and refinement to be an ornament to society, qualified by education to rear her daughters to lives of honor and usefulness, how it must have wrung her heart to allow her little ones to go unprotected into a wilderness of strangers. But she could not leave her husband to die alone. Rather solitude, better death, than desert the father of her children. O, Land of the Sunset! let the memory of this wife's devotion be ever enshrined in the hearts of your faithful daughters! In tablets thus pure, engrave the name of Tamsen Donner.

---

When the June sunshine gladdened the Sacramento Valley, three little barefooted girls walked here and there among the houses and tents of Sutter's Fort. They were scantily clothed, and one carried a thin blanket. At night they said their prayers, lay down in whatever tent they happened to be, and, folding the blanket about them, fell asleep in each other's arms. When they were hungry, they asked food of whomsoever they met. If any one inquired who they were, they answered as their mother had taught them: "We are the children of Mr. and Mrs. George Donner." But they added something they had learned since. It was, "And our parents are dead."

# CHAPTER XIX.

KESEBERG is one of the leading characters in the Donner Party. Usually, his part in the tragedy has been considered the entire story. Comparatively few people have understood that any except this one man ate human flesh, or was a witness of any scene of horror. He has been loathed, execrated, abhorred as a cannibal, a murderer, and a heartless fiend. In the various published sketches which have from time to time been given to the world, Lewis Keseberg has been charged with no less than six murders. His cannibalism has been denounced as arising from choice, as growing out of a depraved and perverted appetite, instead of being the result of necessity. On the fourth of April, 1879, this strange man granted an interview to the author, and in this and succeeding interviews he reluctantly made a statement which was reduced to writing. "What is the use," he would urge, " of my making a statement? People incline to believe the most horrible reports concerning a man, and they will not credit what I say in my own defense. My conscience is clear. I am an old man, and am calmly awaiting my death. God is my judge, and it long ago ceased to trouble me that people shunned and slandered me."

Keseberg is six feet in height, is well proportioned, and weighs from one hundred and seventy-five to one hundred and eighty pounds. He is active, vigorous, and of an erect, manly carriage, despite his years and his many afflictions. He has clear blue eyes, regular features, light hair and beard, a distinct, rapid mode of enunciation, a loud voice, and a somewhat excited manner of speech. In conversing he looks one squarely and steadily in the eye, and appears like an honest, intelligent German. He speaks and writes German, French, Spanish, and English, and his selection of words proves him a scholar. His face generally wears a determined, almost fierce expression, but one is impressed with the thought that this appearance is caused by his habitually standing on the defensive as against his fellow-men. Since he has never before had an opportunity of speaking in his own defense, it is perhaps fitting that his statement should be given in his own language:

"My name is Lewis Keseberg. I was born in the city of Berleburg, Province of Westphalia, in the Kingdom of Prussia, on the twenty-second of May, 1814. I am therefore almost sixty-three years of age. I was married June 22, 1842, came to the United States May 22, 1844, and emigrated to California in 1846 with the Donner Party. I never have made a statement concerning my connection with that Party to any one connected with the press. It is with the utmost horror that I revert to the scenes of suffering and unutterable misery endured during that journey. I have always endeavored to put away from me all thoughts or recollections of those terrible events. Time is the best physician, and would, I trusted, heal the wounds produced by those days of torture; yet my mind to-day recoils with undiminished horror as I endeavor to speak of this dreadful subject. Heretofore I have never attempted to refute the villainous slanders which have been circulated and published about me. I feel it my duty to make this statement, however, because I am convinced of your willingness to do justice to all who were concerned in that dreadful affair, and heretofore I have been treated with gross injustice.

"If I believe in God Almighty having anything to do with the affairs of men, I believe that the misfortune which overtook the Donner Party, and the terrible part I was compelled to take in the great tragedy, were predestined. On the Hastings Cut-off we were twenty-eight days in going twenty-one miles. Difficulty and disaster hovered about us from the time we entered upon this cut-off.

"One day, while we were traveling on Goose Creek, we saw so many wild geese that I took my shotgun and went hunting. Ordinarily I am not superstitious, but on this morning I felt an overwhelming sense of impending calamity. I mentioned my premonitions to Mrs. Murphy before starting on the hunt. Becoming excited with the sport, and eagerly watching the game, I stepped down a steep bank. Some willows had been burned off, and the short, sharp stubs were sticking up just where I stepped. I had on buckskin moccasins, and one of these stubs ran into the ball of my foot, between the bones and the toes. From this time, until we arrived at Donner Lake, I was unable to walk, or even to put my foot to the ground. The foot became greatly swollen and inflamed, and was exceedingly painful. One day, at Donner Lake, one of my companions, at my earnest request, lanced my foot on the top.   It discharged freely, and some days afterwards, in washing it, I found a hard substance protruding from the wound, and obtaining a pair of forceps, succeeded in extracting a piece of the willow stub, one and a half inches in length.   It had literally worked up through my foot.   I mention this particularly, because I have been frequently accused of remaining at the Donner cabins from selfish or sinister motives, when in fact I was utterly unable to join the relief parties."

It is proper to mention, in corroboration of Keseberg's statement regarding his lameness, that several of the survivors remembered, and had related the circumstance prior to the interview.   It is a well-authenticated fact that he was very lame, and could not walk, yet, as a specimen of the abuse which has been heaped upon the man, a quotation is introduced from Thornton's "Oregon and California."   In speaking of the departure of Foster and Eddy, Thornton says: "There were in camp Mrs. Murphy, Mr. and Mrs. George Donner, and Keseberg—the latter, it was believed, having far more strength to travel than others who had arrived in the settlements.   But he would not travel, for the reason, as was suspected, that he wished to remain behind for the purpose of obtaining the property and money of the dead."   Keseberg's statement continues:

"When we reached the lake, we lost our road, and owing to the depth of the snow on the mountains, were compelled to abandon our wagons, and pack our goods upon oxen. The cattle, unused to such burdens, caused great delay by 'bucking' and wallowing in the snow.   There was also much confusion as to what articles should be taken and what abandoned.   One wanted a box of tobacco carried along; another, a bale of calico, and some one thing and some another.   But for this delay we would have passed the summit

and pressed forward to California. Owing to my lameness,
I was placed on horseback, and my foot was tied up to the
saddle in a sort of sling. Near evening we were close to the
top of the dividing ridge. It was cold and chilly, and everybody was tired with the severe exertions of the day. Some
of the emigrants sat down to rest, and declared they could
go no further. I begged them for God's sake to get over the
ridge before halting. Some one, however, set fire to a pitchy
pine tree, and the flames soon ascended to its topmost
branches. The women and children gathered about this fire
to warm themselves. Meantime the oxen were rubbing off
their packs against the trees. The weather looked very
threatening, and I exhorted them to go on until the summit
was reached. I foresaw the danger plainly and unmistakably.
Only the strongest men, however, could go ahead and break
the road, and it would have taken a determined man to induce the party to leave the fire. Had I been well, and been
able to push ahead over the ridge, some, if not all, would
have followed. As it was, all lay down on the snow, and
from exhaustion were soon asleep. In the night, I felt something impeding my breath. A heavy weight seemed to be
resting upon me. Springing up to a sitting posture, I found
myself covered with freshly-fallen snow. The camp, the
cattle, my companions, had all disappeared. All I could see
was snow everywhere. I shouted at the top of my voice.
Suddenly, here and there, all about me, heads popped up
through the snow. The scene was not unlike what one
might imagine at the resurrection, when people rise up out
of the earth. The terror amounted to a panic. The mules
were lost, the cattle strayed away, and our further progress
rendered impossible. The rest you probably know. We returned to the lake, and prepared, as best we could, for the
winter. I was unable to build a cabin, because of my lame-

14

ness, and so erected a sort of brush shed against one side of Breen's cabin.

"When Reed's relief party left the cabins, Mr. Reed left me a half teacupful of flour, and about half a pound of jerked beef. It was all he could give. Mrs. Murphy, who was left with me, because too weak and emaciated to walk, had no larger portion. Reed had no animosity toward me. He found me too weak to move. He washed me, combed my hair, and treated me kindly. Indeed, he had no cause to do otherwise. Some of my portion of the flour brought by Stanton from Sutter's Fort I gave to Reed's children, and thus saved their lives. When he left me, he promised to return in two weeks and carry me over the mountains. When this party left, I was not able to stand, much less to walk.

"A heavy storm came on in a few days after the last relief party left. Mrs. George Donner had remained with her sick husband in their camp, six or seven miles away. Mrs. Murphy lived about a week after we were left alone. When my provisions gave out, I remained four days before I could taste human flesh. There was no other resort—it was that or death. My wife and child had gone on with the first relief party. I knew not whether they were living or dead. They were penniless and friendless in a strange land. For their sakes I must live, if not for my own. Mrs. Murphy was too weak to revive. The flesh of starved beings contains little nutriment. It is like feeding straw to horses. I can not describe the unutterable repugnance with which I tasted the first mouthful of flesh. There is an instinct in our nature that revolts at the thought of touching, much less eating, a corpse. It makes my blood curdle to think of it! It has been told that I boasted of my shame—said that I enjoyed this horrid food, and that I remarked that human flesh was more palatable than California beef. This is a falsehood. It is a horrible, revolting falsehood. This food was never otherwise than loathsome, insipid, and disgusting. For nearly two months I was alone in that dismal cabin. No one knows what occurred but myself—no living being ever before was told of the occurrences. Life was a burden. The horrors of one day succeeded those of the preceding. Five of my companions had died in my cabin, and their stark and ghastly bodies lay there day and night, seemingly gazing at me with their glazed and staring eyes. I was too weak to move them had I tried. The relief parties had not removed them. These parties had been too hurried, too horror-stricken at the sight, too fearful lest an hour's delay might cause them to share the same fate. I endured a thousand deaths. To have one's suffering prolonged inch by inch, to be deserted, forsaken, hopeless; to see that loathsome food ever before my eyes, was almost too much for human endurance. I am conversant with four different languages. I speak and write them with equal fluency; yet in all four I do not find words enough to express the horror I experienced during those two months, or what I still feel when memory reverts to the scene. Suicide would have been a relief, a happiness, a godsend! Many a time I had the muzzle of my pistol in my mouth and my finger on the trigger, but the faces of my helpless, dependent wife and child would rise up before me, and my hand would fall powerless. I was not the cause of my misfortunes, and God Almighty had provided only this one horrible way for me to subsist."

Did you boil the flesh?

"Yes! But to go into details—to relate the minutiæ—is too agonizing! I can not do it! Imagination can supply these. The necessary mutilation of the bodies of those who had been my friends, rendered the ghastliness of my situation more frightful. When I could crawl about and my lame foot was partially recovered, I was chopping some wood one day and the ax glanced and cut off my heel. The piece of flesh grew back in time, but not in its former position, and my foot is maimed to this day.

"A man, before he judges me, should be placed in a similar situation; but if he were, it is a thousand to one he would perish. A constitution of steel alone could endure the deprivation and misery. At this time I was living in the log-cabin with the fireplace. One night I was awakened by a scratching sound over my head. I started up in terror, and listened intently for the noise to be repeated. It came again. It was the wolves trying to get into the cabin to eat me and the dead bodies.

"At midnight, one cold, bitter night, Mrs. George Donner came to my door. It was about two weeks after Reed had gone, and my loneliness was beginning to be unendurable. I was most happy to hear the sound of a human voice. Her coming was like that of an angel from heaven. But she had not come to bear me company. Her husband had died in her arms. She had remained by his side until death came, and then had laid him out and hurried away. He died at nightfall, and she had traveled over the snow alone to my cabin. She was going, alone, across the mountains. She was going to start without food or guide. She kept saying, 'My children! I must see my children!' She feared she would not survive, and told me she had some money in her tent. It was too heavy for her to carry. She said, 'Mr. Keseberg, I confide this to your care.' She made me promise sacredly that I would get the money and take it to her children in case she perished and I survived. She declared she would start over the mountains in the morning. She said, 'I am bound to go to my children.' She seemed very cold, and her clothes were like ice. I think she had got in the creek in coming. She said she was very hungry, but refused the only food I could offer. She had never eaten the loathsome flesh. She finally lay down, and I spread a feather-bed and some blankets over her. In the morning she was dead. I think the hunger, the mental suffering, and the icy chill of the preceding night, caused her death. I have often been accused of taking her life. Before my God, I swear this is untrue! Do you think a man would be such a miscreant, such a damnable fiend, such a caricature on humanity, as to kill this lone woman? There were plenty of corpses lying around. He would only add one more corpse to the many!

"Oh! the days and weeks of horror which I passed in that camp! I had no hope of help or of being rescued, until I saw the green grass coming up by the spring on the hillside, and the wild geese coming to nibble it. The birds were coming back to their breeding grounds, and I felt that I could kill them for food. I had plenty of guns and ammunition in camp. I also had plenty of tobacco and a good meerschaum pipe, and almost the only solace I enjoyed was smoking. In my weak condition it took me two or three hours every day to get sufficient wood to keep my fire going.

"Some time after Mrs. Donner's death, I thought I had gained sufficient strength to redeem the pledge I had made her before her death. I started to go to the camps at Alder Creek to get the money. I had a very difficult journey. The wagons of the Donners were loaded with tobacco, powder, caps, shoes, school-books, and dry-goods. This stock was very valuable, and had it reached California, would have been a fortune to the Donners. I searched carefully among the bales and bundles of goods, and found five hundred and thirty-one dollars. Part of this sum was silver, part gold. The silver I buried at the foot of a pine tree, a little way from the camp. One of the lower branches of another tree reached down close to the ground, and appeared to point to the spot. I put the gold in my pocket, and started to return to my cabin. I had spent one night at the Donner tents. On my return I became lost. When it was nearly dark, in crossing a little flat, the snow suddenly gave way under my feet, and I sank down almost to my armpits. By means of the crust on top of the snow, I kept myself suspended by throwing out my arms. A stream of water flowed underneath the place over which I had been walking, and the snow had melted on the underside until it was not strong enough to support my weight. I could not touch bottom with my feet, and so could form no idea of the depth of the stream. By long and careful exertion I managed to draw myself backward and up on the snow. I then went around on the hillside, and continued my journey. At last, just at dark, completely exhausted and almost dead, I came in sight of the Graves cabin. I shall never forget my joy at sight of that log-cabin. I felt that I was no longer lost, and would at least have shelter. Some time after dark I reached my own cabin. My clothes were wet by getting in the creek, and the night was so cold that my garments were frozen into sheets of ice. I was so weary, and chilled, and numbed, that I did not build up a fire, or attempt to get anything to eat, but rolled myself up in the bed-clothes and tried to get warm. Nearly all night I lay there shivering with cold; and when I finally slept, I slept very soundly. I did not wake up until quite late the next morning. To my utter astonishment my camp was in the most inexplicable confusion. My trunks were broken open, and their contents were scattered everywhere. Everything about the cabin was torn up and thrown about the floor. My wife's jewelry, my cloak, my pistol and ammunition were missing. I supposed

Indians had robbed my camp during my absence. Suddenly I was startled by the sound of human voices. I hurried up to the surface of the snow, and saw white men coming toward the cabin. I was overwhelmed with joy and gratitude at the prospect of my deliverance. I had suffered so much, and for so long a time, that I could scarcely believe my senses. Imagine my astonishment upon their arrival to be greeted, not with a 'good morning' or a kind word, but with the gruff, insolent demand, 'Where is Donner's money?'

"I told them they ought to give me something to eat, and that I would talk with them afterwards, but no, they insisted that I should tell them about Donner's money. I asked them who they were, and where they came from, but they replied by threatening to kill me if I did not give up the money. They threatened to hang or shoot me, and at last I told them I had promised Mrs. Donner that I would carry her money to her children, and I proposed to do so, unless shown some authority by which they had a better claim. This so exasperated them, that they acted as though they were going to kill me. I offered to let them bind me as a prisoner, and take me before the alcalde at Sutter's Fort, and I promised that I would then tell all I knew about the money. They would listen to nothing, however, and finally I told them where they would find the silver buried, and gave them the gold. After I had done this, they showed me a document from Alcalde Sinclair, by which they were to receive a certain proportion of all moneys and property which they rescued."

The men spoken of by Keseberg, were the fourth relief party. Their names were, Captain Fallon, William M. Foster, John Rhodes, J. Foster, R. P. Tucker, E. Coffeemire, and —— Keyser. William M. Foster had recrossed the mountains the second time, hoping to rescue his wife's mother, Mrs. Murphy. Alas! he found only her mutilated remains.

# CHAPTER XX.

DECEMBER 16, 1846, the fifteen composing the "Forlorn Hope," left Donner Lake. January 17, 1847, they reached Johnson's ranch; and February 5th Capt. Tucker's party started to the assistance of the emigrants. This first relief arrived February 19th at the cabins; the second relief, or Reed's party, arrived March 1st; the third, or Foster's, about the middle of March; and the fourth, or Fallon's, on the seventeenth of April. Upon the arrival of Capt. Fallon's company, the sight presented at the cabins beggars all description. Capt. R. P. Tucker, now of Goleta, Santa Barbara County, Cal., endeavors, in his correspondence, to give a slight idea of the scene. Human bodies, terribly mutilated, legs, arms, skulls, and portions of remains, were scattered in every direction and strewn about the camp. Mr. Foster found Mrs. Murphy's body with one of her limbs sawed off, the saw still lying by her remains. It was such scenes as these which gave this party their first abhorrence for Keseberg. The man was nowhere to be seen, but a fresh track was discovered in the snow leading away from the cabins toward the Donner tents. The party pressed forward to Alder Creek. Captain Tucker writes: "The dead bodies lay moldering around, being all that was left to tell the tale of sorrow. On my first trip we had cut down a large pine tree, and laid the goods of the Donners on this tree to dry in the sun. These goods lay there yet, with the exception of those which Reed's party had taken away."

George Donner was wealthy. His wealth consisted not merely of goods, as many claim, but of a large amount of coin. Hiram Miller, of the relief parties, is authority for the statement that Mr. Donner owned a quarter section of land within the present city limits of Chicago. This land was sold for ten thousand dollars, shortly before Mr. Donner started for California. Mr. Allen Francis, who has been mentioned as the very best authority concerning this family, camped with them on the evening of their first night's journey out of Springfield, Illinois, saw Mr. Donner's money, and thinks there was ten thousand dollars. Mrs. F. E. Bond, of Elk Grove, Sacramento County, California, does not remember the exact amount, but knows that Mr. Donner started with a great deal of gold, because she helped make the belts in which it was to be carried in crossing the plains. The relief parties always understood there was at Donner's camp a large sum of money, estimated at from six to fourteen thousand dollars. It is not disputed that Halloran left about fifteen hundred dollars to this family. Yet Capt. Fallon's party could find no money. It was clear to their minds that some one had robbed the Donner tents.

Remaining over night, thoroughly searching in every place

where the supposed money could be concealed, this party returned to Donner Lake. On their way they found the same
mysterious track, also returning to the cabins. They probably discovered Keseberg in about the manner described. It
is plain to be seen that they regarded him as the murderer
of Mrs. Donner. In forcing him to tell what he had done
with the money, they, too, claim to have choked him, to
have put a rope around his neck, and to have threatened to
hang him. On the other hand, if Keseberg's statement be
accepted as truth, it is easy to understand why he refused to
surrender the money to men who treated him from the outset
as a murderer and a robber.

Let the God to whom Lewis Keseberg appeals be his judge.
It is not the part of this book to condemn or acquit him.
Most of the fourth relief party have already gone before the
bar at which Keseberg asks to be tried. Capt. Tucker is
about the only available witness, and his testimony is far
more lenient than the rumors and falsehoods usually published.

If Keseberg be guilty of any or of all crimes, it will presently be seen that the most revengeful being on earth could
not ask that another drop be added to his cup of bitterness.
His statement continues:

"These men treated me with the greatest unkindness. Mr.
Tucker was the only one who took my part or befriended
me. When they started over the mountains, each man carried two bales of goods. They had silks, calicoes, and de-
laines from the Donners, and other articles of great value.
Each man would carry one bundle a little way, lay it down,
and come back and get the other bundle. In this way they
passed over the snow three times. I could not keep up with
them because I was so weak, but managed to come up to
their camp every night. One day I was dragging myself

slowly along behind the party, when I came to a place which had evidently been used as a camping-ground by some of the previous parties. Feeling very tired, I thought it would be a good place to make some coffee. Kindling a fire, I filled my coffee-pot with fresh snow and sat waiting for it to melt and get hot. Happening to cast my eyes carelessly around, I discovered a little piece of calico protruding from the snow. Half thoughtlessly, half out of idle curiosity, I caught hold of the cloth, and finding it did not come readily, I gave it a strong pull. I had in my hands the body of my dead child Ada! She had been buried in the snow, which, melting down, had disclosed a portion of her clothing. I thought I should go frantic! It was the first intimation I had of her death, and it came with such a shock!

"Just as we were getting out of the snow, I happened to be sitting in camp alone one afternoon. The men were hunting, or attending to their goods. I was congratulating myself upon my escape from the mountains, when I was startled by a snuffling, growling noise, and looking up, I saw a large grizzly bear only a few feet away. I knew I was too weak to attempt to escape, and so remained where I sat, expecting every moment he would devour me. Suddenly there was the report of a gun, and the bear fell dead. Mr. Foster had discovered the animal, and slipping up close to camp, had killed it."

When the party arrived at Sutter's Fort, they took no pains to conceal their feelings toward Keseberg. Some of the men openly accused him of Mrs. Donner's murder. Keseberg, at the suggestion of Captain Sutter, brought action against Captain Fallon, Ned Coffeemire, and the others, for slander. The case was tried before Alcalde Sinclair, and the jury gave Keseberg a verdict of one dollar damages. The old alcalde records are not in existence, but some of the survivors remember the circumstance, and Mrs. Samuel Kyburz, now of Clarksville, El Dorado County, was a witness at the trial. If Keseberg was able to vindicate himself in an action for slander against the evidence of all the party, it is clear that such evidence was not adduced as has frequently appeared in books. For instance, in Captain Fallon's report of this trip, he alleges that "in the cabin with Keseberg were found two kettles of human blood, in all supposed to be over one gallon." Had this been proven, no jury would have found for Keseberg. Fresh blood could not have been obtained from starved bodies, and had the blood been found, Keseberg would have been adjudged a murderer.

Speaking upon this point, Keseberg denies the assertion that any blood was discovered, calls attention to the length of time Mrs. Donner had been dead, to the readiness with which blood coagulates, and adds that not a witness testified to such a circumstance at the trial. Why should Keseberg murder Mrs. Donner? If he wanted her money, it was only necessary to allow her to go out into the mountains alone, without provisions, without any one to point out the way, and perish in the trackless snows. She could not carry any considerable portion of her money with her, and he had only to go back to Alder Creek and secure the treasure. He bears witness that she never tasted human flesh; that she would not partake of the food he offered; how reasonable, then, the story of her death. The fourth relief party expected to find a vast sum of money. One half was to be given them for their trouble. They regarded the man Keseberg as the murderer of George Foster, because of the reports given by the little children brought out by the third relief. The father of this child was with both the third and fourth reliefs. Arriving at the cabins, they were amazed and horrified at the dreadful sights. Hastening to the tents, they found no

LEWIS KESEBERG.

1879.

money. Their idea that Keseberg was a thief was confirmed by his disgorging the money when threatened with death. There was much reason for their hatred of the man who crossed the mountains with them, and this was intensified by their being brought before Alcalde Sinclair and proven slanderers. Out of this hatred has grown reports which time has magnified into the hideous falsehoods which greet the ear from all directions. Keseberg may be responsible for the death of Hardcoop, but urges in his defense that all were walking, even to the women and the children. He says Hardcoop was not missed until evening, and that it was supposed the old man would catch up with the train during the night. The terrible dangers surrounding the company, the extreme lateness of the season, the weakness of the oxen, and the constant fear of lurking, hostile Indians, prevented him or any one else from going back. Keseberg may be responsible for the death of Wolfinger, of George Foster, of James Eddy, of Mrs. Murphy, and of Mrs. Tamsen Donner, but the most careful searcher for evidence can not find the slightest trace of proofs. In his own mournful language, he comes near the truth when he says:

"I have been born under an evil star! Fate, misfortune, bad luck, compelled me to remain at Donner Lake. If God would decree that I should again pass through such an ordeal, I could not do otherwise than I did. My conscience is free from reproach. Yet that camp has been the one burden of my life. Wherever I have gone, people have cried, 'Stone him! stone him!' Even the little children in the streets have mocked me and thrown stones at me as I passed. Only a man conscious of his innocence, and clear in the sight of God, would not have succumbed to the terrible things which have been said of me—would not have committed suicide! Mortification, disgrace, disaster, and unheard-of misfortune

have followed and overwhelmed me. I often think that the
Almighty has singled me out, among all the men on the face
of the earth, in order to see how much hardship, suffering,
and misery a human being can bear!

"Soon after my arrival at the Fort, I took charge of the
schooner Sacramento, and conveyed wheat from Sacramento
to San Francisco, in payment of Capt. Sutter's purchase of
the Russian possessions. I worked seven months for Sutter;
but, although he was kind to me, I did not get my money.
I then went to Sonoma, and worked about the same length
of time for Gen. Vallejo. I had a good position and good
prospects, but left for the gold mines. Soon afterward I was
taken sick, and for eight months was an invalid. I then
went to Sutter's Fort and started a boarding-house. I made
money rapidly. After a time I built a house south of the
Fort, which cost ten thousand dollars. In 1851 I purchased
the Lady Adams hotel, in Sacramento. It was a valuable
property, and I finally sold it at auction for a large sum of
money. This money was to be paid the next day. The
deeds had already passed. That night the terrible fire of
1852 occurred, and not only swept away the hotel, but ruined
the purchaser, so that I could not collect one cent. I went
back to Sutter's Fort and started the Phœnix Brewery. I
succeeded, and acquired considerable property. I finally sold
out for fifty thousand dollars. I had concluded to take this
money, go back to Germany, and live quietly the rest of my
days. The purchaser went to San Francisco to draw the
money. The sale was effected eight days before the great
flood of 1861–2. The flood came, and I lost everything."

Thus, throughout his entire career, have business reverses
followed Lewis Keseberg. Several times he has been wealthy
and honorably situated. At one time he was a partner of
Sam. Brannan, in a mammoth distillery at Calistoga; and

Mr. Brannan is one among many who speak in highest terms of his honesty, integrity, and business capacity. On the thirtieth of January, 1877, Phillipine Keseberg, his faithful wife, died. This was the severest loss of all, as will presently be seen.

Eleven children were born to them, and four are now living. One of these, Lillie, now lives in Sacramento with her husband. Another, Paulina, a widow, resides in San Rafael. Bertha and Augusta live with the father at Brighton, Sacramento County. Both these children are hopelessly idiotic. Bertha is twenty-six years of age, and has never uttered an intelligible word. Augusta is fifteen years old, weighs two hundred and five pounds, and possesses only slight traces of intelligence. Teething spasms, occurring when they were about two years old, is the cause of their idiocy. Both are subject to frequent and violent spasms or epileptic fits. They need constant care and attention. Should Bertha's hand fall into the fire, she has not sufficient intelligence to withdraw it from the flames. Both are helpless as children. The State provides for insane, but not for idiots. Keseberg says a bill setting aside a ward in the State Asylum for his two children, passed the Legislature, but received a pocket veto by the Governor. Sacramento County gives them eighteen dollars a month. Their helplessness and violence render it impossible to keep any nurse in charge of them longer than a few days. Keseberg is very poor. He has employment for perhaps three months during the year. While his wife lived, she took care of these children; but now he has personally to watch over them and provide for their necessities. While at work, he is compelled to keep them locked in a room in the same building. They scream so loudly while going into the spasms that he can not dwell near other people. He therefore lives isolated, in a plain little house back of his brewery.   Here he lives, the saddest, loneliest, most pitiable creature on the face of the earth.   He traces all his misfortunes to that cabin on Donner Lake, and it is little wonder that he says: "I beg of you, insert in your book a fervent prayer to Almighty God that He will forever prevent the recurrence of a similar scene of horror."

# CHAPTER XXI.

Sketch of Gen. John A. Sutter—The Donner Party's Benefactor—The Least and Most that Earth can Bestow—The Survivors' Request—His Birth and Parentage—Efforts to Reach California—New Helvetia—A Puny Army—Uninviting Isolation—Ross and Bodega—Unbounded Generosity—Sutter's Wealth—Effect of the Gold Fever—Wholesale Robbery—The Sobrante Decision—A "Genuine and Meritorious" Grant—Utter Ruin—Hock Farm—Gen. Sutter's Death—Mrs. E. P. Houghton's Tribute.

EALOUS in sending supplies and relief to the suffering Donner Party, earnest in providing shelter, clothing, and food to all who were rescued, Captain John A. Sutter merits more than a passing mention in this history. From the arrival of Stanton at Sutter's Fort with the tidings that a destitute emigrant train was *en route* for California until the return of the fourth relief party with Lewis Keseberg, Captain Sutter's time, wealth, and influence were enlisted in behalf of the party. Actuated only by motives of benevolence and humanity, he gave Stanton and the various relief parties full and free access to whatever he possessed, whether of money, provisions, clothing, mules, cattle, or guides. With all due deference to the generosity of Yerba Buena's citizens, and to the heroic endeavors of the noble men who risked their lives in rescuing the starving emigrants, it is but just and right that this warm-hearted

15

philanthropist should be accorded the honor of being first among the benefactors of the Donner Party. His kindness did not cease with the arrival of the half-starved survivors at Sutter's Fort, but continued until all had found places of employment, and means of subsistance. Pitiful and unworthy is the reward which history can bestow upon such a noble character, yet since he never received any remuneration for his efforts and sacrifices, the reward of a noble name is the least and the most that earth can now bestow. In view of his good deeds, the survivors of the Donner Party have almost unanimously requested that a brief biographical sketch of the man be inserted in these pages.

At midnight on the twenty-eighth of February (or first of March), 1803, John A. Sutter was born in the city of Baden. He was of Swiss parentage, and his father and mother were of the Canton Berne. Educated in Baden, we find him at the age of thirty a captain in the French army. Filled with enthusiasm, energy, and love of adventure, his eyes turned toward America as his "land of promise," and in July, 1834, he arrived in New York. Again breaking away from the restraints of civilized life, he soon made his way to the then almost unknown regions west of the Mississippi. For some years he lived near St. Charles, in Missouri. At one time he entertained the idea of establishing a Swiss colony at this point, and was only prevented by the sinking of his vessel of supplies in the Mississippi River. During this time he accompanied an exploring party into the sultry, sand-covered wastes of New Mexico. Here he met hunters and trappers from California, and listened to tales of its beauty, fertility, and grandeur which awoke irresistible longings in his breast. In March, 1838, with Captain Tripp, of the American Fur Company, he traveled westward as far as the Rocky Mountains, and thence journeying with a small party of trappers, finally reached Fort Vancouver. Finding no land route to California, he embarked in a vessel belonging to the Hudson Bay Company, which was ready for a voyage to the Sandwich Islands. From Honolulu he thought there would be little difficulty in finding passage in a trading vessel for the Coast of California. Disappointed in this, he remained at the Islands some months, and finally shipped as supercargo of a ship bound for Sitka. In returning, the vessel entered the Bay of San Francisco, but was not allowed to land, and Monterey was reached before Sutter was permitted to set foot upon California soil. From Governor Alvarado he obtained the right of settling in the Sacramento Valley. After exploring the Sacramento, Feather, and American Rivers, finally, on the sixteenth of August, 1839, he landed near the present site of Sacramento City, and determined to permanently locate. Soon afterward he began the construction of the famous Sutter's Fort. He took possession of the surrounding country, naming it New Helvetia. One of the first difficulties to be overcome was the hostility of the Indian tribes who inhabited the Sacramento and San Joaquin valleys. Kindness and humane treatment were generally sufficient to cause these Indians to become his allies, yet in more than one instance he was obliged to resort to arms. Considering the size of his army, there is a sort of grim heroism in the fact that he successfully waged at times a defensive and at times an aggressive warfare. His entire army was composed of six white men, who had been collected from different parts of the world, and eight Kanakas.

Dunbar, in describing Sutter's situation, says: "This portion of upper California, though fair to look upon, was peculiarly solitary and uninviting in its isolation and remoteness from civilization. There was not even one of those cattle ranches, which dotted the coast at long intervals, nearer to Sutter's locality than Suisun and Martinez, below the mouth of the Sacramento. The Indians of the Sacramento were known as 'Diggers.' The efforts of the Jesuit Fathers, so extensive on this continent, and so beneficial to the wild Indians wherever missions were established among them, never reached the wretched aborigines of the Sacramento country. The valley of the Sacramento had not yet become the pathway of emigrants from the East, and no civilized human being lived in this primitive and solitary region, or roamed over it, if we (34) except a few trappers of the Hudson Bay Company."

Out of this solitude and isolation, Sutter, as if with a magician's wand, brought forth wealth and evolved for himself a veritable little kingdom. Near the close of the year. 1839, eight white men joined his colony, and in 1840 his numbers were increased by five others. About this time the Mokelumne Indians became troublesome, and were conquered. Other tribes were forced into submission, and Sutter was practically monarch of the Sacramento and San Joaquin. The old pioneers speak with pride of the wonderful power he exerted over these Indians, teaching them the arts of civilization, forming them into military companies, drilling them in the use of fire-arms, teaching them to till the soil, and making them familiar with the rudiments of husbandry. The vast herds of cattle which in process of time he acquired, were tended and herded principally by these Indians, and the cannon which ultimately came into his possession were mounted upon the Fort, and in many instances were manned by these aborigines. Hides were sent to Yerba Buena, a trade in furs and supplies was established with the Hudson Bay Company, and considerable attention was given to mechanical and agricultural pursuits.

In 1841, Sutter obtained grants from Governor Alvarado of the eleven leagues of land comprised in his New Helvetia, and soon afterwards negotiated a purchase of the Russian possessions known as "Ross and Bodega." By this purchase, Sutter acquired vast real and personal property, the latter including two thousand cattle, one thousand horses, fifty mules, and two thousand five hundred sheep. In 1845 Sutter acquired from Gov. Manuel Micheltorena the grant of the famous *Sobrante*, which comprised the surplus lands over the first eleven leagues included within the survey accompanying the Alvarado grant.

As early as 1844 a great tide of emigration began flowing from the Eastern States toward California, a tide which, after the discovery of gold, became a deluge. Sutter's Fort became the great terminal point of emigration, and was far-famed for the generosity and open-heartedness of its owner. Relief and assistance were rendered so frequently and so abundantly to distressed emigrants, and aid and succor were so often sent over the Sierra to feeble or disabled trains, that Sutter's charity and generosity became proverbial. In the sunny hillslopes and smiling valleys, amidst the graceful groves and pleasant vineyards of this Golden State, it would be difficult to find localities where pioneers have not taught their children to love and bless the memory of the great benefactor of the pioneer days, John A. Sutter. With his commanding presence, his smiling face, his wealth, his power, and his liberality, he came to be regarded in those days as a very king among men. What he did for the Donner Party is but an instance of his unvarying kindness toward the needy and distressed. During this time he rendered important services to the United States, and notably in 1841, to the exploring expedition of Admiral Wilkes. The *Peacock*, a vessel belonging to the expedition, was lost on the Columbia bar, and a part of the expedition forces, sent overland in consequence, reached Sutter's Fort in a condition of extreme distress, and were relieved with princely hospitality. Later on he gave equally needed and equally generous relief to Colonel Fremont and his exploring party. When the war with Mexico came on, his aid and sympathy enabled Fremont to form a battalion from among those in Sutter's employ, and General Sherman's testimony is, "that to him (Sutter) more than any single person are we indebted for the conquest of California with all its treasures."

In 1848, when gold was discovered at Sutter's Mill, near Coloma, quoting again from Dunbar: "We find that Captain Sutter was the undisputed possessor of almost boundless tracts of land, including the former Russian possessions of Ross and Bodega, and the site of the present city of Sacramento. He had performed all the conditions of his land grants, built his fort, and completed many costly improvements. At an expense of twenty-five thousand dollars he had cut a mill-race three miles long, and nearly finished a new flouring mill. He had expended ten thousand dollars in the erection of a saw-mill near Coloma; one thousand acres of virgin soil were laid down to wheat, promising a yield of forty thousand bushels, and extensive preparations had been made for other crops. He owned eight thousand cattle, two thousand horses and mules, two thousand sheep, and one thousand swine. He was the military commander of the district, Indian agent of the territory, and Alcalde by appointment of Commodore Stockton. Respected and honored by all, he was the great man of the country."

Subsequently he was a member of the Constitutional Convention at Monterey, and was appointed Major General of militia. Would that the sketch of his life might end here; but, alas! there is a sad, sad closing to the chapter. This can not be told more briefly and eloquently than in the language of the writer already mentioned:

"As soon as the discovery of gold was known, he was immediately deserted by all his mechanics and laborers, white, Kanaka, and Indian. The mills were abandoned, and became a dead loss. Labor could not be hired to plant, to mature the crops, or reap and gather the grain that ripened.

"At an early period subsequent to the discovery, an immense emigration from overland poured into the Sacramento Valley, making Sutter's domains their camping-ground, without the least regard for the rights of property. They occupied his cultivated fields, and squatted all over his available lands, saying these were the unappropriated domain of the United States, to which they had as good a right as any one. They stole and drove off his horses and mules, and exchanged or sold them in other parts of the country; they butchered his cattle, sheep, and hogs, and sold the meat. One party of five men, during the flood of 1849–50, when the cattle were surrounded by water, near the Sacramento river, killed and sold $60,000 worth of these—as it was estimated—and left for the States. By the first of January, 1852, the so-called settlers, under pretense of pre-emption claims, had appropriated all Sutter's lands capable of settlement or appropriation, and had stolen all of his horses, mules, cattle, sheep, and hogs, except a small portion used and sold by himself.

"There was no law to prevent this stupendous robbery; but when law was established, then came lawyers with it to advocate the squatters' pretensions, although there were none from any part of Christendom who had not heard of Sutter's grants, the peaceful and just possession of which he had enjoyed for ten years, and his improvements were visible to all.

"Sutter's efforts to maintain his rights, and save even

enough of his property to give him an economical, comfortable living, constitute a sad history, one that would of itself
filll a volume of painful interest.   In these efforts he became
involved in continuous and expensive litigation, which was not
terminated till the final decision of the Supreme Court in
1858–59, a period of ten years.   When the United States
Court of Land Commissioners was organized in California,
Sutter's grants came up in due course for confirmation.
These were the grant of eleven leagues, known as New Helvetia, and the grant of twenty-two leagues, known as the
*Sobrante.*   The land commissioners found these grants perfect.   Not a flaw or defect could be discovered in either of
them, and they were confirmed by the board, under the provisions of the treaty of Guadalupe Hidalgo.

"The squatter interest then appealed to the United States
District Court for the Northern District of California.   This
court confirmed the decision of the land commissioners.
Extraordinary as it may appear, the squatter interest then
appealed both cases to the Supreme Court of the United
States at Washington, and still more extraordinary to relate,
that court, though it confirmed the eleven-league grant, decided that of the *Sobrante*—twenty-two leagues—in favor of
the squatters.   The court acknowledged that the grant was a
"genuine and meritorious" one, and then decided in favor of
the squatter interest on purely technical grounds.

"Sutter's ruin was complete, and its method may be thus
stated: He had been subjected to a very great outlay of
money in the maintenance of his title, the occupancy and the
improvement of the grant of New Helvetia.   From a mass
of interesting documents which I have been permitted to
examine, I obtained the following statement relative to the
expenses incurred on that grant:

From a Photo by Sarony, New York, Jan. 19, 1878.

Expenses in money, and services which formed the original consideration of the grant................................................. $50,000
Surveys and taxes on the same................................... 50,000
Cost of litigation extending through ten years, including fees to eminent
counsel, witness fees, traveling expenses, etc.................... 125,000
Amount paid out to make good the covenants of deeds upon the grant,
over and above what was received from sales...................... 100,000
$325,000

"In addition, General Sutter had given titles to much of
the *Sobrante* grant, under deeds of general warranty, which,
after the decision of the supreme court of the United States
in favor of the squatter interest, Sutter was obliged to make
good, at an immense sacrifice, out of the New Helvetia grant;
so that the confirmation of his title to this grant was comparatively of little advantage to him. Thus Sutter lost all his
landed estate.

"But amid the wreck and ruin that came upon him in
cumulative degree, from year to year, Sutter managed to save,
for a period, what is known as Hock farm, a very extensive
and valuable estate on the Feather River. This estate he
proposed to secure as a resting-place in his old age, and for
the separate benefit of his wife and children, whom he had
brought from Switzerland in 1852, having been separated
from them eighteen years. Sutter's titles being generally
discredited, his vast flocks and herds having dwindled to a
few head, and his resources being all gone, he was no longer
able to hire labor to work the farm; and as a final catastro-
phe, the farm mansion was totally destroyed by fire in 1865,
and with it all General Sutter's valuable records of his pioneer
life." As difficulties augmented, Hock farm became incum-
bered with mortgages, and ultimately it was swallowed up in
the general ruin.

For some years he received a small allowance from the
State of California; but after a time this appropriation expired,

and was never thereafter renewed. The later years of the
pioneer's life were passed at Litiz, Lancaster County, Pennsylvania, and his time was devoted to endeavoring to obtain
from Congress an appropriation of $50,000, as compensation
for the expenditures he made for the relief of the early settlers of California. His death occurred at Washington, D.
C., on the eighteenth day of June, 1880, and his remains were
laid at rest in Litiz, Pennsylvania. The termination of this
grand, heroic life, under circumstances of abject poverty and
destitution, forms as strange and mournful a story as can be
found in the annals of the present age.

In concluding this chapter, it may not be inappropriate to
quote from a private letter written by Mrs. S. O. Houghton,
*née* Eliza P. Donner, immediately after the General's death.
It aptly illustrates the feeling entertained toward him by the
members of the Donner Party. Writing from San Jose, she
says:

" I have been sad, oh ! so sad, since tidings flashed across
the continent telling the friends of General Sutter to mourn
his loss. In tender and loving thought I have followed the
remains to his home, have stood by his bier, touched his icy
brow, and brushed back his snowy locks, and still it is hard
for me to realize that he is dead; that he who in my childhood
became my ideal of all that is generous, noble, and good; he
who has ever awakened the warmest gratitude of my nature,
is to be laid away in a distant land ! But I must not yield to
this mood longer. God has only harvested the ripe and
golden grain. Nor has He left us comfortless, for recollection, memory's faithful messenger, will bring from her treas-
ury records of deeds so noble, that the name of General
Sutter will be stamped in the hearts of all people, so long as
California has a history. Yes, his name will be written in
letters of sunlight on Sierra's snowy mountain sides, will be

traced on the clasps of gold which rivet the rocks of our State, and will be arched in transparent characters over the gate which guards our western tide. All who see this land of the sunset will read, and know, and love the name of John A. Sutter, who fed the hungry, clothed the naked, and comforted the sorrowing children of California's pioneer days."

# CHAPTER XXII.

WITH the arrival of the emigrants at places of safety,
this history properly closes. The members of the
Donner Party were actively and intimately associ-
ated with all the early pioneer history of the State.
The life of almost every one would furnish foundation for a most interesting biographical sketch. Ninety
names were mentioned in the first chapter. Of these, forty-
two perished. Mrs. Sarah Keyes, Halloran, John Snyder,
Hardcoop, Wolfinger and William M. Pike did not live to
reach the mountain camps. The first victim of starvation,
Baylis Williams, died in the Reed cabin. About this time
Jacob Donner, Samuel Shoemaker, Joseph Rhinehart and
James Smith perished at Alder Creek. The five deaths last
mentioned occurred within one week, about the middle of
December. During the journey of the "Forlorn Hope,"
the fifteen were reduced to seven by the deaths of C. T.

Stanton, F. W. Graves, Antoine, Patrick Dolan, Lemuel Murphy, Jay Fosdick, Lewis, and Salvador. Meantime, enrolled on the death-list at Donner Lake, were the names of Charles Burger, Lewis Keseberg, Jr., John Landrum Murphy, Margaret Eddy, Harriet McCutchen, Augustus Spitzer, Mrs. Eleanor Eddy, Milton Elliott, and Catherine Pike.

During the journey of the first relief party, Ada Keseberg, John Denton, and William Hook perished, and with the second relief party died Mrs. Elizabeth Graves, Isaac Donner, and F. W. Graves, Jr. About this time, at the tents, died Lewis Donner, Mrs. Elizabeth Donner, and Samuel Donner, George Foster and James Eddy. No deaths occurred in the party of the third relief, and no names are to be added to the fatal list save Mrs. Lavina Murphy, George Donner, and Mrs. Tamsen Donner.

Out of the Donner Party, forty-eight survived. Walter (35) Herron reached California with James F. Reed, and did not return. Of the "Forlorn Hope," Mary A. Graves, Mrs. Sarah Fosdick, Mrs. Amanda M. McCutchen, Mrs. Harriet F. Pike, Mrs. S. A. C. Foster, William M. Foster, and W. H. Eddy lived. The two last mentioned returned and again braved the dangers which encompassed the emigrants. The first relief party rescued Mrs. Margaret W. Reed, Virginia E. Reed and James F. Reed, Jr., Elitha C. Donner, Leanna C. Donner, George Donner, Jr., Wm. G. Murphy, Mary M. Murphy, Naomi L. Pike, W. C. Graves, Eleanor Graves, Lovina Graves, Mrs. Phillipine Keseberg, Edward J. Breen, Simon P. Breen, Eliza Williams, Noah James, and Mrs. Wolfinger.

The second relief succeeded in reaching the settlements with only Solomon Hook, Patty Reed, and Thomas K. Reed. With this party were its Captain, James F. Reed, and William McCutchen. Those who were brought to Starved Camp by the second relief, and saved by a portion of the third relief, were Patrick Breen, Mrs. Margaret Breen, John Breen, Patrick Breen, Jr., James F. Breen, Peter Breen, Isabella M. Breen, Nancy Graves, Jonathan Graves, Elizabeth Graves, and Mary M. Donner. The remainder of the third relief rescued Simon P. Murphy, Frances E. Donner, Georgia A. Donner, Eliza P. Donner, and John Baptiste. W. H. Eddy remained in the valleys after making this journey. Wm. M. Foster traversed the snow-belt no less than five times—once with the "Forlorn Hope," twice with the third relief, and twice with the fourth. The fourth relief rescued Lewis Keseberg.

General Kearney visited the cabins at Donner Lake on the twenty-second of June, 1847. Edwin Bryant, the author of "What I Saw in California," was with General Kearney, and says: "A halt was ordered for the purpose of collecting and interring the remains. Near the principal cabins I saw two bodies entire, with the exception that the abdomens had been cut open and the entrails extracted. Their flesh had been either wasted by famine or evaporated by exposure to the dry atmosphere, and they presented the appearance of mummies. Strewn around the cabins were dislocated and broken skulls (in some instances sawed asunder with care, for the purpose of extracting the brains), human skeletons, in short, in every variety of mutilation. A more revolting and appalling spectacle I never witnessed. The remains were, by an order of General Kearney, collected and buried under the superintendence of Major Swords. They were interred in a pit which had been dug in the center of one of the cabins for a cache. These melancholy duties to the dead being performed, the cabins, by order of Major Swords, were fired, and with everything surrounding them connected with this horrid and melancholy tragedy were consumed. The body of George Donner was found at his camp, about eight or ten miles distant, wrapped in a sheet. He was buried by a party of men detailed for that purpose."

To carefully lay out her husband's body, and tenderly enfold it in a winding-sheet, was the last act of devotion to her husband which was performed by Tamsen Donner.

With varying incidents and episodes, the immigrants all reached Sutter's Fort. One very attractive young lady received a proposal of marriage while doing her best to manage the rebellious mule on which she was riding. The would-be lover pleaded his case well, considering the adverse circumstances, but the young lady gave not her consent.

Twenty-six, and possibly twenty-eight, out of the forty-eight survivors, are living to-day. Noah James is believed to be alive, and John Baptiste was living only a short time since, at Ukiah, Mendocino County, California. Besides these two, there are twenty-six whose residences are known. William McCutchen, who came from Jackson County, Missouri, is hale and strong, and is a highly-respected resident of San Jose, California. Mr. McCutchen is a native of Nashville, Tennessee, was about thirty years old at the time of the disaster, and has a clear, correct recollection of all that transpired. Lewis Keseberg's history has been pretty fully outlined in his statement. He resides in Brighton, Sacramento County, California.

In May, 1847, Mary A. Graves married Edward Pile. He was murdered by a Spaniard in 1848, and this Spaniard was the first person hanged in California under the laws of the United States. In 1851 or 1852 Mrs. Pile married J. T. Clarke. Their children are: Robert F., born in 1852, who is married and living at White River, Tulare County Cal.; Mattie, born in 1854, and now the wife of P. Bequette, Jr., of Visalia; James Thomas, born in 1857; an infant, who died soon after birth; Belle, born in 1860, and died in 1871; Alexander R., born in 1865, and Daniel M., born in 1872.   Mrs. M. A. Clarke's address is White River, Tulare County, California.

Eleanor Graves married William McDonnell about the first of September, 1849.   Their children are: Ann, born September, 1850; Charles, born in 1852; Mary, born in 1855, married to Lester Green, January 2, 1878, and now living on the Sacramento River, about seventeen miles below the city; Lillie, born April 14, 1857, died in February, 1873; Franklin, born in 1860, died in March, 1873; Henry, born July, 1864; Eleanor, born July, 1868; Leslie, born October, 1872, died March, 1873; Louisa, born in 1878.   Mrs. Eleanor McDonnell and family reside in Knights Valley, Sonoma County.   Their address is Calistoga, California.

Lovina Graves married John Cyrus June 5, 1856.   Their children are: Henry E., born April 12, 1859; James W., born February 16, 1861; Mary A., born April 26, 1863; Sarah Grace, born December 11, 1866; and Rachel E., born January 27, 1873.   Their address is Calistoga.

Nancy Graves married Rev. R. W. Williamson in 1855. Their eldest, George, is an artist in Virginia City; Emily is teaching school in Knights Valley; Kate, Frederick, and Lydia Pearl are residing with their parents at Los Gatos, Santa Clara County, Cal.

William C. Graves is a blacksmith, living at Calistoga.   He visited Truckee this spring, examined the sites of the different cabins, and has rendered most valuable assistance in the preparation of this history.

The Murphys have always been well and favorably known in the best society of California.   Mrs. Harriet F. Pike was married at Sutter's Fort, in 1847, by Alcalde Sinclair, to M. C. Nye.   Prior to the discovery of gold, they lived about three

miles above Marysville, which, at this time, bore the name of
Nye's Ranch. Mrs. Nye died in 1872, at Dalles, Oregon,
and her remains were brought to Marysville and laid in the
city cemetery. Naomi L. Pike was married, in 1865, to Dr.
Mitchell, of Marysville, moved to Oregon, became a widow,
and is now the wife of John L. Schenck. Her address is,
The Dalles, Wasco County, Oregon.

Mary M. Murphy was married, in 1848, to C. Covillaud,
then of Nye's Ranch, Cal. In 1850 the city of Marysville
was laid out, and was named in honor of Mrs. Mary Covillaud. After lives of distinguished honor, Mr. and Mrs. Covillaud died, but there are now living five of their children.
Mary Ellen is married to a prominent stock dealer, of Dalles,
Oregon; Charles J., a very bright and promising young man,
is in the law office of his uncle, William G. Murphy; William P., Frank M., and Naomi S., are all living at Dalles,
Oregon. William G. Murphy resided at Marysville until
1849, when he went east to receive an education. He grad-
uated with high honors at the State University of Missouri.
He was married in Tennessee, returned to the Pacific Coast
in 1858, and in 1863 was duly admitted a member of the bar
of the Supreme Court of Nevada. He resided and practiced
his profession at Virginia City until in the fall of 1866, when
he returned to Marysville, Cal. He now holds the position
of City Attorney, and has an excellent and remunerative
practice. He has a beautiful and charming home, and his
family consists of himself, his wife, and seven children. His
eldest, Lulie T., was born in the Territory of Nevada, and
his second child, Kate Nye, was born in Nevada subsequent to its admission as a State. William G., Jr., Charles
Mitchell, Ernest, Harriet F., and Leander B. were born in
Marysville.

Simon P. Murphy went back to Tennessee, and married at
16

his old home.  He served in the Union army.  He died in 1873, leaving a wife and five children.

William M. Foster gave his name to Foster's Bar, on the Yuba River.  He died in 1874, of cancer.  Of the children of Mr. and Mrs. Foster, there are now living, Alice, born in 1848; Georgia, born in 1850; Will, born in 1852; Minnie, born in 1855; and Hattie, born in 1858.  Mrs. S. A. C. Foster has been residing in San Francisco, but her present address is, care of her brother, Wm. G. Murphy, Marysville.

Mr. and Mrs. Reed settled with their family in San Jose, California.  Mrs. Margaret Reed died on the twenty-fifth of November, 1861, and her husband, James F. Reed, on the twenty-fourth of July, 1874.  They are buried side by side, their coffins touching.  Mrs. Reed died with her entire family gathered about her bedside, and few death-bed scenes ever recorded were more peaceful.  As she entered the dark waters, all about her seemed suddenly bright.  She spoke of the light, and asked that the windows be darkened.  The curtains were arranged by those about her, but a moment afterward she said, "Never mind; I see you can not shut out the bright light which I see."  Looking up at the faces of her husband and children, she said very slowly, "I expect, when I die, I will die this way, just as if I was going to sleep.  Wouldn't it be a blessing if I did?"  The last words were uttered just as the soul took its flight.  Thomas K. Reed and James F. Reed, Jr., reside in San Jose, Cal.  The latter was married March 16, 1879, to Sarah Adams.  Virginia E. Reed was married on the twenty-sixth of January, 1850, to J. M. Murphy.  Their children's names are, Mary M., Lloyd M., Mattie H., John M., Virginia B., J. Ada, Dan James, Annie Mabel, and T. Stanley.  Lloyd, Mattie, and Mabel are sleeping in Oak Hill Cemetery, at San Jose, Cal.  Mary was married to P. McAran, June 28, 1869.  Mr. Mc-

Aran is one of the directors of the Hibernia Bank, and resides in San Francisco. John M. Murphy, Jr., was married April 1, 1880, to Miss Hattie E. Watkins. Martha J. (Patty) Reed was married at Santa Cruz, Cal., December 25, 1856, to Mr. Frank Lewis. They had eight children: Kate, born October 6, 1857; Margaret B., born June 6, 1860; Frank, born March 22, 1862; Mattie J., born April 6, 1864; James Frazier, born August 31, 1866; a babe, born May 30, 1868, who died in infancy; Carrie E., born September 15, 1870; and Susan A., born December 31, 1873. Mr. Lewis died June 18, 1876. Mrs. Lewis and her children reside at San Jose.

Wm. H. Eddy married Mrs. F. Alfred, at Gilroy, California, in July, 1848. They had three children: Eleanor P., James P., and Alonzo H. Eleanor married S. B. Anderson, in 1871, and resides in San Jose. James married in 1875, and with his wife and two children resides in San Jose. Alonzo is a physician in Monument, Colorado. In 1854, Mr. and Mrs. Eddy separated, and in 1856 he married Miss A. M. Pardee, of St. Louis. Mr. Eddy died December 24, 1859, at Petaluma, California.

Patrick Breen removed with his family from Sutter's Fort early in 1848, and permanently settled at the Mission of San Juan Bautista, in San Benito County, California. Mr. Breen lived to see all his children grow to maturity and become happily established in life. On the twenty-first of December, 1868, he peacefully closed his eyes to this world, surrounded by every member of his family, all of whom he preceded to the tomb.

All the surviving members of the Breen family are still residing at or near San Juan. John Breen married in 1852. His family, consisting of his wife and ten children, are all living. His children's names are: Lillie M., Edward P., John J., Thomas F., Adelaide A., Kate, Isabelle, Gertrude,

Charlotte, and Ellen A. Breen. Edward J. Breen married in 1858. His wife died in 1862, leaving the following children: Eugene T., Edward J., and John Roger. Patrick Breen, Jr., married in 1865; his wife is living, and their children are Mary, William, Peter, Eugene. Simon P. Breen married in 1867; his wife is living; their children are Geneva and Mary. James F. Breen, the present Superior Judge of San Benito County, married in 1870; his wife is living; their only surviving children are Margaret and Grace. Peter Breen died, unmarried, on July 3, 1870, by accidental death. Isabella M. Breen was married in 1869, to Thomas McMahon, and with her husband resides at Hollister, San Benito County. William M. Breen, whose portrait appears in the group of the Breen family, was born in San Juan in 1848, and was not of the Donner Party. He married in 1874, leaving a widow, and one child, Mary.

Margaret Breen, the heroic woman, devoted wife, and faithful mother, had the satisfaction of living to see her infant family, for whose preservation she had struggled so hard and wrought so ceaselessly, grow to manhood and womanhood. In prosperity, as in adversity, she was ever good, kind, courageous, and "affable to the congregation of the Lord." She was always self-reliant, and equal to the most trying emergencies; and yet, at all times, she had a deep and abiding faith in God, and firmly relied on the mercy and goodness of Him to whom she prayed so ardently and confidently in the heavy hours of her tribulation. The hope of her later years was that she might not be required to witness the death of any of her children; but it was willed differently, as two of them preceded her to the grave. April 13, 1874, ripe in years, loved by the poor, honored and respected by all for her virtues and her well-spent life, she quietly and peacefully passed from the midst of her sorrowing family to the other and better shore.

WILLIAM M<sup>c</sup>CUTCHEN,

1880.

The following lines from the pen of Miss Marcella A. Fitz-
gerald, the gifted poetess of Notre Dame Convent, San Jose,
were published in the San Francisco Monitor, at the time of
Mrs. Breen's death:

### IN MEMORIAM.

#### MRS. MARGARET BREEN.

The spring's soft light, its tender, dreamy beauty
  Veils all the land around us, and the dome
Of the blue skies is ringing with the music
  Of birds that come to seek their summer home.

But one whose heart this beauty often gladdened
  No more shall see the fragrant flowers expand;
For her no more of earth—but fairer portion
  Is hers, the beauty of the Better Land;

The beauty of that land to which with yearning
  Her true heart turned in faith and trust each day;
The land whose hope a glorious bow of promise
  Illumed her path across life's desert way.

A loving wife; a fond, devoted mother;
  A friend who reckoned friendship not a name;
A woman who with gentle influence brightened
  The hearts of all who to her presence came.

A halo of good deeds her life surrounded;
  Her crown of years was bright with deeds of love;
Hers was a gift of charity whose merits
  A golden treasure waiteth her above.

Out of the wealth the Master gave unto her
  She clothed the needy and the hungry fed;
The poor will mourn a true friend taken from them—
  Above her will the orphan's tear be shed.

The orphan's prayer, a prayer of power unbounded,
  In grateful accents shall for her ascend,
And strength and consolation for her children
  Down from the Savior's pitying heart descend;

For over death the Christian's faith doth triumph—
   The crown of victory shines above the Cross;
Hers is the fadeless joy and ours the sorrow—
   Hers is the gain and ours the bitter loss.

And while the hearts of kindred ache in sadness,
   And gloom rests on her once fair home to-day,
As a true friend who mourns a loved one taken,
   This simple wreath upon her grave I lay.

# CHAPTER XXIII.

NUSUAL interest attaches to the three little orphan children mentioned in a preceding chapter. Frances, Georgia, and Eliza Donner reached Sutter's Fort in April, 1847. Here they met their two elder sisters, who, in charge of the first relief party, had arrived at the Fort a few weeks earlier. The three little girls were pitiable-looking objects as they gathered around the blazing fire, answering and asking questions respecting what had taken place since they parted with their sisters at their mountain cabins.

Among the first to stretch forth a helping hand to clothe the needy children was that noble philanthropist, Capt. John A. Sutter. Other newly-found friends gave food from their scanty supplies, and the children would have been comfortable for a time, had not some pilfering hand taken all that had been given them. They were again obliged to ask for

food of those whom they thought would give. As the
weather became warmer it had a cheering influence over
them. They forgot their wish for heavier clothing; but
oftener repeated the more heartfelt one—"If mother would
only come!"

Those who have suffered bereavement under similar circumstances can understand how fully these little girls realized
their situation when they were told that their mother was
dead.

Not long after it became known that their parents were
dead, Georgia and Eliza enlisted the sympathies of a kind-
hearted Swiss couple, Christian and Mary Brunner, who
lived a short distance from the Fort. Mrs. Brunner brought
them bread, butter, eggs, and cheese, with the kind remark
to those in whose hands she placed the articles: "These are
for the little girls who called me grandma; but don't give
them too much at a time." A few days later, upon inquiring
of them how they liked what she brought, grandma was told
they had not had anything, and was so surprised that she decided to take Georgia home with her for a week. Georgia
was more delicate than her younger sister. Eliza was promised that she should be treated as kindly upon Georgia's
return. The week passed, and Georgia returned, looking
stronger. She told such wonderful stories about the many
cows! lots of chickens! two sheep that would not let her
pass unless she carried a big stick in sight! about the kindness grandma, grandpa, and Jacob, his brother, had shown
to her, that it seemed to Eliza the time would never come
when she and grandma were to start to that enchanting
home! Such a week of pleasure! Who but that little girl
could describe it! Grandma's bread and milk gave strength
to her limbs and color to her cheeks. She chased the chickens, and drove the cows; she brought chips for grandma,

rode the horse for Jacob, and sat upon grandpa's knee so
cheerfully, that they began to feel as if she belonged to them.
But her week had come to an end!  Grandma, all dressed
for a walk to the Fort, sought the little girl, who was busy at
play, and said: "Come, Eliza, I hear that Georgia is sick,
and I am going to take you back, and bring her in your
place."  The sweet little girl looked very grave for a moment,
then glancing up with her large black eyes into that dear old
face, she took courage, and asked, with the earnestness of an
anxious child: "Grandma, can't you keep both of us?"

This simple question provided a home for both until after
Hiram Miller was appointed their guardian.  He was intrusted
with their money, obtained from Keseberg and from other
sources.  The little sisters were then again separated.  Frances had found a home in Mrs. Reed's family.  Georgia was
to go with grandpa, who was about to remove to Sonoma.
Eliza went to her eldest sister, who was now married and living on the Cosumnes River.  Here she remained until winter.  Then, hearing that Mr. Brunner's family and Georgia
desired her return, she became so homesick that her sister
consented to her going to them.  Fortunately, they heard of
two families who were to move to Sonoma in a very short
time, and Eliza was placed in their charge.  This journey
was marked with many incidents which seemed marvelous to
her child-mind.  The one which impressed itself most forci-
bly occurred upon their arrival at the bank of the Sonoma
River.  She was told that Jacob would meet her here and
take her to grandma's, and was delighted that her journey
was so nearly over.  Imagine her disappointment at finding
the recent rains had raised the river until a torrent flowed
between her and her anxious friends.  For days Jacob sought
the slowly-decreasing flood and called across the rushing
stream to cheer the eager child.  Finally, an Indian, who

understood Jacob's wish, offered to carry her safely over for a silver dollar.  Never did silver look brighter than that which Jacob held between his fingers, above his head, that sunny morning, to satisfy the Indian that his price would be paid when he and his charge reached the other bank.

What a picture this scene presents to the mind!   There is the Indian leading his gray pony to the river's side!   He examines him carefully, and puts the blanket on more securely!  He waits for the approaching child.  How small she is—not five years old!  How she trembles with dread as the swift current meets her eye!  Yet she is anxious to go.  One pleading look in the Indian's face, and she is ready.  He mounts; she is placed behind him; her little arms are stretched tightly around his dusky form!  He presses his elbows to his sides to made her more secure, and, by signs, warns her against loosening her grasp, or she, like the passing branches, will be the water's prey!  They enter the stream.  Oh! how cold the water is!  They reach the middle; her grasp is tighter, and she holds her breath with fear, for they are drifting with the current past where Jacob stands!  But joy comes at last.  They have crossed the river.  There stands the pony shaking the water from his sides.  The Indian takes his dollar with a grunt of satisfaction, and Jacob catches up the little girl, mounts his horse, and hurries off to grandpa's, where grandma, Leanna, and Georgia are waiting to give her a warm welcome.

Months passed pleasantly, but gradually changes occurred.  The war with Mexico ended, and gold was discovered.  All the men who were able to go, hurried off to the mines to make a fortune.  The little girls gave up their plays, for grandma was not able to do all the work, and grandpa and Jacob were away.  They spent seven years with Mr. and Mrs. Brunner.  They were kindly treated, but their education was neglected. In 1854, their eldest sister, Elitha, and her husband, came to Sonoma, and offered them a home and an opportunity of attending school. This kind offer was accepted. For six years Eliza remained in Sacramento, in the family of her sister, Elitha. To her she was indebted for the opportunity she enjoyed of attending, for one year, with her sister Frances and afterwards Georgia, St. Catherine's Academy, at Benicia, and the public schools of Sacramento.

Elitha C. Donner married Perry McCoon, who was subsequently killed by a runaway horse. On the eighth of December, 1853, Mrs. McCoon was married to Benj. W. Wilder. They reside on the Cosumnes River, a few miles from Elk Grove, Sacramento County, Cal., and have six children. Leanna C. Donner was married September 26, 1852, to John App. They now reside in Jamestown, Tuolumne County, Cal., and their family consists of Rebecca E., born February 9, 1854; John Q., born January 19, 1864; and Lucy E., born August 12, 1868, who reside with their parents.

Frances E. Donner was married November 24, 1858, to William R. Wilder, and now resides at Point of Timber, Contra Costa County, Cal. Their children are: Harriet, born August 24, 1859; James William, born May 30, 1863; Frances Lillian, born July 17, 1867; Asaph, born May 7, 1870; and Susan Tamsen, born September 3, 1878. Georgia A. Donner was married November 4, 1863, to W. A. Babcock. Their family consists of Henry A., born August 23, 1864; Frank B., born June 29, 1866; and Edith M., born August 24, 1868. Their address is Mountain View, Santa Clara County, Cal.

Eliza P. Donner, on the tenth of October, 1861, was married to Sherman O. Houghton. Mr. Houghton was born in New York City, April 10, 1828, served in the Mexican war, was Mayor of San Jose in 1855 and 1856, represented California in the Forty-second and Forty-third Congress, and is at present a prominent member of the San Jose bar.   Mr. and Mrs. Houghton have six children.   The youngest living was born in Washington, D. C., at which city his family resided during the four years he served as member of Congress. Their children are: Eliza P., Sherman O., Clara H., Charles D., Francis J., and Stanley W.   Their youngest born, Herbert S., died March 18, 1878, aged twenty months.   Mary M. Donner, daughter of Jacob Donner, was adopted into the family of Mr. James F. Reed, in 1848.   She continued a member of this family until her marriage with Hon. S. O. Houghton, of San Jose, August 23, 1859.   June 21, 1860, Mrs. Mary M. Houghton died, leaving an infant daughter, Mary M., who is now a young lady, and a member of the family of Mr. and Mrs. Houghton.

George Donner, Jr., son of Jacob Donner, married Miss Margaret J. Watson, June 8, 1862.   Their children now living are: Mary E., Cora J., George W., John C., Betty L., and Frank M.   Albert, their eldest, died in 1869, and an infant son died in 1875.   George Donner, Jr., died at Sebastopol, February 17, 1874.   Mrs. Donner now lives with her children on their farm near Sebastopol, Sonoma County, California.

# CHAPTER XXIV.

ERBA BUENA'S citizens, shortly after the arrival
of George and Mary Donner, contributed a fund
for the purpose of purchasing for each of them a
town lot. It happened that these lots were being
then distributed among the residents of the town.
Upon the petition of James F. Reed, a grant was made to
George Donner of one hundred vara lot number thirty-nine, (36)
and the adjoining lot, number thirty-eight, was granted to
Mary. The price of each lot was thirty-two dollars, and both
were paid for out of the fund. The grants were both entered
of record by the Alcalde, George Hyde. The grant made to
George was signed by the Alcalde, but that made to Mary
was, through inadvertence, not signed. A successor of Hyde,

as Alcalde, regranted the lot of Mary Donner to one Ward, who discovered the omission of the Alcalde's name to her grant. This omission caused her to lose the lot. In 1851, a number of persons squatted on the lot of George Donner, and in 1854 brought suit against him in the United States Circuit Court to quiet their title. This suit was subsequently abandoned under the belief that George Donner was dead. In 1856, a suit was instituted by George Donner, through his guardian, to recover possession of the lot. Down to the spring of 1860, but little progress had been made toward recovering the possession of the lot from the squatters. The attorneys who had thus far conducted the litigation on behalf of George Donner, were greatly embarrassed because of their inability to fully prove the delivery of the grant to him, or to some one for him, the courts of the State having, from the first litigation concerning similar grants, laid down and adhered to the rule that such grants did not take effect unless the original grant was delivered to the grantee. Such proof was therefore deemed indispensable.

After such proofs upon this point as were accessible had been made, the proceedings had ceased, and for several months there had been no prospect of any further progress being made. During this time, one Yontz, who had undertaken to recover possession of the lot at his own expense for a share of it, had the management of the case, and had employed an attorney to conduct the litigation. Yontz became unable, pecuniarily, to proceed further with the case, and informed Donner of the fact, whereupon the latter induced his brother-in-law, S. O. Houghton, to attempt to prosecute his claim to some final result. Mr. Houghton applied to the court to be substituted as attorney in the case, but resistance was made by the attorney of Yontz, and the application was denied. Houghton then applied to the Supreme Court for a

THE "BIG ROCK".—SITE OF THE MURPHY CABIN.
1880.

writ of mandate to compel the judge of the court before
which the suit was pending, to order his substitution as attorney of record for Donner.   This writ was granted by the
Supreme Court, and in January, 1861, Mr. Houghton became
the attorney of record.   This suit had been brought by Green
McMahon, who had been appointed Donner's guardian for
that purpose, and after a full examination of the case, Mr.
Houghton dismissed it, and immediately commenced another in the name of George Donner, who was then of age.
In the following year, February, 1862, it was brought to trial
before a jury, and after a contest which lasted ten days, a
verdict was rendered in favor of Donner.

The squatters appealed to the Supreme Court of the State
where the verdict of the jury was set aside, a new trial ordered, and the case sent back for that purpose.   This new
trial was procured by means of an amendment of the law
regulating trials by jury in civil cases.   This amendment was
passed by the Legislature, at the instance of the squatters,
after the verdict had been rendered.   A new trial was had in
1864, before a jury, and resulted in another verdict for Donner.   The first trial had attracted much attention, and was
frequently mentioned in the newspapers of San Francisco,
and thus several persons who were present when the grant
was made had their attention called to the controversy, and
to the difficulty encountered in proving a delivery of the
grant.   They communicated to Donner the fact that it was
delivered for him to William McDonald, the man with whom
he lived at the time.   They also narrated the circumstances
attending the delivery of the grant.   This information, however, came too late for the purposes of the trial.   Prior to the
second trial, the written testimony of all these witnesses was
procured and in readiness for use when required, but it was
never required.   Mr. Houghton and the attorneys whom he

had called upon to aid in the case, determined to rest its decision upon another ground.   They concluded to insist that,
as it was a grant issuing from the government through its instrument, the Alcalde, who was invested with authority for
the purpose, no delivery of the grant was necessary, and that
none was possible, as the entry on the record book of the
Alcalde was the original, it bearing his official signature and
being a public record of his official act.   This was a bold attack upon the rule which the courts had long established to
the contrary.   After a full argument of the question at the
second trial, the court sustained the view of the law taken by
Mr. Houghton and his associates, and, on appeal, the decision
was sustained by the Supreme Court of the State, and subsequently affirmed by the Supreme Court of the United States,
before which the question was carried by writ of error.

Donner's attorneys adopted this course because, at the
first trial, the squatters had produced the copy of the grant
which had actually been issued and delivered.   This they
had obtained possession of and mutilated, and then had sur-
reptitiously placed it in the office of the County Clerk of San
Francisco, who was the custodian of the records of the
office of the Alcaldes of San Francisco.   Their purpose was
to make it appear that it had never been signed or issued by
the Alcalde, but had been transferred with the other papers
and records of that office to the office of the County Clerk.
This document was written on paper having the same water-
marks as numerous other grants to other persons, admitted
to be genuine, made about the same time as the grant to
Donner.   The body of this instrument was in the hand-
writing of the then clerk of the Alcalde, and the certificate
that the Alcalde's fees had been paid bore the genuine signature of the clerk.   There was, however, no signature or
name where the signature of the Alcalde should have been;

but there was, instead, a plain, palpable erasure, easily seen by holding the paper to the light.

George Donner lived to see his property become very valuable, but the vexatious litigation above described was not terminated until after his death.   Meantime, however, he sold his interest, receiving therefor a considerable sum of money.

In conclusion it may be proper to speak of the many interesting relics which have recently been found under the former sites of the cabins of the Donner Party.   When the last relief party left Donner Lake, all articles of minor value were left scattered here and there about the floors and door-yards.   Soon afterward the tide of emigrant travel turned principally to other routes, and the Donner Lake road was comparatively deserted.   Years passed, and the loose soil, the wind-blown dust, the grass and fallen leaves covered the articles from sight.   It was twenty years before men began to search for the sites of the cabins, and to carry away little mementos of the mournful place.   Nothing at this time remained in sight save a few charred logs, and a few score of tall, unsightly stumps.   Even the old pioneers had great difficulty in pointing out the location of more than one or two of the cabins.   After the preparation of this history began, the author induced several of the survivors to visit Donner Lake, and to assist in definitely determining the location and boundaries of the cabins.   Digging in the earth which thirty-two years ago formed the cabin floors, the most interesting relics were found.   A collection of over five hundred of these articles is in the author's possession.   There are spoons which are bent and rust-eaten, some of which are partially without bowls, and some destitute of handles, the missing portions being vaguely shadowed in the rust-stained earth in which they were imbedded.   Knives there are whose

17

blades are mere skeleton outlines of what they formerly
were, and which in some instances appear to be only thin
scales of rust. The tines of the forks are sometimes pretty
well preserved, sometimes almost entirely worn away by the
action of rust.

Among the relics found at the Breen cabin are numerous
pieces of old porcelain, and china-ware. These fragments
are readily distinguished by painted flowers, or unique de-
signs enameled in red, blue, or purple colors upon the pure
white ground-surface of the china-ware. This ware is celebrated for the durability of its glaze or enamel, which can
not be scratched with a knife, and is not acted upon by
vegetable acids. The relics unearthed were found at a depth
of from one to six inches beneath the ground which formed
the floor. A fragment of this ware, together with an old-
fashioned gun-flint, was sent to Hon. James F. Breen, who
wrote in reply:

"The relics, piece of chinaware and gun-flint, are highly
appreciated. The chinaware was at once recognized by my
brother. In fact, there is one piece of the china set (a cream
pitcher) still in the possession of my brother. The piece
sent is recognizable by the decoration figures, which corre-
spond exactly with those on the pitcher."

There is less of the "ghastly" and "horrible" among the
relics thus far discovered than would be supposed. There
are many, like the beads and arrow-heads, which were evidently treasured by members of the party as relics or curiosities collected while crossing the plains. There are pieces of
looking-glass which reflected the sunken, starved features of
the emigrants. Among the porcelain are pieces of pretty
cups and saucers, and dainty, expensive plates, which in
those days were greatly prized. Bits of glassware, such as
tumblers, vials, and dishes, are quite numerous. Bolts, nails,

screws, nuts, chains, and portions of the wagon irons, are almost unrecognizable on account of the rust. The nails are wrought, and some of them look as if they might have been hammered out by the emigrants. One of these nails is so firmly imbedded in rust alongside a screw, that the two are inseparable. Metallic buttons are found well preserved, a sewing awl is quite plainly distinguishable, and an old-fashioned, quaint-looking bridle-bit retains much of its original form. Some of the more delicate and perishable articles present the somewhat remarkable appearance of having increased in size by the accumulations of rust and earth in which they are encased. This is especially the case with a darning-needle, which has increased its circumference in places nearly one half, while in other places it is eaten away until only a mere filament of steel remains. The sharp point of a curved sewing-awl has grown with rust until it is larger than the body of the awl. Several fish-hooks have been found, all more or less rust-eaten. A brass pistol, single-barreled, apparently a century old, was found under the Graves cabin, and near it was an old flint-lock. In the corner of the fire-place of the Reed cabin were found several bullets and number two shot. Gun-flints, ready for use or in a crude form, were found in each of the cabins.

W. C. Graves visited the site of his father's cabin on the twenty-first of April, 1879, and many articles were dug up in his presence which he readily recognized. A large number of the leading citizens of Truckee were present, and assisted in searching for the relics. Among other things was a cooper's inshave, which belonged to his father, who was a cooper by trade. An iron wagon-hammer was also immediately recognized as having been used in their wagon. A small tin box, whose close-fitting cover was hermetically sealed with rust, was found, and while it was being examined, one of the

gentlemen, Mr. Frank Rabel, tapped it lightly with his knife-
handle. The side of the box crushed as easily as if it had
been an egg-shell. The wonderful fact connected with this
relic, however, is that Mr. Graves said, before the box was
crushed, that his mother kept oil of hemlock in this box, and
that upon examination a distinct odor of oil of hemlock was
found remaining in the box.

A whetstone, or what might more properly be called an
oil-stone, was discovered at the Breen cabin. On this stone
were the initials "J. F. R.," which had evidently been cut
into its surface with a knife-blade. Mrs. V. E. Murphy and
Mrs. Frank Lewis, the daughters of James F. Reed, at once
remembered this whetstone as having belonged to their
father, and fully identified it upon examination.

A great many pins have been found, most of which are
the old-fashioned round-headed ones. A strange feature in
regard to these pins is that although bright and clean, they
crumble and break at almost the slightest touch. The metal
of which they are made appears to be entirely decomposed.
One of the most touching relics, in view of the sad, sad history, is the sole of an infant's shoe. The tiny babe who
wore the shoe was probably among the number who perished
of starvation.

The big rock against which the Murphy cabin stood is
half hidden by willows and by fallen tamaracks, whose
branches are interlaced so as to form a perfect net-work above
the place where the cabin stood. Under the floor of this
cabin the remains of the poor victims are supposed to have
been buried. Nature appears to have made every effort to
conceal the spot. In addition to the bushes and the fallen
trees there is a rank growth of marsh grass, whose rootlets
extend far down in the soil, and firmly resist either shovel or
spade. Until very late in the summer this mournful spot is

still further protected by being inundated by the waters of Donner Creek. It is hardly necessary to remark that no relics have ever been found under the site of the Murphy cabin. The tall stumps which surround this rock, and the site of the Graves and Reed cabin, and which are particularly numerous around the site of the Donner tents at Alder Creek, are of themselves remarkable relics. Many of them were cut by persons who stood on the top of very deep snow. They are frequently ten, fifteen, and twenty feet in height. Time and the action of the elements have caused them to decay until, in some instances, a child's hand might cause them to totter and fall. In a few years more they all will have disappeared.

# EDITORS' NOTES

(1). Page 20, **Milton Elliott.** The familiar "Milt" was a contraction of Elliott's Christian name, Milford.

(2). Page 32, **Pike.** McCutchen, not Pike, was the third member, on the authority of Reed himself ("The Snow-Bound, Starved Emigrants of 1846," *Pacific Rural Press,* March 25, 1871).

(3). Page 35, **was buried.** A manuscript diary, bearing the names of Hiram Miller and Milton Elliott and now at Sutter's Fort Historical Museum, gives August 25 as the date of burial (near some trees at Twenty Wells, at a fork in the trail). The detail and consistency of most of the diary's entries seem to establish its authority in the matter. A grave, assertedly that of Halloran, was discovered near this point in 1927 by Charles E. Davis (*Sacramento Bee,* October 11, 1927). Julia Cooley Altrocchi identifies the pier site at Sunset Beach as Halloran's burial place (*The Old California Trail,* p. 241).

(4). Page 38, **cache.** The remains of an emigrant cache closely resembling the typical one described in the text were discovered on the Salt Lake Desert in 1927 by Charles E. Davis (*Sacramento Bee,* April 11, 1927). See also the issue of July 30, 1927, for Davis' explorations and discoveries along the Coldstream trail.

(5). Page 40, **humanity.** In the first edition these men are designated as the "forlorn hope." The phrase was subsequently dropped in view of its close association with the later attempts of the snowshoe party.

(6). Page 41, **tragedy.** Chapter iv in the first edition makes much of the "betrothal" of Snyder and Mary Graves. In omitting all reference to it in his revision, McGlashan apparently sacrificed romance to fact. The circumstance, if true, would have gone far to explain the obvious partisanship of W. C. Graves in his account of the Reed-Snyder affair.

(7). Page 44, **Gravelly Ford.** Gravelly Ford lay at a point nine miles east of the present railroad station of Palisade,

Nevada. The fact that the Reed-Snyder affair could not have occurred here is fairly obvious, even without the testimony of the "Miller-Elliott" cited above. This document terminates abruptly with the entry (a single word, "Still—") for October 4, the day before Snyder's death. In view of the preceding entries, the site would have to be a point some thirty-five miles west of Gravelly. If we grant the authority of the diary, the entry confirms George Stewart's correction of McGlashan's location (*Ordeal by Hunger,* p. 313 n.).

(8). Page 44, **hot words.** Graves' account states that Snyder struck Reed three times with a whipstock *after* Reed had run him through the heart with a six-inch blade, "cutting off two ribs" [*sic!*]. McGlashan enjoyed a close friendship with Graves, and his rejection of the testimony shows unusually cautious regard for the laws of probability.

(9). Page 53, **No one.** The first edition has: "Keseberg made no attempt to return and find the poor old fellow." The revision of the sentence in the second edition excludes the opinions of several witnesses as calculated to blacken Keseberg's reputation.

(10). Page 53, **occurred.** The statement may or may not be true. Older accounts do not clearly trace Wolfinger's movements, and Graves' narrative confuses the incident with that of Hardcoop. Hardcoop was certainly abandoned, although Breen and Graves must have shared any guilt with Keseberg in the matter. Wolfinger had lost his own cattle and had been obliged to proceed on foot as best he could. The sequence of events is clearly set forth by Thornton (*Oregon and California in 1848,* II, 100 ff.).

(11). Page 56, **was discharged.** The exploded barrel of a brass pistol (not necessarily that which killed Pike) was one of the relics later recovered from the soil at the Graves cabin site (see p. 259 of the text).

(12). Page 62, **Alder Creek Valley.** Survivors and members of relief parties generally agreed in placing this camp site at a distance of from five to seven miles from Donner Lake. Alder Creek Valley is an area four miles northeast of Truckee terminating at the confluence of Alder and Prosser creeks and embracing Sections 25-26, 35-36, of Township 18, North Range, 16 East. In the manuscript diary of John Markle, the valley is mentioned in the entry for August 20, 1849. On that date Markle and his companions halted to investigate the remains of the Donner camp, which he placed at a distance of seven miles from Truckee Lake (Donner Lake) and one mile from the emigrant trail in a northerly direction. McGlashan's statement (see also p. 67) substantially agrees with this early testimony. In 1879 McGlashan visited the spot, once with Nicholas Clark and once with W. C. Graves, and P. M. Wedell subsequently marked it following conversations with McGlashan. For a clear account of the chain of evidence, see Wedell's "Location of the Donner Family Camp," in *California Historical Society Quarterly,* Vol. XXIV, No. 1 (March 1945), pp. 73–77.

(13). Page 63, **frequently seen.** The failure of the emigrants' attempts to catch fish has long formed a subject for debate. Any experienced native of the district can testify that lake fish may be taken easily (if illegally) during the winter months. The facts seem to indicate that members of the party failed to catch fish chiefly because they lacked experience and equipment and because they were too bewildered and dispirited to acquire them.

(14). Page 67, **camped with them.** The first edition has: "a short distance above." The explicit statement in the edition of 1880 seems to indicate later and more specific testimony from a survivor familiar with the district.

(15). Page 71, **they encamped.** The first day's camp was made on December 16, 1846. The following log of "The Forlorn Hope" is based upon a collation of evidence advanced by Reed, Bryant, Thornton, and Stewart, and is designed to clarify the chronology in chapters vi, vii, and ix of the McGlashan history.

| DATE | | OCCURRENCE | MCGLASHAN PAGE |
|---|---|---|---|
| 1846 | | | |
| December | 16 | Departure from the lake and first day's camp. | 71 |
| December | 17 | Party makes six miles | 71 |
| December | 18 | Party makes five miles | 72 |
| December | 19 | Snowblindness afflicts party; Mary Graves sights the "smoky gorge" (see p. 79); Stanton weakens | 73 |
| December | 20 | Stanton falls behind and halts | 73 |

(16). Page 93, **"Truckey."** For a valuable compilation of data on the name, see *Gold Rush: the Journals, Drawings, and Other Papers of J. Goldsborough Bruff,* edited by Georgia Willis Read and Ruth Gaines (New York: Columbia University Press, 1944), Vol. I, pp. 551, 552–53; Vol. II, pp. 1081, 1089. Donner Lake was misnamed "Truckee Lake" by early travelers and cartographers, who missed the junction of Donner Creek and the Truckee River and concluded that Donner Lake was the source of the latter.

(17). Page 101, **this stump.** The tall stumps have had a continuous tradition since the time of the Donner party disaster. The emigrant Lemuel McKeeby first noted them in 1849 ("Memoirs," *California Historical Society Quarterly,* 1924, III, 137). Several stumps were standing at Donner Lake in 1880 and of these two remained at the turn of the century. Others still stood in the more hospitable soil at the Alder Creek camp site as late as 1910, and three ancient specimens with well-defined undercuts are still intact there.

(18). Page 101, **blanks which occur.** McGlashan used the version of Breen's diary published in the *Nashville* (Tenn.) *Whig*, and he could not know that the various refinements were peculiar to the printed transcript. Breen certainly did not make his entries with a view to publication, and many of the comments in his manuscript are extremely outspoken. The entry for "Jan. 21" has: "Mrs. Reid sent her back to live or die on them."

(19). Page 102, **seized . . . . goods.** The entry for "Jan. 30" has: "Mrs. Graves seized on Mrs. Reids goods."

(20). Page 104, **refused . . . . hides.** The entry for "Feb. 15" has: "Mrs. Graves refused to give Mrs. Reid any hides."

(21). Page 110, **Johnson's Ranch.** Johnson's Ranch lay three miles east of the present town of Wheatland.

(22). Page 112, **R. S. Mootrey.** The name is "Moultry" in the records of the relief.

(23). Page 117, **Mule Springs.** Mule Springs lay within the boundaries of the present Maguire Ranch, midway between the Bear River and Steephollow Creek and due north of the town of Dutch Flat.

(24). Page 128, **Perry McCan.** The name is "McCoon" in other records.

(25). Page 149, **famous mining camps.** See "Three Deserted Villages," in W. F. Edwards' *Tourists' Guide and Directory of the Truckee Basin,* pp. 100–102. For other topographical features, see *Topographical Map of Lake Tahoe and Surrounding Country,* by Ferdinand von Leicht and J. D. Hoffman (San Francisco: G. T. Brown, 1874).

(26). Page 152, **Reed-Snyder tragedy.** The first edition makes no reference to the Reed-Snyder affair at this point in the narrative. By 1880 the fierce partisanship of survivors had forced McGlashan to emphasize fate rather than passion in his treatment of the killing and banishment.

(27). Page 152, **original diary.** The first edition does not include the extracts from Reed's manuscript diary which is now in Sutter's Fort Historical Museum.

(28). Page 161, **Joseph Jondro.** A corruption of "Gendreau." **Hiram Miller** had left Fort Bridger with six other emigrants on July 20, arriving at Johnson's Ranch on August 30 (H. H. Bancroft, *History of California,* Vol. V, p. 528).

(29). Page 161, **distress . . . . was extreme.** McGlashan says nothing of the sinister reminders of cannibalism which Reed's party found at the Alder Creek camp. This reticence arises from neither ignorance nor false delicacy but from the author's fixed practice of reporting facts in the main body of the narrative solely from the point of view of the characters immediately concerned. Far more deeply rooted distaste for such realistic detail was shown by Reed himself in his published recollections. The scenes are fully described by Jessy Quinn Thornton in his *Oregon and California in 1848* (New York, 1849, Vol. II) and by George Stewart (*op. cit.,* chapter xxiv).

(30). Page 162, **behind a large rock.** On May 14, 1891, Edward Reynolds, a miner from Sierra Valley, discovered a large number of silver coins while prospecting at a point midway along the north shore of Donner Lake. Reynolds, with McGlashan and one Amos Lane, made a systematic search and finally recovered a total of one hundred and ninety-one coins of various denominations and of American, Spanish, Mexican, French, and German mintage. The hoard was found at a point less than thirty feet from the large rock which tradition had identified for half a century as Mrs. Graves' hiding-place. No coin was dated later than 1845, and many of the pieces were badly corroded. For a detailed account of the discovery, see *The San Francisco Examiner,* May 24, 1891.

(31). Page 165, **justify these men.** After the third relief, charges of looting and cowardice were freely brought against Cady, Stone, and Clark; and McGlashan must have heard and read them. From a mass of wholly hearsay evidence, a single fact emerges—that the three men quit their posts. The circumstances are fully discussed by Thornton (*op. cit.,* II, 224 *et seq.*) and by Stewart (*op. cit.,* chapters xxvi, xxviii, xxix).

(32). Page 175, **following description.** Eliza Farnham, author of *California In Doors and Out,* the work from which the quotations are taken.

(33). Page 199, **Samuel Donner.** Samuel Donner was probably still alive at this time, according to a report in the *California Star,* April 3, 1847.

(34). Page 228, **"Company."** Quoted from Edward E. Dunbar's *The Romance of the Age.*

(35). Page 237, **survived.** Beneath the vital statistics of the survivors of the Donner party, there are some curious facts which deserve notice. The women generally outlived the men by considerable periods. Of eight women survivors who died after 1920, four reached the age of ninety, three were well over eighty, and one was in her late seventies. Four of these were Donners (Leanna, Elitha, Frances, and Eliza) and two were Reeds (Martha and Virginia)—children of the two leading families of the expedition. Two others were Naomi Pike and Isabella Breen. Elitha Donner (Wilder) and Martha Reed (Lewis) died on the same day. Isabella Breen was the last to die, ending the final chapter of a history the most desperate moments of which had been chronicled by her father. Naomi Pike, Isabella Breen, and Eliza's cousin, Mary Donner, had been literally snatched from death as infants: Naomi had been abandoned at Donner Lake, Isabella had lain unseen in the fire-pit at "Starved Camp," and Mary had almost frozen to death (she died later, in childbirth). In recent years, an ironic epilogue was added to the history when a direct descendant of the Breens, Kathleen Trevethick, died of exposure and hunger in a snowbound automobile in western Nevada.

(36). Page 253, **one hundred *vara* lot number thirty-nine.** This lot embraced an area southeast of the intersection of Second and Folsom streets in San Francisco. For a comprehensive view of the complicated legal action involving the property, see the transcript of appeal in the case of *Donner* vs. *Palmer, et al.* (California Supreme Court Records, Vol. 42), and the report in the *Sacramento Union,* February 8, 1862.

(37). **Interesting relics.** Recent acquisitions of important *ana* and relics of the Donner Party now in Sutter's Fort Historical Museum are listed and described in *Tahoe Topics,* Vol. I, No. 1 (May 17, 1946), p. 9.

# BIBLIOGRAPHY

NOTE.—The following classified list includes all recognized works dealing directly with the Donner party. No attempt has been made to trace all of the more recent periodical and newspaper articles on the subject; for the most part, these offer little fresh information, and they are usually summaries of well-known works.

## I. THE STORY AS A WHOLE: NARRATIVES AND BRIEF NOTICES PUBLISHED AFTER 1880

BANCROFT, HUBERT HOWE. *History of California.* San Francisco: The History Company, 1884–1890. Vol. V (1886), chap. xx, pp. 524–58

———. *California Inter Pocula.* San Francisco: A. L. Bancroft Company, 1888. Pp. 93–109

BURNETT, PETER HARDEMANN. *Recollections and Opinions of an Old Pioneer.* New York: D. Appleton & Co., 1880. Pp. 275–82

CLELAND, ROBERT GLASS. "A Tragedy of the Trail," *Pathfinders.* Los Angeles: Powell Publishing Company, 1929. Chap. xiv, pp. 347–68

CONMY, PETER THOMAS. *The Donner Party, 1846.* San Francisco: California Historical Board, N.S.G.W. (mimeographed), 1937

EDWARDS, W. F. "Donner Lake," *Tourists' Guide and Directory of the Truckee Basin.* Truckee: W. F. Edwards, 1883. Pp. 61–67

ELDREDGE, ZOETH SKINNER. *The Beginnings of San Francisco,* San Francisco: Z. S. Eldredge, 1912. 2 vols. Vol. II, p. 627

———. *History of California.* New York: The Century History Company, 1915. 5 vols. Vol. III, chap. iii, pp. 120–49

FOOTE, H. S. (ed.). *Pen Pictures from the Garden of the World.* Chicago: Lewis Publishing Company, 1888. Pp. 58–63

*Grass Valley Morning Union.* Series of articles by Edmund G. Kenyon. June 26, July 10, September 4, September 11, 1938

*Grizzly Bear.* "History of the Donner Party." June 1907
———. "Remarkable Story of the Sufferings and Experiences of the Historical Donner Party." January 1908
HITTELL, THEODORE HENRY. *History of California.* San Francisco: N. J. Stone & Co., 1885. 4 vols. Vol. II, pp. 678–81
HOUGHTON, ELIZA P. DONNER. *The Expedition of the Donner Party and Its Tragic Fate.* Chicago: A. C. McClurg & Co., 1911
JAMES, GEORGE WHARTON. "The Great-Hearted Hero of the Snows, Charles T. Stanton," *Heroes of California.* Boston: Little, Brown & Co., 1910. Pp. 56–64
———. "The Midnight Heroine of the Plains, Virginia Reed," *Heroes of California.* Boston: Little, Brown & Co., 1910. Pp. 64–75
1929. Chap. xiv, pp. 347–68
McGLASHAN, C. F. *History of the Donner Party.* San Francisco: A. L. Bancroft Company, 1880
NORTON, HENRY KITTREDGE. *The Story of California from the Earliest Days to the Present.* Chicago: A. C. McClurg & Co., 1913. Pp. 169–75
ROYCE, JOSIAH. *California, from the Conquest in 1846 to the Second Vigilance Committee in San Francisco.* Boston and New York: Houghton, Mifflin Company, 1886. Pp. 43–45, 197
*San Francisco Call.* General account. October 3, 1880
———. Sketch by Virginia Reed Murphy. July 5, 1891
———. Description by Juan B. Truxedo. October 11, 1891
*San Francisco Chronicle.* General accounts. January 1, 1889; September 7, 1890
*San Francisco Examiner.* General accounts. August 21, 25, 1884; January 26, 1890
STEWART, GEORGE. *Ordeal by Hunger.* New York: Henry Holt & Co., 1936
TRIPLETT, FRANK. *Conquering the Wilderness.* New York and St. Louis: N. D. Thompson Publishing Company, 1886. Chaps. xv–xvi, pp. 645–60

II. IMAGINATIVE WORKS INSPIRED BY THE STORY
ALTROCCHI, JULIA COOLEY. *Snow Covered Wagons.* New

York: The Macmillan Company, 1936

BIRNEY, HOFFMAN, *Grim Journey*. New York: Milton Balch & Co., 1934

MABIE, MARY LOUISE. *The Long Knives Walked*. Indianapolis: Bobbs-Merrill Company, 1932

McCARTHY, JOHN RUSSELL. "Hunger in the Snow," *Westways*, November, 1937. P. 19

III. PRIMARY SOURCES: RECORDS OF SURVIVORS; ACCOUNTS AND BRIEF NOTICES BY CONTEMPORARIES

BREEN, JOHN. "Pioneer Memoirs," Manuscript in Bancroft Library, University of California

BREEN, PATRICK. Diary. Manuscript in Bancroft Library, University of California

———. *Diary of Patrick Breen*. Ed. Frederick Teggart. Berkeley: University of California Press, 1910

BRYANT, EDWIN. *What I Saw in California.* Philadelphia: D. Appleton & Co., 1848. Chap. xx, pp. 249–65

CRONISE, TITUS FEY. *The Natural Wealth of California*. San Francisco and New York: H. H. Bancroft & Co., 1868. Pp. 52–53

DEGROOT, HENRY. "The Donner Party," *Overland Monthly.* Vol. V, (o.s.) July 1870, pp. 38–43

DONNER, TAMSEN. Letter written from Independence, Missouri, to her sister, May 11, 1846. Manuscript in Huntington Library

DUNBAR, EDWARD E. *The Romance of the Age*. New York: D. Appleton & Co., 1867. P. 65

FARNHAM, ELIZA. "Narrative of the Emigration of the Donner Party to California in 1846," *California In Doors and Out*. New York: Dix, Edwards & Co., 1856. Pp. 380–457

FROST, JOHN. "The Wonderful Fortitude of Female Emigrants," *Pioneer Mothers of the West*. Boston: Lee & Shepard, 1875. Pp. 239–68

GRAVES, WILLIAM C. "Crossing the Plains in '46," *The Russian River Flag* (Healdsburg). April 26, May 3, 10, 17, 1877; December 30, 1875

HARLAN, JACOB WRIGHT. *California, '36 to '48*. San Francisco: The Bancroft Company, 1888. Pp. 40–73

KERN, EDWARD M. Letter summarizing experiences of the Donner party, January, 1847. Manuscript in Huntington Library

McCLELLAN, ROLLANDER GUY. *The Golden State.* Philadelphia: W. Flint & Co., 1872. Pp. 144–46

McDOUGAL, FRANCES H. "The Donner Tragedy," *Pacific Rural Press.* January 21, April 29, 1871

McGLASHAN, C. F. "History of the Donner Party" (serial numbers), *Truckee Republican.* January–June, 1879

———. *History of the Donner Party.* Truckee: Crowley & McGlashan, 1879

MURPHY, VIRGINIA REED. "Deeply Interesting Letter," *Illinois Journal* (Springfield). December 16, 1847

———. *A Happy Issue: the Hitherto Unpublished Letter of a Child, Virginia Elizabeth B. Reed.* Privately printed, 1935

———. Letters to C. F. McGlashan. Manuscript in possession of McGlashan Estate

———. "Across the Plains in the Donner Party (1846)," *Century Magazine,* July 1891. Pp. 409–26

OWEN, ROBERT DALE. *Footfalls on the Boundary of Another World.* Philadelphia: J. B. Lippincott & Co., 1877. P. 457

POWER, JOHN CARROLL. *History of the Early Settlers of Sangamon County, Illinois.* Springfield: E. A. Wilson & Co., 1876. Pp. 258–60

QUIGLEY, HUGH. *The Irish Race in California.* San Francisco: A. Roman & Co., 1878. Pp. 210–15

REED, JAMES FRAZIER. "From a California Emigrant," *Sangamo Journal* (Springfield). November 5, 1846

———. "Narrative of the Sufferings of a Company of Emigrants in the Mountains of California, in the Winter of '46 and '7," *Illinois Journal* (Springfield). December 9, December 23, 1847

———. "The Snow-Bound, Starved Emigrants of 1846," *Pacific Rural Press.* March 25, April 1, 1871

———. Statement by James F. Reed, *San Jose Pioneer.* April 28, 1877

*Sacramento Union.* General accounts. September 27, October 1, October 8, 1866

*San Francisco Bulletin.* General account. March 25, 1864

*San Jose Pioneer.* George Donner's letter. November 10, 1877

Soule, Frank. *The Annals of San Francisco.* New York: D. Appleton & Co., 1855. Pp. 188–91

Thornton, Jessy Quinn. *Oregon and California in 1848.* New York: Harper & Brothers, 1849. 2 vols. Vol. II, chaps. vii–xvii, pp. 95–246

## IV. PRIMARY SOURCES: RECORDS OF THE RELIEF

*California Star* (Yerba Buena–San Francisco). Various accounts of the plight of the emigrants and of the organization and progress of the relief. January 16, February 6, February 13, February 27, March 20, April 10, 1847

Fallon, W. O. "Extracts from a Journal Written by a Member of the Party Latest from the California Mountains," *California Star.* June 5, 1847

McCutchen, William. "Statement of William McCutchen," *Pacific Rural Press.* April 1, 1871

McKinstry, George. "Documents for the History of California." Manuscript in Bancroft Library, University of California

————. Letter, *California Star.* March 13, 1847

Moutry (Moultry), Riley. Petition for compensation for services in relief party; affidavits by James Reed, Wm. McCutchen, and Edward Pyle. 1872. Manuscript in Huntington Library

Rhoads, Daniel. "Relief of the Donner Party, 1846." Statement transcribed by W. R. Grimshaw. Manuscript in Bancroft Library, University of California

*Sacramento Bee.* Account of Joseph Gray's claims to a role in the relief of the Donner party. December 12, 1884

Stokes, Frank. "The Last Man Out," *Touring Topics,* February 1929. Pp. 22–50

Sutter, John A. "Personal Reminiscences." Manuscript in Bancroft Library, University of California

Swords, Thomas. *Report of a Journey from California by the South Pass to Fort Leavenworth in 1847.* No. 557 Ex. Doc. 1 of H.R., 30th Cong., 2d Sess. (1848). Pp. 226–36

*Transcript of the Fort Sutter Papers, together with the Historical Commentaries Accompanying Them.* Published by Edward Eberstadt, n.d. Vols. XXVI–XXVII

WISE, HENRY AUGUSTUS. *Los Gringos: or an Inside View of Mexico and California, with Wanderings in Peru, Chili, and Polynesia.* London: Richard Bentley, 1849. Pp. 64–66

WOODWORTH, SELIM. Letter, *California Star.* April 3, 1847

## V. ROUTES, TRAILS, AND CAMP SITES

ALTROCCHI, JULIA COOLEY. *The Old California Trail: Traces in Folklore and Furrow.* Caldwell, Idaho: Caxton Printers, 1945

CLAYTON, WILLIAM. "The Latter-Day Saints' Emigrants' Guide," *A Journal of the Birmingham Emigrating Company.* Salt Lake: The Legal Printing Company, 1928. Pp. 137–76

CLYMAN, JAMES. "Diaries and Memoranda of a Journey through the Far West" (Ed. Charles L. Camp), *California Historical Society Quarterly.* Vol. IV, No. 2 (1925), pp. 105–41, 307–61

DORNIN, MAY. "The Emigrant Trails into California." Unpublished Master's thesis in History, University of California, 1921

MILLER-ELLIOTT DIARY. Unpublished Manuscript Diary. In Sutter's Fort Historical Museum, Sacramento, California

MCKINSTRY, GEORGE. "Documents for the History of California." Manuscript in Bancroft Library, University of

JEFFERSON, T. H. *Map of the Emigrant Road from Independence, Mo., to St. Francisco, California.* With an Introduction and Notes by George Stewart. San Francisco: California Historical Society, 1945

KELLY, CHARLES. *Salt Desert Trails.* Salt Lake: The Western Printing Company, 1930. Chap. ix, pp. 81–95

MCGLASHAN, C. F. "The Donner Party Cabin-Sites," letter addressed to the Historical Landmarks Committee, N.S.-G.W., Oakland, California, 1920. (14 pp.)

NORTH, ARTHUR W. "The Cut-Off," *Sunset Magazine,* December 1915. Pp. 1095–1104 (map)

PERKINS, ELISHA DOUGLAS. "Sketches of a Trip from Marietta, Ohio, to the Valley of the Sacramento in the Spring and Summer of 1849." Holograph manuscript in Huntington Library

PROUTY, ANNIE ESTELLE. "The Development of Reno in Relation to Its Topography," *Nevada State Historical Papers.* Vol. IV (1923–1924), pp. 28–189. Maps: "Trails Across Nevada" (p. 40); "Fremont's Expeditions" (p. 48); "The Hastings Cut-Off" (p. 54)

RENSCH, H. E. and E. G., and HOOVER, MILDRED BROOKE. *Historic Spots in California. Valley and Sierra Counties.* Stanford University Press, 1933. Pp. 152, 210–16, 309–12, 513, 542, 544, 560

WAGGONER, W. W. "The Donner Party and Relief Hill," *California Historical Society Quarterly.* Vol. X, No. 4 (December 1931), pp. 347–52

WARREN, G. K. (LIEUT.). *Map of the Territory of the United States from the Mississippi to the Pacific Ocean.* Ex. Doc. No. 78, Vol. XI, U.S. 33d Cong., 2d Sess. (1855)

WEDELL, P. M. "Location of the Donner Family Camp." *California Historical Society Quarterly.* Vol. XXIV, No. 1 (March 1945), pp. 73–77

WEDELL, P. M. "Map of Historic Emigrant Road." San Jose, 1930. Bancroft Library, University of California

WILKES, CHARLES. *Narrative of the United States Exploring Expedition during the Years 1838, 1839, 1840, 1841, 1842.* Philadelphia: Lee & Blanchard, 1845. 5 vols. and atlas

## VI. LEGENDS AND TRAVELERS' TALES

BIGLER, H. W. "Diary of H. W. Bigler," *Overland Monthly,* September–October, 1887. P. 240

BUSHNELL, HORACE. "Dream about the Donner Party," *Nature and the Supernatural.* New York: Scribner & Co., 1858. Pp. 475–76

CORDUA, THEODOR. "Memoirs of Theodor Cordua," translated by Erwin C. Gudde, *California Historical Society Quarterly.* Vol. XII, No. 4 (December 1933), p. 293

MARKLE, JOHN A. "The Travell of a Gold Digger Enroute," Manuscript in possession of Auburn Parlor, N.S.G.W.

"C. M." "Reminiscences of a Forty-Niner," *Santa Barbara Press.* January 31, 1881

MCKEEBY, LEMUEL CLARKE. "Memoirs," *California Historical Society Quarterly.* Vol. III, Nos. 1 and 2 (1924), p. 137

*Solano Democrat.* "Strange History Connected with the Donner Party." December 23, 1871

TAYLOR, BAYARD. *Eldorado.* New York: George P. Putnam, 1850. 2 vols. Vol. I, p. 228


## VII. SURVIVORS AND DESCENDANTS

GENEALOGICAL RECORDS OF CALIFORNIA PIONEERS. Compiled by the California Society, Daughters of the American Revolution. Various volumes. California State Library

PIONEER RECORD AND INDEX. California State Library

*Sacramento Bee.* Donner Party Obituary File. Library, *Sacramento Bee* (Sacramento, California)


## VIII. RELICS OF THE DONNER PARTY

McGLASHAN, C. F. Inventory of Donner Party Relics. Manuscript in possession of Bliss McGlashan Hinkle

*Sacramento Bee* (Sacramento, California). May 30, 1891; April 11, July 30, October 11, 1927

*Sacramento Union.* September 27, 1866; May 17, 1879; February 23, 1894

*San Francisco Call.* July 12, 1891

*San Francisco Examiner.* May 24, 1891

*San Jose Pioneer.* November 15, 1879

*Tahoe Topics,* "New Material on the Donner Party Discovered Lately." (Tahoe, California). Vol. I, No. 1 (May 17, 1946). p. 9

# INDEX